Civilizing War

FLASHPOINTS

The FlashPoints series is devoted to books that consider literature beyond strictly national and disciplinary frameworks, and that are distinguished both by their historical grounding and by their theoretical and conceptual strength. Our books engage theory without losing touch with history and work historically without falling into uncritical positivism. FlashPoints aims for a broad audience within the humanities and the social sciences concerned with moments of cultural emergence and transformation. In a Benjaminian mode, FlashPoints is interested in how literature contributes to forming new constellations of culture and history and in how such formations function critically and politically in the present. Series titles are available online at http://escholarship.org/uc/flashpoints.

SERIES EDITORS:

Ali Behdad (Comparative Literature and English, UCLA), Founding Editor; Judith Butler (Rhetoric and Comparative Literature, UC Berkeley), Founding Editor; Michelle Clayton (Hispanic Studies and Comparative Literature, Brown University); Edward Dimendberg (Film and Media Studies, Visual Studies, and European Languages and Studies, UC Irvine), Coordinator; Catherine Gallagher (English, UC Berkeley), Founding Editor; Nouri Gana (Comparative Literature and Near Eastern Languages and Cultures, UCLA); Susan Gillman (Literature, UC Santa Cruz); Jody Greene (Literature, UC Santa Cruz); Richard Terdiman (Literature, UC Santa Cruz)

A complete list of titles begins on page 249.

Civilizing War

Imperial Politics and the Poetics of National Rupture

Nasser Mufti

NORTHWESTERN UNIVERSITY PRESS | EVANSTON, ILLINOIS

THIS BOOK IS MADE POSSIBLE BY A COLLABORATIVE GRANT
FROM THE ANDREW W. MELLON FOUNDATION.

Northwestern University Press
www.nupress.northwestern.edu

Printed in the United States of America

10 9 8 7 6 5 4 3 2 1

Library of Congress Cataloging-in-Publication Data [to come]

Names: Mufti, Nasser, author.
Title: Civilizing war : imperial politics and the poetics of national rupture / Nasser Mufti.
Other titles: FlashPoints (Evanston, Ill.)
Description: Evanston, Illinois : Northwestern University Press, 2018. | Series: FlashPoints |
    Includes bibliographical references.
Identifiers: LCCN 2017014831| ISBN 9780810136038 (cloth : alk. paper) | ISBN
    9780810136021 (pbk. : alk. paper) | ISBN 9780810136045 (e-book)
Subjects: LCSH: English fiction—19th century—History and criticism. | English fiction—
    20th century—History and criticism. | Civil war in literature. | Imperialism in literature.
    | Great Britain—Colonies—Civilization.
Classification: LCC PR830.W37 M84 2018 | DDC 820.9/3581—dc23
LC record available at https://lccn.loc.gov/2017014831

♾ The paper used in this publication meets the minimum requirements of the American
National Standard for Information Sciences—Permanence of Paper for Printed Library
Materials, ANSI Z39.481992.

For Dodo, Abba, and Yasser
(pay no attention to the epigraph!)

Whatever brotherhood human beings may be capable of has grown out of fratricide.

—HANNAH ARENDT, *On Revolution*

Contents

Acknowledgments

These pages could not exist had it not been for the sheer luck of the academic job market. This afforded me the time and institutional support to make this book what it is. Who or what to thank for this, or whether gratitude is even appropriate in this context, I don't know.

Much easier to know is whom to thank for their guidance, skepticism, humor, feedback, patience, tough love, and goodwill. Sunil Agnani, Dina Al-Kassim, Étienne Balibar, Tamara Beauchamp, Carolyn Betensky, Adrienne Brown, Nick Brown, Mark Canuel, Joey Carnie, Alicia Christoff, Jeff Clapp, Pete Coviello, Mark Cunningham, Brock Cutler, Madhu Dubey, Harris Feinsod, Leah Feldman, Lisa Freeman, Sharareh Frouzesh, Richard Godden, Harvey, Rachel Havrelock, Kim Icreverzi, Anna Kornbluh, Lee Laskin, Andrew Leong, Walter Benn Michaels, Gianna Mosser, Aamir Mufti, Jessica Ostrower, R. Radhakrishnan, Sina Rahmani, Ringo, Roger Reeves, Zach Samalin, Chris Taylor, Rei Terada, Sonali Thakkar, Irene Tucker, Urchin, Ken Yoshida, the two anonymous readers of the manuscript, and the series editors at FlashPoints made these pages what they are. Conversations at the Chicagoland Junior Faculty Writing Group, the Chicagoland Junior Faculty Writing Splinter Group, the NAVSA Junior Faculty Writing Group, and the Institute for the Humanities Workshop at UIC helped make shots in the dark into rough drafts, and rough drafts into drafts. I am also grateful to Stuart Brisley and Maya Balcioglu for use of *The Missing Text: Interregnum I (6 May–12 May), 2010* for the cover of this book.

If the list above is relatively easy to compile, then acknowledging Kim is a no-brainer.

An early version of Chapter 5 was published as "Kipling's Art of War," *Nineteenth Century Literature* 70, no. 4 (2016): 496–519.

Civilizing War

Introduction

"These people never fight civilized wars, do they? So much for calling it a civil war."[1] Such is the evaluation of the Nigerian Civil War by Susan Greville-Pitts, a British ex-patriot in Chimamanda Ngozi Adichie's novel *Half of a Yellow Sun* (2006). It is easy to dismiss Susan's statement as racist, or even defend it as anachronistic cultural insensitivity (the novel is set in the 1960s). Too easy. For at the heart of her comment is the affinity between "civil," "civil war," and "civilized." All three have their etymological origin in the Latin word *civis*, which is also the root for citizen, city, civil, civility, and civilization.[2] Susan's claim is that the *incivility* of Nigeria's civil war undermines its status as a *civil* war. For the conflict to be a *civilized* civil war, Nigerians would have to fight like civilized people—which, according to Susan, they are as yet incapable of doing. Susan's wordplay makes it possible to think of the project of civilizing, otherwise known as imperialism, as the project of making civil war a possibility in places not yet civilized—namely, the colonies. In context, the Nigerian Civil War was the country's first civil war as a postcolonial nation-state. But the logic of Susan's statement erases the "post" in "postcolonial" because it calls for continued civilizing of "these people," which, as the phrase suggests, means more than merely Nigerians, but all "these people" not yet civilized, not yet civil, not yet capable of fighting civilized civil wars.

Still too easy. For an identical conjuncture of incivility and civil war proliferates in the rhetoric of today's most prominent imperial institutions. In 2003, the World Bank completed a study on civil war, the outcome of which was a policy report titled *Breaking the Conflict Trap: Civil War and Development Policy*. In the report's foreword, Nicholas Stern, chief economist of the World Bank at the time, states that ever since World War II, "the risk of civil war is much higher in low-income countries than middle-income countries."[3] Civil war, according to Stern, happens exclusively in the developing world and is inextricably linked to the forces of modernization. The report cites examples of civil wars in countries as diverse as Peru, El Salvador, Angola, the Democratic Republic of Congo, Burundi, Cambodia, Rwanda, Somalia, and Sudan, all of which are collapsed into a single paradigm that is unique to the non-West. These civil wars, Stern argues, create "development in reverse" because they are "not just a problem *for* development, but a failure *of* development."[4] Civil war is a problem unique to the developing world, which in turn prohibits this world from ever becoming modern. As such, civil war is both a cause (a failure *of* development) and an effect (a problem *for* development)—disease *and* symptom. As a later chapter in the World Bank's study explains, "Once a country has stumbled into conflict powerful forces—the conflict trap—tend to lock it into a syndrome of further conflict."[5] Clumsy countries who know nothing about the art of modern statecraft "stumble" at the thresholds of modernity into "the conflict trap." These traps are so powerful that it takes a benevolent institution like the World Bank (which has complete confidence in its ability to tell apart victims from perpetrators) to rescue such states by setting them free into the domain of Western modernity. In the name of development and with the alibi of civil war, the World Bank takes on the burdens of an uncannily familiar *mission civilisatrice* to "break the trap" of the developing world's self-destructiveness. Hence the report proclaims: "The international community . . . has a legitimate role as an advocate for those who are victims."[6] Within the space of a few sentences, one of the world's most powerful men in one of the most powerful international organizations produces an ontology of the Global South in which civil war is located at the center.

Such claims never come out of a vacuum. Social scientific disciplines have been the backbone to the World Bank's geopolitical order of things. Beginning in the mid-1990s, an explosion of scholarship in the political sciences laid much of the groundwork for the World Bank's report. These studies define civil war through positivistic lenses such as casualties, rate of casualties, perpetrators of violence, levels of organization, and the status of sovereignty.[7] Within these institutional debates, definitions of what exactly a civil war is range from "one thousand deaths per conflict" to "two hundred deaths per conflict" to "one thousand deaths per conflict year."[8] Some define civil war as involving two governments, while others say that it can be between any two organized groups in a singular territory. Civil wars, we learn, last seven years on average.[9] Within one such time span, the social sciences produced a vast field of abstract knowledge about civil war complete with quantified graphs, trees, and an implicit map that consistently separates the West from the non-West.[10] If classical Orientalism took civility as its *topos*, its modern-day incarnation anchors itself in a knowledge of civil war. Indeed, to know civil war today is to know the developing world. Integral to this knowledge is also the solution to civil war's incivility. For within this discourse, foreign intervention, whether through military strikes, economic stimulation, or internationally induced reform, is never *not* the answer to civil war.[11] Academic disciplines work in concert with neoimperial conglomerates like the World Bank and take part in discourses that not only echo but reproduce the procedures of nineteenth-century imperialism by, as Edward Said put it long ago, "making statements about it, authorizing views of it, describing it, by teaching it, settling it, ruling over it."[12] When it comes to civil war, Orientalism is alive and well.

Most recently, civil war has become synonymous with the figure of the refugee. The movement of millions of stateless individuals within the Middle East and the influx of hundreds of thousands into Europe over the last few years have made civil war into an undeniably international event. Alongside these transnational movements away from crumbling nation-states has been the return of a vividly xenophobic nationalism within the West that is entirely at home in the language of wars of civilization, civilizing missions, and civility. The rhetoric of barbarism and a clash of the civilizations is always near at hand in popular and political debates surrounding the civil wars in the Middle East and Africa, which routinely equate the postcolonial refugee with the terrorist and sometimes Islam as such. The resurgence of far-Right nationalism within Europe and the United States, which derives its energy from a perceived "attack" on Western values and society by migrants and refugees, has revived, and in some cases ushered in, nationalist organizations and political parties like Patriotische Europäer gegen die Islamisierung des Abendlandes (PEGIDA) in Germany, the English Defense League and UK Independence Party in Britain (a party at the vanguard of the breakup of the European Union, no less), the National Front in France, Golden Dawn in Greece, the Sweden Democrats, the Danish People's Party, and the Finns Party. Far from developmental regression in the Global South, the far Right claims the Islamic State in Syria and Iraq is waging a "global civil war" (the vector of which is the refugee) that threatens to return Europe to medieval times. Thus in Europe and the United States it has become routine to hear calls for the closing off of borders to protect national identity, security, and the domestic labor market, while at the same time advocating for military intervention in the Middle East and North Africa under the moniker of "peacekeeping" or "humanitarian" missions with no cognizance of the long imperial history of benevolent interventionism.

This book is about how civil war came to figure so prominently in the politics of empire. As the readings above suggest, the resonance of Europe's civilizing missions in today's rhetoric of civil war necessitates an understanding of national rupture that attends to its prehistory in the nineteenth century as well as the global context in which it operates. Seen in this comparative light, we learn that the contemporary assumption that civil war is a demodernizing force emanating out of the global periphery is a relatively new one. For in nineteenth-century Britain, civil war was understood as a distinctly metropolitan problem rather than a crisis unique to the peripheries. Conflicts like the Indian Mutiny or the Morant Bay Rebellion were not seen by Victorians as civil wars but instead as acts of colonial treachery. In Charles Dickens's famously incendiary response to the Mutiny, he expresses his desire to "exterminate the Race upon whom the stain of the late cruelties rested" and "to blot it out of mankind and raze it off the face of the Earth."[13] In contrast, conflicts in the West like the American Civil War were understood to be essential to the globalization of industrial modernity. Karl Marx characterized the civil war in the United States as "nothing but a struggle between two social systems, between a system of slavery and the system of free labor," while John Stuart Mill equated the conflict to a civilizational war between the "barbarizing power" of the Confederacy and the "crusade of civilized Europe."[14] Britain's own class struggles were routinely described as latent civil wars between the middle class and the industrial proletariat. While capitalism is today seen as the solution to civil war, nineteenth-century Britons as diverse as Marx, Elizabeth Gaskell, and Thomas Carlyle saw capitalism to itself be a civil war between the rich and the poor that was waged under peaceful conditions. Instead of an uncivil affair justifying imperial intervention as it does today, civil war in the Victorian imagination described those antagonisms that were said to properly belong to places already civilized, where capitalist modernity had already arrived. In nineteenth-century Britain the logic was: *we* are at civil war, and it must be *our* civil war for it does not include the uncivilized colonies. Today the logic in the West is: *they* are at civil war, meaning we can intervene in their uncivilized conflicts as benevolent actors.

At the heart of *Civilizing War* is the historical transformation of civil war from a civil affair into an uncivil crisis. In the context of my study, civility and incivility are not markers of cultivation or conduct but geopolitical signposts of national boundaries in an imperial milieu.[15] The close relationship between civility and the civilizing mission is evident in early sociological texts like Norbert Elias's *The Civilizing Process* (1938).[16] Although Elias's text is primarily concerned with the self-cultivation of society, he nevertheless recognizes how such processes are inherently Orientalist in the modern age. This is in large part because in the context of the modern nation-state, socialization of one's own people operates through a will-to-difference with a more or less cultivated outside. The idea of civilization, Elias explains, "expresses the self-consciousness of the West. One could even say: national consciousness. It sums up everything in which Western society of the last two or three centuries believes itself superior to earlier societies or 'more primitive' contemporary ones."[17] With Elias in mind, Étienne Balibar elaborates that "the term 'civilization' is not easily dissociated from the idea that there are barbarians and savages who have to be 'civilized' (that is to say, in practice, subjected to the worst violence)."[18] It is this "nationalized" and "imperialized" idea of civility and civilization that interests me here, specifically how they are made legible through narratives of civil war.

The chapters that follow track the shift in the idea of civil war within the West from describing an Occidental affair to an Oriental crisis from the mid-nineteenth to the late twentieth centuries.[19] Instead of an expansive account of this period—a task better left to a historian—my study examines the efflorescence of tropes, narratives, and metaphors of civil war at three salient moments in the biography of the modern nation-state.[20] Part 1, "Civility," looks at how narratives of latent civil war were essential to the ways in which early Victorians first articulated the idea of English nationality during the 1840s, not coincidentally nineteenth-century England's most tumultuous decade. Part 2, "Civilizing Mission," is a transitionary section that looks at how narratives of civil war shifted from describing a civil affair to a barbaric conflict during the British empire's most ambitious years, the dawn of New Imperialism at the turn of the century. It was during these years that civil war emerged as the alibi for international intervention and economic development, the twentieth-century equivalent of nineteenth-century civilizing missions. And finally, Part 3, "Incivility," examines the continued conjuncture of civil war and the civilizing mission in the age of decolonization, and its centrality to how writers have articulated the historicity of the postcolonial. These three themes organize the historical arc of this book and chart civil war's projection from the Occident out to the Orient. In the coda, I look at how the recent international refugee crisis has returned the threat of civil war to Europe by undermining the classical geopolitical coordinates of the West and the Middle East and North Africa. Approaching the conjuncture of civil war and imperialism in such a comparative framework helps us see how, despite representing the domestic crisis par excellence, civil war in fact allows us to think *across* national literatures, national borders, and the thresholds of historical periodization. Consistent across these geopolitical, historical, and cultural boundaries is how the idea of civil war has been complicit with and integral to nationalist discourse and its sibling projects, imperialism and decolonization.

Taken together, the assemblage of texts I examine in this book can be understood to be a counter to the social scientific epistemology of civil war I outlined earlier in the opening pages of this introduction.[21] Rather than speak of specific historical civil wars like the American Civil War or the Spanish Civil War, or pin down a concept of civil war, I am interested in civil war as a discourse of power. To borrow from Michel Foucault, "Civil war is not a sort of antithesis of power, what exists before or reappears after it. Civil war and power are not mutually exclusive. Civil war takes place on the stage of power."[22] Moreover, civil war must be seen as a "matrix within which elements of power come to function, are reactivated. . . . There is no civil war without the work of power and work on power."[23] Essential in making these matrices visible is what I call a "poetics of national rupture." This poetics takes on a variety of textual and narrative forms—figures, metaphors, tropes (and most important for this book), plot, and closure—all of which play a crucial role in making the nation legible in the age of empire, be it for the ends of consolidating political community or questioning its limits. I choose the term "poetics" because the literary discourse discussed in this book manifests across genres, including political essays, social analysis, travelogues, historiography, and novels. By attending to national rupture as a textual effect rather than a historical episode or a crisis to sovereignty, we learn that nationalism doesn't only desire or presuppose unity but often valorizes its internal antagonisms and disunity for articulating and realizing its imperial and postcolonial ambitions.

THE POETICS OF NATIONAL RUPTURE

Such a study must begin by questioning our basic assumptions about the national imagination. Over the last four decades, it has become commonplace to think of nations as products of "imaginations," "fictions," "fantasies," "narratives," "myths," "specters," and "dreams." That almost anyone trained in the humanities can recognize at least one of the above-mentioned descriptors of nationalist discourse attests to just how familiar the nation has become as a category of analysis and critique. The lexicon of illusion, conjuring, and reverie doesn't discount the nation as false or a delusion, nor does it question the authenticity of a nation's claims to unity, but calls attention to the procedures through which the nation is produced and reproduced. The means of such reproduction involve a range of apparatuses and institutions like language, literature, historiography, the press, and the school system—to name only a handful. If there is something that unifies the studies mentioned above, it is that nations exist within and function through an array of representations; nations are produced out of representations, but this production takes place within the representative domain of the nation. Balibar calls this "the self-manifestation of the national personality."[24]

Less well understood, if understood at all, is how nations dissolve. If nations are widely seen to be institutional inventions produced out of a range of discursive matrixes, then why are civil wars only ever described as discrete historical episodes? Can one imagine communal antagonisms just as one conjures national bonds? Does civil war inhabit the same historical sensibility of the nation—filling "empty homogeneous time"—or something different? If nations are indeed imagined, fictive, fantasized, and narrated, then is their dissolution in civil war equally so? One of Benedict Anderson's most persuasive claims about the "reality" and ideological force of nationalism is that over the last two centuries, nationalism has made it possible for "so many millions of people, not so much to kill, as willingly die for such limited imaginings."[25] Anderson's point is not that nations are necropolitical—a power over death—or that death proves or actualizes nationality but that the national imagination can be so powerful that millions have willingly sacrificed their own lives for individuals they have never met: their fellow-countrymen.[26] What happens to the national imagination in civil war when the "willingness *to die for*" one's countrymen is simultaneously a "willingness *to kill*" one's countrymen? If "colossal sacrifices" in war demonstrate the tenacity of imagined bonds, then does the willingness to die demonstrate the "reality" *of the absence* of fraternity in civil war? If critics have become well-versed in the poetics of nationalism, what might a poetics of national rupture look like?

Before answering these questions, it is important to recognize how historical instances of national rupture are always highly contested. Consider, for example, the "English Civil War" vs. the "English Interregnum," "American Civil War" vs. the "war of Northern aggression," the "Russian Revolution" vs. the "Russian Civil War," the "Nigerian Civil War" vs. "The Biafran War of Independence," "The Rwandan Civil War" vs. "The Rwandan Genocide," "The Sri Lankan Civil War" vs. "The Tamil Eelam Liberation Struggle," "The Syrian Civil War" vs. "Global Jihad." In each case, the name of a conflict has a transformative effect on its perceived content. Hence the plasticity of "civil war" as a term, whose meaning can encompass revolution, rebellion, insurrection, and genocide.[27] Because one citizen's civil war is another's secession, independence, colonization, liberation, or statelessness, usage of the term (one way or another) is always contested and implicitly entails what Mahmood Mamdani calls a "politics of naming."[28]

This book argues that integral to the politics of naming is a politics of narration. In a rarely discussed chapter in the revised edition of *Imagined Communities*, Anderson argues that the periodization of civil war is integral to the historical imagination of the nation. He points out the odd syntax of Ernst Renan's infamous statement that "every French citizen has to have already forgotten Saint Bartholomew, or the massacres that took place in the Midi in the thirteenth century."[29] Implicit is the citizen's obligation *to have already* forgotten ancient civil wars. National belonging is premised on a commitment to forget the falsity of the national bond in advance, to foreclose the possibility of ever remembering ancient fratricides. Such an injunction plays a pedagogical role in producing the historical consciousness of a nation in a counterintuitive way—what Anderson calls the "reassurance of fratricide."[30] The ideological function of civil war within nationalist discourse complements his original thesis that "a sociological organism moving calendrically through homogenous, empty time is a precise analogue of the idea of the nation, which also is conceived as a solid community moving steadily down (or up) history."[31] Remembering to forget a past civil war suggests an opposite movement, one in which the ancient fratricide bears upon the present, threatening to reveal the fiction of ethnic bonds, thereby halting historical movement.[32] For Anderson, to forget is to re-place the nation's internal contradictions into the distant past as something not resonant within the present or future. Civil wars are therefore always narrated as static episodes detached from the present, fixed in the past, *against which* the nation pushes off, as it were, to move forward through the empty homogeneous time of history. Anderson's implicit suggestion is that memories of forgotten fratricides energize nationalism by their episodic quality—"we fought then, our unity is now." So while civic discord might contradict the existence of an imagined community, its periodization as a bygone event renders it memorable in the service of the nation.[33] To encounter civil war as a historical episode is to encounter it as the product of nationalism. As an integral unit of the national narrative, civil war's "episodization" enables citizens to forget and defang their most divisive moments by relegating these events to the distant past.

While *Civilizing War* builds on Anderson's suggestion that civil war is part of the narrative work of nationalist discourse, it also finds that such conflicts have a life beyond the episode. Not only did nineteenth-century writers describe civil war as an ongoing, epochal, and often nonviolent process, writers in the twentieth century proliferated narratives of national rupture as a way to represent modernity in the colonial and postcolonial peripheries. Far from something to be forgotten, the writers I am interested in produce narratives of national rupture as a way to think the nation. As I discuss in Part 1 of this book, Victorians often described England's class divisions as a latent war between fellow-countrymen. Thinkers as diverse as Friedrich Engels, Thomas Carlyle, Elizabeth Gaskell, and Benjamin Disraeli drew on what Michel Foucault calls the discourse of "race war" to frame the "Condition of England" question as fundamentally about internal divisions and antagonisms. Foucault's genealogy of war, delivered as lectures at the Collège de France in 1976, argues that late eighteenth- and nineteenth-century historiography reinvented war from a violent confrontation between states to an analytic of power in its rawest form. For historians like Augustin Thierry, François Guizot, and Montlossier, histories of peoples looked more and more like histories of struggles between them. Importantly, this discourse of war depicted antagonists as bound in an epochal conflict spanning centuries, and that was so pervasive that it saturated all aspects of civil life. Moreover, it relocated war from the state to everyday power relations, making war conceivable within societies during periods of assumed peace. The historical imagination of the period thus inverted Carl von Clausewitz's famous formulation that "war is politics by other means" to "politics is war by other means."[34] Early Victorians turned to this very discourse in their treatments of the national question. As I discuss in Chapter 3, Benjamin Disraeli's Young England novel *Sybil, or, The Two Nations* depicts industrial modernity as having resurrected the Norman Conquest in the shape of a "Norman" bourgeoisie and "Saxon" proletariat. Disraeli's historical revisionism folds the tropes of the Norman Conquest into narratives of class antagonism, supplanting French conquerors and vanquished Saxons with fellow-Englishmen. This "invasion" is represented in the novel as entirely nonviolent, taking the form instead of a protracted institutional usurpation of property and civic institutions by one class over another from the sixteenth century onward. Far from a crisis, or even a bygone scandal, Disraeli narrates civil war as a protracted affair that is crucial to the national-historical imagination of his novel. Rather than an episode in the distant past of national history, Disraeli presents a latent civil war *as* England's history.

The example of *Sybil* makes two salient features of the poetics of national rupture vividly clear. The first is that the poetics of national rupture offers a lens into the relations of power both within and between nations. This is because inscribed into the modern narrative of civil war is a tension between race and class. "Few ideologies," Hannah Arendt tells us in *The Origins of Totalitarianism*, "have won enough prominence to survive the hard competitive struggle of persuasion, and only two have come out on top and essentially defeated all others: the ideology which interprets history as an economic struggle of classes, and the other that interprets history as a natural fight of races."[35] These two ideologies are always operative in the poetics of national rupture. Disraeli's novel, for example, casts the industrial proletariat as dispossessed "Saxons" and the ruling class as conquering "Normans," and in doing so makes it impossible to distinguish class struggle from race struggle. Furthermore, these class/race struggles were often complicated by the presence of colonial subjects within the metropole. Thus Disraeli and his contemporaries went to great lengths to distinguish the class war between rich and poor Englishmen from the antagonisms between the English and Irish working classes. That is to say, early Victorian narratives of national rupture, which relied on the discourse of race and class struggles, were also inflected by the imperial milieu within which they were situated. And far from a nineteenth-century phenomenon, narratives of civil war in the twentieth century continue to draw on the affinity between race and class. The Second Anglo-Boer War, for example, was in large part an effort by the British empire to solidify territorial and economic control of the Cape colony, which had recently yielded its subterranean treasures of gold and diamonds and created the need for a disenfranchised labor force. And yet, the war was celebrated by British jingoists like Arthur Conan Doyle and Rudyard Kipling as between the "blood brotherhood" of the empire, a formulation of racial filiation of Britain's settler colonies that excluded colonized subjects from the conflict.[36] More recently, narratives of master-servant relations in the context of highly racialized civil wars saturate postcolonial historical fiction about conflict in sub-Saharan Africa. V. S. Naipaul's *A Bend in the River* (1979), Nadine Gordimer's *July's People* (1981), and Adichie's *Half of a Yellow Sun*—to name just a few—thematize shifting class relations in the domestic sphere against backdrops of civic unrest in sub-Saharan Africa. The fact that today's Right in Europe and North America describes the influx of refugees as corrupting national character on the one hand and draining the state's resources in an age of austerity on the other attests to the continued affinity between race and class in contemporary conjuncture of what is sometimes referred to as a "global civil war." In all of these cases, civil war might name a crisis of national identity, but it does so by showing the forms of domination at work both inside and between political communities.

The second feature of the poetics of national rupture that *Sybil* exemplifies is how some of the very mechanisms and institutions that typically imagine communities also make their disunity conceivable and palpable. Novels, for example, have played a central role in imagining political community.[37] Importantly, the novel does not create the nation but, as Jonathan Culler reminds us, is "a formal condition of imagining the nation—a structural condition of possibility."[38] As a genre, the novel narrativizes a space and time in which seemingly detached (and I would add, even antagonistic) individuals can be thought of as belonging to the same society. To put it simply: the novel makes the nation *possible*.[39] My argument in this book is that literary texts, especially novels, also carve a space (and time) for the reader to un-imagine the bonds between fellow-countrymen in civil war. If the novel, to recall Culler, creates the condition of possibility for the nation, then I find that it also creates the condition for the nation's *impossibility*. It is this *negative* aspect of the novel's involvement in the horizon of legibility of nationhood that will mostly concern me here.

Especially adept at giving this negativity a narrative form is the historical novel. It is no coincidence that all the novels I discuss in this book fall within this genre. Even the nonfictional works I discuss, such as Engels's *The Conditions of the Working Class in England* (1844), Carlyle's *Chartism* (1839) and *Past and Present* (1842), and J. R. Seeley's *The Expansion of England* (1883), are committed to understanding the present through its prehistory—which according to György Lukács is essential to the historical novel's temporal sensibility. In his account, the historical novel, a child of the French Revolution, "made history a mass experience" by linking history to the "inner life of the nation."[40] The emergence of a new national sensibility at the end of the eighteenth century made it possible for "men to comprehend their own existence as something historically conditioned, for them to see in history something which deeply affects their daily lives and immediately concerns them."[41] The genre played an important part in Europe's emergent civil societies because in addition to historical man it sought to make historical communities legible to its readers. If the novel makes social relations legible, the historical novel makes society legible as a product of history.

Why and how can this genre, widely understood to have been integral to the birth of national feeling in the late eighteenth and early nineteenth centuries, narrate *the opposite* of political community: civil antagonism? How can one of the foundational institutions of nationalism even represent, let alone narrate, civil war? As the case of *Sybil* suggests, Disraeli follows the very same protocols of nationalist historiography, only supplants a narrative of fraternity with that of an extended fratricide. The common history of Englishmen, we learn, is not energized by racial or ethnic filiation but domestic conquest, intranational strife, and civil war that persist over centuries. If, as Balibar argues, race is the "symbolic kernel" of national identity and history, then Disraeli's novel teaches us that *race war* can function as this core.[42] That is to say, fraternity is always already inscribed into a novelistic history of fratricide.

But if in Disraeli's time civil war was the motor of history, then what does the historical novel look like in the twentieth century, when civil war is said to *reverse* development? How does a historical novel narrate the prehistory of the present if historical development is stagnant or regressive? Parts 2 and 3 of this book consider these questions in the colonial and postcolonial contexts of the twentieth century. Jed Esty's important intervention in *Unseasonable Youth* shows how the genre of the bildungsroman, especially in its encounter with modernism, allegorized uneven development in a globalized world.[43] In the contexts I examine in this book, arrested development and endless youth look more like what the World Bank calls the "conflict trap": the historical paralysis caused by the persistence of civil war in the colonial and postcolonial world. Integral to this sensibility is literary modernism, which having been shaped by the asymmetries of colonial modernity sought to recast the historical novel's emplotment toward an accomplished future. In novels like William Henry Hudson's *The Purple Land* (1885) and Joseph Conrad's *Nostromo* (1904), Latin American countries are bewitched by cycles of civil war and dictatorships. And toward the end of the twentieth century, writers like V. S. Naipaul, Nadine Gordimer, and Michael Ondaatje produced historical fictions in which African and Asian postcolonies are similarly paralyzed by the persistence of brutal regimes and civic conflict. What interests me is how these writers formalize the conflict trap into a kind of narrative trap, producing historical novels that stall the *telos* of historical transition. By formalizing the conflict trap via narratives of impasse, their poetics of national rupture tell tales of endless transition. So rather than stories of "unseasonable youth," as Esty calls them in reference to the bildungsroman, I read narratives of "development in reverse."

My point throughout this book is that the poetics of national rupture offers an unintuitive lens into nationalist discourse in the age of empire. In an account of empire that has become routine, the nation emerges out of a will-to-difference with an outside (colonies for the metropole, metropole for the colonies). And in this account, the nation reproduces itself as a singular, unified political community by endlessly differentiating itself from the extranational, what Anderson calls "official nationalism."[44] This book illustrates how nationalism's will-to-difference also draws its ideological energy by articulating and often valorizing the nation's internal contradictions. With this in mind, it becomes possible to revisit nationalism as a discourse whose "self-manifestation," to recall Balibar once more, occurs not only through its self-perpetuation but also through its *self-division*. The premise of this study is that we must confront the fact that imagining community has been coextensive to un-imagining it. To read against the grain of nationalist discourse in this manner reveals how the most *intra*national of all conflicts, civil war, is in fact entirely woven into the *extra*national politics of imperialism and decolonization.

how

STATES OF UNEXCEPTION

By locating my study within the domain of national culture, my account of civil war is markedly different from that of the Hobbesian tradition in political theory, which in recent years has gained significant currency in the American academy by way of Giorgio Agamben. While Agamben's work is most commonly associated with studies of sovereignty, what is all too often ignored is the centrality of civil war in his political philosophy. In *State of Exception* he calls civil war "the opposite of normal conditions" because "it lies in the zone of undecidability with respect to the state of exception, which is the state power's immediate response to the most extreme internal conflicts."[45] Such formulations illustrate Agamben's debt to Thomas Hobbes and Carl Schmitt, both of whom oppose civil war to conditions of peace and security. For example, one of the sole tasks of Hobbes's Leviathan, a "Mortal God," is to prevent civil war: "It belongeth therefore to him that hath the Soveraign Power, to be Judge, or constitute all Judges of Opinions and Doctrines, as a thing necessary to Peace, thereby to prevent Discord and Civill Warre."[46] Carl Schmitt inherits Hobbes's opposition between sovereignty and civil war, while also adapting it for the modern state. Civil war, Schmitt argues, is a "self-laceration" of the state because it triggers the "dissolution of the state as an organized political entity, internally peaceful, territorial enclosed, and impenetrable to aliens."[47] Civil war undermines Schmitt's entire concept of the political, which is premised on the state's ability to differentiate between friend and enemy.

Elsewhere, however, Agamben questions the opposition between civil war and sovereignty. When discussing the aporetic concept of the "people" in Western political thought, he in fact departs from Schmitt: "the people always contains a division more originary than that of friend-enemy, an incessant civil war that divides it more radically than every conflict and, at the same time, keeps it united and constitutes it more securely than any identity."[48] For Agamben, the "secure unity" of the identity in question is between two vertically oriented strata, the state and civilians, sovereigns and subjects: "It is as if what we call 'people' were in reality not a unitary subject but a dialectical oscillation between two opposites poles: on the one hand, the set of the People as a whole political body, and on the other, the subset of the people as a fragmentary multiplicity of needy and excluded bodies . . . at one extreme, the total state of integrated and sovereign citizens, and at the other, the preserve . . . of the wretched, the oppressed, and the defeated."[49] The antagonism between the "People" and the "wretched" is, according to Agamben, more primordial than Schmitt's famous opposition between friend and enemy. Still another understanding of civil war in Agamben's political philosophy can be found in his recently published lectures on the Greek notion of *stasis*—classical Greece's word for civic discord—which he explains "constitutes a zone of indifference between the unpolitical space of the family and the political space of the city. . . . *This means that in the system of Greek politics civil war functions as a threshold of politicisation and depoliticisation, through which the house is exceeded in the city and the city is depoliticised in the family.*"[50] While much could be said about each of these accounts of civil war, what I want to note is how this entire Hobbesian tradition sees civil war as relating to questions of sovereignty and the state.

My study is concerned with a very different conception of internal conflict. Rather than a state of emergency, the suspension of law, or a citizenry's declaration of war against "the wretched," the writers I examine locate civil war within the domain of national culture, that is to say, within civil society. To put it differently, I study what civil war means after, as Foucault once put it, the head of the king has been cut off.[51] Consequently, in my study civil war is not an exceptional moment at all but entirely imbedded within the everyday life of the nation. This book's first task is to reorient the Hobbesian tradition of thinking about civil war away from the state toward political community. I do so by reconciling Foucault's genealogy of race war in *"Society Must Be Defended"* with theories of nationalism—Anderson's and Balibar's in particular. This constellation helps me recast the Victorian decades, often referred to as the "age of equipoise" when English nationhood first crystalized, as a period preoccupied with national rupture. Part 1 of this book looks at how Victorians turned to war as a field of intelligibility into everyday life. Rather than imagining itself as a singular people, England's national unity was often articulated through its internal antagonisms. I illustrate this paradoxical logic of the nation in

Chapters 1, 2, and 3 by looking at a range of texts in different genres, paying close attention to the early writings of Marx and Engels, in particular the latter's study of England's industrial cities in *The Conditions of the Working Class in England*, Thomas Carlyle's writings on the condition of England question in *Chartism* and *Past and Present*, and Benjamin Disraeli's *Sybil, or, The Two Nations*. Rather than a historical episode, early Victorians described a latent war to saturate all aspects of English civic life. This war, importantly, had been ushered in by the advent of capital, which Victorians consistently describe as the motor of their own history. In stark contrast to development in reverse, the "civil wars" that preoccupied the Victorian national imagination were narrated as development as such. And so rather than states of exception, this early Victorian poetics of national rupture describes neither a void of sovereign power nor the conflation of politics with non-politics but rather the quotidian aspects of modern life and nationhood. Engels, for example, sees war in the organization of neighborhoods, in the sanitary conditions of laboring districts, and even in the postures of the homeless. Carlyle claims that capitalist money-relations are akin to the original fratricide: Cain's murder of Abel. And Disraeli sees a latent civil war to have undergirded English social relations since Henry VIII's reign. If civil war is the condition of possibility for the state of exception, then I find Victorian narratives of national rupture to be entirely *unexceptional*. Approaching British nationalist thought in this manner revises a truism within literary criticism and historiography that the early Victorian years saw, as Mary Poovey has put it, the "making of a social body" and, as Linda Colley has argued in *Britons*, the crystallization of British nationality.[52] In contrast, I argue that at the very moment it became possible to speak of a British nation, it became both possible and necessary to tell stories of its internal wars.

Part 2 is a transitionary section that looks at how narratives of national rupture are projected outward to the colonies at the turn of the century. In its journey from the center to the periphery, the poetics of national rupture increasingly describes a crisis of modernization rather than the motor of industrial modernity. That is to say, civil war transforms into something "uncivilized" and the occasion for the civilizing mission. Chapter 4 tracks what happens to narratives of civil war during the British empire's most ambitious years, when it saw Britain and its settler colonies as belonging to a global nation-state, most commonly referred to as "Greater Britain." The apex of this national-imperial imagination came with the outbreak of the Second Anglo-Boer

War, which jingoists like Arthur Conan Doyle and Rudyard Kipling celebrated as a civil war because South Africa and Britain were said to belong to the same imperial nation-state. Hence the characterization of the Boer War as "the last of the gentleman's wars" or a "sahibs' war," because it was said to be fought between the civilized fellow-citizens of "Greater Britain." But Kipling, especially in his short story "A Sahibs' War" (1902), also had to confront the fact that British and Boer tactics were decidedly "ungentlemanly" at the war front, and so conflated the South African conflict with anticolonial uprisings in Afghanistan and Burma, which in his mind were barbaric frontier conflicts. This historical conjuncture makes visible, on the one hand, how civil war was the zenith of Britain's expansion around the world and, on the other hand, how this highest stage of civilization looked uncannily like the barbarism of the colonies.

While for early Victorians capitalism poised fellow-Englishmen in fratricidal antagonism, capitalism is figured as the solution to fratricide in the twentieth century. Chapter 5 examines how the civilizing mission was discussed in political treatises by J. A. Hobson and Lord Cromer as well as the fiction of William Henry Hudson, but focuses in particular on Joseph Conrad's historical novel *Nostromo*, where civil war is described as a distinctly non-Western phenomenon and symptomatic of a lack of development. Far from civil, gentlemanly, and something to be feared in England, civic discord is egoistic, moblike, vengeful, barbaric, and unique to the non-West. And built into Conrad's novel is the solution to such uncivil civil wars: economic development, the seed of which can only ever come from the West. Incapable of truly saving itself, the fictional South American country of Costaguana must be saved by a class of foreign investors, industrialists, and statesmen. By detaching the civilizing mission from the official British empire, Conrad actually extends the *imperium*'s reach to anywhere in the world.

Part 3 argues that the postcolonial historical novel has both anticipated and displaced the contemporary truism that civil war hinders progress. Rather than describe the past as the prehistory of the present (as Lukács's account of the genre stipulates), postcolonial historical fiction emplots the historically regressive effects of civil war—what the World Bank calls "development in reverse." Chapter 6 discusses a range of postcolonial historical fiction but focuses on V. S. Naipaul's *A Bend in the River*. Naipaul's emplotment of "development in reverse," I argue, doesn't justify international intervention but instead highlights the colonial origins of Western benevolence and how in its efforts to stop civil war in the Global South, development projects in fact fore-close the very future they promise. My final chapter looks at a late colonial manifestation of the poetics of national rupture in apartheid South Africa. Civil war is the backdrop to a number of late apartheid novels, such as Gordimer's *July's People*, J. M. Coetzee's *The Life and Times of Michael K* (1983), and André Brink's *States of Emergency* (1988), all of which situate their narratives in the midst of revolutionary historical transition out of apartheid. The turn to civil war as a narrative category, I argue, allowed white South African novelists who were writing against apartheid to narrate historical transitions to the postcolonial while at the same time disavow prescribing the trajectory of such a transition. Gordimer's novel explicitly calls this impasse an "interregnum"—a concept she borrows from Antonio Gramsci's prison writings. More than the thematic content of the novel, *July's People* formalizes the temporality of the interregnum in its plot, producing a narrative structure that cannot arrive at its destination. Gordimer's turn to the interregnum, a species of civil war, as a narrative category shows how postcolonial nationhood must not be understood as a departure from colonial rule but as a period of suspended transit—what I call a "postcolonial interregnum."

Having been projected out to the colonies by the advent of capitalist modernity, civil war seems today to have returned to the "birthplace" of the modern civilization, of the citizen, of modern civil war. If nineteenth-century Europe was the origin of civility and civil war, and the Global South its recipient in the twentieth century, then contemporary civil war discourse is questioning these boundaries and their meanings in an unprecedented way. In the coda to this book, I discuss the current refugee crisis in Europe and the United States and the rhetoric of civil war and civility that surrounds it. My hope is that the chapters that follow situate this current conjuncture of civil war in the long, braided history of civil war and the civilizing mission.

PART I

Civility

A binary structure runs through society.

—FOUCAULT, "Society Must Be Defended"

No theorist transformed our understanding of nineteenth-century Britain more than Michel Foucault. The foundational texts of British literary criticism, Edward Said's *Orientalism* and *Culture and Imperialism*, D. A. Miller's *The Novel and the Police*, Catherine Gallagher's *The Industrial Reformation of English Fiction*, and Nancy Armstrong's *Desire and Domestic Fiction* (to name just a few), have all brought questions Foucault posed about the emergence of civil society in the Enlightenment to the realm of nineteenth-century British literary studies. Among Foucault's numerous studies into epistemology, medicine, and psychiatry, *Discipline and Punish* and *The History of Sexuality, Volume 1* have been especially important and influential to the abovementioned critics.[1] Far less influential have been the lectures Foucault delivered at the Collège de France between the publication of *Discipline* and *The History* in 1976, titled *"Society Must Be Defended."*[2] The lectures differ from the two published books in that their focus is not on the world of right and discipline but the discourse of conflict. Rather than scientific knowledge, Foucault looked to historical knowledge. Rather than the prison, the nation. Rather than the body, the body politic. Rather than power, war.

Foucault's lectures track how historians, sociologists, and jurists in the eighteenth and nineteenth centuries reinvented the concept of war as a lens for sociological analysis and understanding national history. A common misunderstanding of Foucault's argument is that his

21

lectures concern actual warfare and approach war as a historical event. In fact, he is far more interested in thinking about *how* the Enlightenment invented war *as* historical truth. That is to say, how war was a form of historico-political knowledge, not an act of violence. This knowledge, Foucault explains, afforded a "field of visibility" that illuminated power in its rawest form. Such "wars" were not singular historical events but were depicted as saturating national history and civic life. At the broadest level, the lectures could be understood to be about the invention of the Hegelian dialectic and its centrality in shaping modern civil society. Importantly, Foucault in no way sees Hegel or the Hegelian dialectic to have invented the idea of social warfare. Rather, he sees the dialectic as a philosophical appropriation of much older discourse of "race war," which must "be understood as philosophy and right's colonization and authoritarian colonization of a historico-political discourse that was both a statement of fact, a proclamation, and a practice of social warfare."[3] Foucault argues that the "dialectic is born" the day royal power was challenged by aristocratic and middle classes.[4] "Basically," he explains, "the dialectic codifies struggle, war, and confrontation into a logic, or so-called logic, of contradiction; it turns them into the twofold process of the totalization and revelation of a rationality that is at once final but also basic, and in any case irreversible."[5] This bellicose vision of the world was dualistic through and through, and constitutive of a distinctly Enlightenment worldview: "The great pyramidal description that the Middle Ages or politico-philosophical theories gave of the social body, the great image of the organism or the human body painted by Hobbes . . . is being challenged by a binary conception of society."[6] Rather than a homogeneous whole, the national imagination of Europe's emergent civil societies saw themselves as a split society—Franks and Gauls, Normans and Saxons, bourgeois and proletariat. The stuff of history "was no longer the discourse of sovereignty, or even race, but a discourse about races, about a confrontation between races, about the race struggle that goes on within nations and within laws."[7] It is important to clarify that "race" in "race war" refers to the most general anthropological sense of "group," "camp," or "people," not in the biological sense that it came to have in the later nineteenth century.[8] Instead of producing the biography of a single people, Foucault argues that historians like Augustin Thierry, Francois Guizot, and Comte de Boulainvilliers narrated how intranational divisions were animated by mutual antagonism: the races "form a unity and a single polity only as a result of wars, invasions, victories, and defeats, or in other words, acts of violence. The only link between them is the link established by the violence of war. And finally, one can say that two races exist when there are two groups which, although they coexist, have not become mixed because of the differences, dissymmetries, and barriers created by privileges, customs, and rights, the distribution of wealth, or the way in which power is exercised."[9] War thus emerges not as an event but as an entire field of analysis, whose object of interpretation was the modern nation-state rooted in internal dualisms, inequality, asymmetries of power, and conflict.

Foucault's genealogy of war and nationalism has had little traction in nineteenth-century British literary and cultural studies, which have instead focused almost exclusively on his final lecture on the invention of biopolitics.[10] This seems to be a significant oversight because Foucault's lectures have much more to say about the concept of war than forms of biological governance (though the two are, of course, genealogically related).[11] Why have these interstitial lectures on war and nationhood, nestled perfectly between the publication of *Discipline and Punish* and *The History of Sexuality*, proven so unproductive to scholars of nineteenth-century Britain? Theorizing war was obviously important for helping Foucault think through the transition from the tactics of policing and discipline to the regulation of biological life. So why has the category of war not resonated with scholarship on nineteenth-century Britain?[12] If war, as Foucault argues, was understood to be the condition of Europe's emergent civil societies, then where might we find such tumult in Victorian England, a period often referred to as "the age of equipoise"?[13]

The "two nations" trope, of course, was widespread in Victorian treatments of the "Condition of England" question.[14] In *Oliver Twist* (1837), Fagin's little community of thieves stands in sharp contrast to Brownlow's benevolence, while Nancy's proletarian desperation is contrasted to Rose's bourgeois empathy. In a review of Henry Mayhew's *London Labour and the London Poor* (1851), the *Christian Observer* referred to the poor as "this nation within a nation—living among us, trading with us, amenable to the same laws, but not speaking the same language, nor using the same amusements; influenced by no religion, holding a conventional code of morality, and bound up in the prejudices of a mode of life of which they acknowledge the miseries, but from the magic circle of which they are unable and unwilling to escape."[15] Mayhew himself characterized this class as a "parasitic" race that fed off the propertied classes. As Mayhew's example suggests, class difference was often described in the language of "races" and "nations," and even invoked colonial difference. Thus in Dickens's *Sketches by Boz* (1836), Boz "meditates" on a slum, Monmouth Street, and describes its inhabitants as "a distinct class; a peaceable and retiring race . . . who seldom come forth into the world, . . . a happy troop of infantile scavengers."[16] While these texts span a range of genres and concerns, they, and numerous others, share a thesis about England's intranational bifurcation.

Reviving Foucault's orphaned genealogy of war in the context of nineteenth-century British culture opens up a constellation of writers across the political spectrum who saw England as a fractured society whose internal divisions were antagonistic. Radicals like Friedrich Engels, liberals like Elizabeth Gaskell, conservative Tories like Benjamin Disraeli, and even those who were all three of these—namely, Thomas Carlyle—saw England to be saturated in conflict. These writers extend the "two nation" thesis to one about civil war, for they see these "nations" to be intertwined in a latent conflict. Engels, for example, claims that "the working class has gradually become a race wholly apart from the English bourgeoisie."[17] But he also notes that both of these "races" were intertwined in a "social war" that raged beneath the surface of society.[18] Reflecting on the same problem of wage labor, Carlyle describes the class war between the between factory owner and his worker as akin to Cain's murder of his kin Abel. In a different key but to a similar end, Disraeli's second Young England novel *Sybil, or, The Two Nations* understands this class war as akin to primordial events in English history like the Norman Conquest and Henry VIII's campaign against the monasteries. While the title of Elizabeth Gaskell's *North and South* suggests that England is geographically and ethnographically divided into a pastoral South and industrial North, the true division at the heart of the novel is the "battle" between factory owners and their workers.[19] In all of these cases, writers were not describing an actual state of war but turning to war as a figure to describe English society in times of assumed peace. So while *Oliver Twist*'s Rose and Nancy are separated by the Thames, they are never antagonistically poised as Engels suggests London's rich and poor are. Or when Mayhew describes the "wandering tribes" of the poor who feed off the rich, these tribes have not "conquered" and "plundered" each other for centuries as they have in Disraeli's *Sybil*. War, this discourse claims, is the permanent social relation of England.

This constellation of texts, illuminated by Foucault's lectures on war and society, recasts the early Victorian period as not merely preoccupied with, as Mary Poovey has famously put it, "making a social body" but interested in thinking about how social bodies are divided, rent apart in two, and un-made in civil war. Literary critics and historians alike have understood the early nineteenth century as the moment when representations of English society as a "single mass culture" first crystallized. Benedict Anderson's thesis about nationalism, widely accepted within the fields and disciplines of literary criticism, anthropology, and history, rests on the idea that of the many institutions upon which the nation rests, two of the most important are the newspaper and the novel. Franco Moretti pinpoints Jane Austen's novels, and specifically their narrativization of the marriage market, as an important mechanism by which England's and Britain's national imagination was first made legible.[20] In the Foucauldian tradition of D. A. Miller, Catherine Gallagher, and those who have followed, techniques of discipline and regulation are seen to have created a social body that was, above all else, governable because the field of governance had shifted from the state to civil society. Mary Poovey claims that "material innovations like affordable transportation, cheap publications, and national museums, these technologies of representation simultaneously brought groups that had rarely mixed into physical proximity with each other and represented them as belonging to the same, increasingly undifferentiated whole."[21] In a different methodological key but with similar historical coordinates, Linda Colley's *Britons* argues that British national identity was an outgrowth of centuries of war with France, which culminated in a cohesive idea of British nationality around the ascension of Queen Victoria.[22]

The early Victorian discourse of race war calls the "solidity" of England's imagined community into question. This discourse (which manifests in a range of genres beyond the confines of the newspaper and realist novel, including political essays, social analysis, and ethnographic studies) operates under the same temporal-historical framework as the imagined community, but its ideological effect is a divided community. That is to say, the discourse of race war follows the very same protocols of national-historical time, only to create the condition of possibility of an antagonistically split society. The cumulative effect is not the dissolution of community as such but the institution of a community united by a paradoxical "bond of division." Not only do Victorians like Engels, Gaskell, and Disraeli find England in a state of antagonistic disunity, but the "war" they see everywhere is civil in all senses of the term: it is entirely nonviolent, it is between fellow-Englishmen, and it is the tragic consequence of capitalist modernity. What is hard to conceptualize, and which is the focus of the following three chapters, is how disunity can be conceived as a form of unity. The dualisms early Victorians see as running through English society are the very divisions that, paradoxically, hold England together. My point here is not to refute the claim that English nationhood, with all its disciplinary mechanisms, did not emerge as the privileged form of affiliation and governance. Rather, I want to argue that it is no coincidence that at the moment it became possible to speak of an English nation, it became conceivable and productive to speak of its fractures, divisions, and internal wars.

CHAPTER I

A Glimpse of Social War

"The flaneur still stands on the threshold—of the metropolis as of the middle-class. Neither has him in its power yet. In neither is he at home. He seeks refuge in the crowd."[1] This is Walter Benjamin's praise for Charles Baudelaire's Paris. But it is also, albeit to a lesser degree, directed toward Friedrich Engels, whom Benjamin saw as a proto-flaneur. The text Benjamin has in mind, of course, is Engels's first book, *The Conditions of the Working Class in England*, whose city is not Paris but England's "great towns": London and Manchester. A mixture of sociology, travelogue, city guide, and polemic on the disastrous effects of industrial capitalism on the metropolis and its inhabitants, *The Conditions* is best known as a text about the industrial city. As Ira Katznelson puts it, Engels's book "introduced urban space . . . into the core of Marx's macroscopic historical materialism and into Marx's account of the logic of capitalist accumulation by utilizing the organization and reorganization of the urban built-form to show how city space defines a dynamic, changing terrain: the city appears at once in his work as absolute space . . . , as relative space . . . , and as relational space."[2] The reason *The Conditions* has been so influential for Marxist thought is because rather than mere descriptions of London and Manchester, it offers what Henri Lefebvre calls a "spatial architectonics" of the industrial city. Lefebvre explains that spaces "are products of an activity which involves the economic and technical realms but which extends well beyond them, for these are also political products, and strategic spaces."[3] "Social space" is "polyvalent" because while it is "a *product* to be used, to be consumed, it is also a *means of production*; networks of exchange and flows of raw materials and energy fashion space and are determined by it."[4] In a similar vein, Engels's text provides an analytic for studying how capitalist forms of production shape and organize everyday life in the industrial metropolis, but also how the city becomes a site for contesting that very order.

Engels's first impression of London is from the Thames. Staggered by the sheer number and velocity of trading vessels in the river, he calls London the "commercial capital of the world" whose "colossal centralization, this heaping together of two and a half millions of human beings at one point has multiplied the power of this two and a half millions a hundredfold."[5] England's imperial might is unmistakable when viewed from the Thames, which is surrounded by "masses of buildings, the wharves on both sides . . . the countless ships along both shores, crowding ever closer and closer together, until, at last, only a narrow passage remains in the middle of the river, a passage through which hundreds of steamers shoot by one another" (36). So imposing is this vista that Engels admits to being "lost in the marvel of England's greatness before he sets foot upon English soil" (ibid.). Once firmly planted on London's soil, however, Engels realizes that the zenith of capitalist modernity goes hand in hand with barbaric conflict. He describes his first moments in London as stepping into a Hobbesian "war of each against all," where "people regard each other only as useful objects; each exploits the other, and the end of it all is, that the stronger treads the weaker under foot, and that the powerful few, the capitalists, seize everything for themselves, while to the weak many, the poor, scarcely a bare existence remains" (37). Despite "the colossal centralization" and modernization of England's industrial cities, its populace is reduced to a primitive state of nature: "What is true of London, is true of Manchester, Birmingham, Leeds, is true of all great towns. Everywhere barbarous indifference, hard egotism on one hand, and nameless misery on the other, everywhere social warfare, every man's house in a state of siege, everywhere reciprocal plundering under the protection of the law and all so shameless, so openly avowed that one shrinks before the consequences of our social state as they manifest themselves here undisguised, and can only wonder that the whole crazy fabric still hangs together" (ibid.). A barbaric war, Engels suggests, lies beneath the surface of modern civilization.

The conjuncture of industrialism and barbarism was a common trope in writings on the transformations brought on by capitalism. In his travels through England some years earlier, Alexis de Tocqueville stated that in Manchester "humanity attains its most complete development and its most brutish; here civilisation works its miracles, and civilised man is turned back almost into a savage."[6] And Henry Mayhew's famous ethnography of the working poor opens by describing the working classes as a "wandering tribe" that feeds off the rich. Basing his claim on ethnologic studies of Southern Africa, Mayhew explains that "we, like the Kafirs, Fellahs, and Finns, are surrounded by wandering hordes—the 'Sonquas' and the 'Fingoes' of this country—paupers, beggars, and outcasts, possessing nothing but what they acquire by depredation from the industries, provident, and civilized portion of the community."[7] Engels differs in that he sees a nonviolent war to be at the heart of this slippage from modernity to barbarity. Such "peaceful" war involves no swords or cannons, entails no bloodshed, and is fought between civilians rather than armies.[8] This conflict is conducted "under the protection of the law," meaning the state is not the agent of warfare but its sanction. And rather than typical instruments of warfare, capital "is the weapon with which this social warfare is carried on" (37–38). As peaceful as the industrial city might seem, as civil as it might appear, Engels sees war everywhere. Seemingly banal activities in the modern city like begging and police harassment take on a bellicose hue: "armies of workers" and "armies of beggars" crowd the streets, against whom "the police carry on perpetual war" (96, 98). Civil society, by his account, is the other means of war. Paradoxically, the "openness" of this war conceals its actual bellicosity, for the conflict manifests latently in the very gestures of the unemployed masses: "The starving workmen, whose mills were idle, whose employers could give them no work, stood in the streets in all directions, begged singly or in crowds, *besieged* the sidewalks in *armies*, and appealed to the passers-by for help; they begged, not cringing like ordinary beggars, but threatening by their numbers, their gestures, and their words" (100; emphasis added). The untrained eye might see beggary, but Engels perceives an "army" laying siege. Similarly, acts of petty resistance look like organized conquest: "And he among the 'surplus' who has courage and passion enough openly to resist society, to reply with declared war upon the bourgeoisie to the disguised war which the bourgeoisie wages upon him, goes forth to rob, plunder, murder, and burn!" (98). Instead of an incursion by a foreign army, the "conquest" that saturates the city is between fellow-countrymen.[9] Even actual instances of resistance like strikes "are the military school of the working men in which they prepare themselves for the great struggle which cannot be avoided" (232). Everyday life is but a preparation for all-out war.

If, as Katznelson argues, Engels inscribed the city into the core of Marxism, he did so by making war integral to his urban optic. War, of course, has always been an important analytic in the history of Marxist thought. The "social war" (*soziale Krieg*) described in *The Conditions* is an early iteration of concepts like "class struggle" (*Klassenkampf*) and "civil war" (*bürgerkrieg*) that entered Engels's and Marx's vocabulary later in the 1840s, all three of which are used interchangeably in the early writings. These early formulations of war don't describe a violent confrontation between two groups as much as a relation of force that is nonviolent and encodes itself into everyday life. Rather than view war as a singular and nameable historical event, early Marxist conceptions of war see it as a protracted process that gives shape to modern forms of sociality.[10] Importantly, the idea of a latent war was not invented by Marx and Engels. As Balibar explains, "While Marxism could not invent a concept of war, it could re-create it, so to speak—that is, introduce the question of war into its own problematic."[11] This is why Marx and Engels's analysis of class struggle is heavily indebted to the discourse of race war that was invented by the waning French nobility of the late eighteenth and nineteenth centuries. In his study of the historical imagination of nineteenth-century Europe, Lukács explains that "the working-class movement does not develop in a vacuum, but surrounded by all the ideologies of decline of bourgeois decadence," meaning histories by figures like Augustin Thierry were deeply influential to the formulation of the class struggle: "The counterposing of the Saxons and Normans in England and of the Franks and Gauls in France forms no more than a transition to the analysis of the class struggles between the rising 'third estate' and the nobility in the history of the Middle Ages and modern times. Thierry did not succeed in unravelling the complicated tangle of national and class antagonisms during the rise of the modern nations, but his theory of the struggles of races was the first step towards a coherent and scientific history of progress."[12] So direct was this influence that in a letter to Engels in 1854, Marx refers to Thierry as "*le père* of the 'class struggle.'"[13]

The reason race war discourse was so useful for an analysis of class was because the former was at its core an analytic of power. One of Foucault's most suggestive claims in "*Society Must Be Defended*" is that the discourse of race war inverted Carl von Clausewitz's famous statement that "war is a continuation of politics by other means" into "politics is the continuation of war by other means."[14] Clausewitz's insight was to revise the classical distinction between war and political peace by suggesting that the ends of politics can be pursued through war when peace is no longer an option. Because of his complete faith in the rationality of the state to utilize violence for political ends, Clausewitz conceives of war as an alternative to political peace, not its antithesis; the form changes, but the content remains the same.[15] However, race war, as conceived by conservative historians like Guizot and Thierry and later by their radical counterparts like Marx and Engels, had no need to be violent because it saturated and energized everyday life in times of assumed peace.[16] In race war discourse, war doesn't look like war at all but is instead a relation of force that suffuses society in peaceful conditions: "War is the motor behind institutions and order. In the smallest of its cogs, peace is waging a secret war. . . . We have to interpret the war that is going on beneath peace; peace itself is a coded war. . . . A battlefront runs through the whole society, continuously and permanently."[17] To perceive war is to engage in a kind of symptomatic reading, to look beneath the surface of civil society, and lay bare its true conditions of tumult. That is to say, war emerged as a field of intelligibility that decoded the hidden political content of social relations in everyday life.[18]

The polemical content of race wars was to render visible that which was hidden in plain sight. In this mode of critique, "*Politics* in the essential sense would precisely concern the transition from one phase to the other, the *becoming visible* of the latent struggle (therefore also its becoming conscious, organized)—perhaps also the reverse."[19] Thus in the *Manifesto* class struggle is a "more or less veiled civil war," in which "oppressor and oppressed, stood in constant opposition to one another, carried on an uninterrupted, now hidden, now open fight."[20] When Marx and Engels witnessed actual revolutions and counterrevolutions, specifically those of 1848, these events shaped their understanding that class struggle was not necessarily an unhindered historical force. Balibar notes how the People's Spring displayed "actual civil wars" rather than social wars, "in which the proletariat was not only defeated, but experienced the inadequacies of the relationship between crises and class politics: the polarization worked in the opposite direction of communism. It also experienced the insufficiency of its understanding of state power and the state apparatus."[21] Indeed, in their reflections on actual violent instances of war, such as the Indian Mutiny or the American Civil War, "war" emerged as an analytic for thinking historical transition and its limits. Marx argued that the latter was a world-historical event: "The struggle has broken out because the two systems can no longer live peacefully side by side on the North American continent. It can only be ended by the victory of one system or the other."[22] In Marx's eyes, the conflict initiated a historical transition between the two economic systems of slavery and capitalism. While certainly diminished, the analytical language of civil war remains active within Marx's thought as late as *Capital* (1867), where in a famous passage he discusses the struggle for the working day as "a more or less concealed civil war between the capitalist and the working class."[23]

The question concerning the role of the state in class struggle became one of Marxism's central debates at the turn of the century, most notably between Eduard Bernstein and Georges Sorel. Bernstein's *The Preconditions of Socialism* (1899) interpreted Engels's introduction to the 1895 edition of Marx's *The Class Struggles in France* (1850) as proving that the need for violent class war had passed, and advocated instead for the Left's engagement with the state through political representation.[24] In contrast, Sorel's *Reflections on Violence* (1908) takes direct aim at Bernstein and argues for the importance of violence in the furthering of class struggle, specifically through the mass strike.[25] A decade later, Rosa Luxemburg reread the general strike as a product of historically determined and identifiable forces. Her essay "The Mass Strike" (1906) characterizes seemingly isolated acts of violence, strikes, and sabotage in the lead-up to the Russian Revolution as episodes within a much longer, linear historical narrative of class struggle.[26] The meaning of such acts of violence and resistance, she argues, is only legible when situated within the longer historical arc of class warfare. When the Russian Revolution finally erupted, V. I. Lenin embraced the category of "civil war" for the proletarian struggle, claiming it to be class war at its most developed stage.[27] Some years later, Walter Benjamin's enigmatic essay "Critique of Violence" (1921) returned to the early Marxian analysis of politics as the continuation of violence to show how (almost) all violence is committed to either preserving the law or creating new laws, and therefore a means to the end of peace.[28] Conversely, all conditions of peace, Benjamin argues, point to the prevalence of legal violence by other means. And some of Gramsci's most rewarding contributions to Marxism (and arguably also postcolonial historiography) can be found in his distinction between the "war of maneuver" and "war of position," wherein the former describes open class conflict, and the latter is a latent struggle often taking place within institutions.[29] In a very different key, Mao Zedong adapted the idea of the class struggle to describe a "protracted war of partisans" in *On Protracted War* (1967), a text Carl Schmitt identifies as first introducing the idea of a "global civil war."[30] At the dawn of Algeria's independence from French rule, Frantz Fanon returned again to the original Marxist notion of war as a relation of force in his studies of colonial domination in *Black Skin White Masks* (1952) and *The Wretched of the Earth* (1961). Most recently, Balibar's writings on the refugee crisis and terrorist attacks in Paris argue that the world, especially Europe, is engulfed in an "international civil war" whose front lines are not conflicts in the Middle East but the borders (economic as well as territorial) between Western nation-states and the non-West.[31] In all these cases, the category of war functions as a field in intelligibility into social and political life. As Balibar explains, "The concepts of *class struggle* and *revolution* are *not* political; they anticipate the 'end of the political state,' or they suppress the *autonomy* of the political sphere. Conversely, at the end, the combination of 'war' and 'revolution' as realizations of, and obstacles to, the class struggle appear to be profoundly *unpolitical*."[32] Because of Marxism's understanding of war as a force of history, and the class struggle's inevitable *telos* toward revolution, Marxism's concept of war contains within it the seeds for an end to (Marxism's idea of) politics as such. This is what Balibar refers to as the "deconstructive effect" of the concept of war on the idea of politics within Marxism.[33]

SPATIAL STORIES OF WAR

Engels's *The Conditions* is an inaugural moment in this morphology of class war. If for Marxism war is a lens into the modern condition, then for Engels war and the industrial city are dialectically related. Inhabiting the modern city makes visible the war that saturates it, which in turn helps Engels understand a city that is otherwise entirely confounding to him. His framing of the social war as an object of interpretation is linked to how the modern metropolis, especially the industrial city, is itself something to be "read." As Alan Robinson argues, "'Reading' was a metaphor applied not only to the spectator's 'excursive' visual experience of landscape gardens and paintings, but also to the city. As a cultural practice, it implied the stroller's semiotic competence to decode the signs on the streets."[34] This is why visual metaphors are essential to the interpretive work Engels undertakes in *The Conditions*. "Society is already in a state of visible dissolution," Engels explains,

> It is impossible to pick up a newspaper without seeing the most striking evidence of the giving way of all social ties. I look at random into a heap of English journals lying before me; there is the *Manchester Guardian* for October 30, 1844. . . . [It reports that] the workers in a mill have struck for higher wages without giving notice. . . . A *Times* of September 12, 1844, falls into my hand, which gives a report of a single day, including theft, an attack on the police, a sentence upon a father requiring him to support his illegitimate son, the abandonment of a child by its parents, and the poisoning of a man by his wife. Similar reports are found in all the English papers. . . . But it may very well surprise us that the bourgeoisie remains so quiet and composed in the face of the rapidly gathering storm-clouds, that it can read all these things daily in the papers without, we will not say indignation at such a social condition, but fear of its consequences, of a universal outburst of that which manifests itself symptomatically from day to day in the form of crime. (142–43)

What baffles Engels is how despite society's "visible dissolution," newspapers fail to relay what should need no relaying.[35] Reportage on crime, attacks on police, and strikes are all proof of the social war's material existence in the industrial city, but bourgeois readers fail to connect the dots into a legible image. Instead of fearing the "rapidly gathering storm-clouds" of revolution, the middle classes are merely "indignant" about the proliferation of crime, unable to see it as representative of a longer trajectory of class warfare. Although all the evidence of the social war is perfectly "evident" everywhere—it is literally under the noses of the middle class—the warlike quality of civic life is strangely invisible. Louis Althusser's famous rereading of *Capital* insists that Marx was demonstrating how the "visible field" of classical political economy created the conditions for its own blindness.[36] In a similar fashion but much earlier, Engels's *The Conditions* extends ocular tropes to an entire theory of urban space in which urban optics are blind to their own production of space. If Engels's polemic in *The Conditions* was about the hidden violence of industrial capitalism, then his intervention was to make this latent violence visible.

Finding journalism insufficient to make English society's internal warfare visible, Engels takes to the streets. After all, he wanted "more than abstract knowledge" of the condition of England: "I wanted to see you [Working Men] in your own homes, to observe you in your everyday life, to chat with you on your condition and grievances, to witness your struggles against the social and political power of your oppressors" (9). Although "abstract knowledge" in the form of Blue books and statistical studies like Edwin Chadwick's *Report on the Sanitary Conditions of the Labouring Classes in Great Britain* (1842), Peter Gaskell's *Manufacturing Population of England* (1833), and Philip Kay's *The Moral and Physical Condition of the Working Class* (1832) (to name only the most famous of such texts) pepper the pages of *The Conditions*, Engels sought to make everyday life in urban space the subject of sociological analysis. And Engels was not alone in this task. Charles Dickens's *Sketches by Boz* and Henry Mayhew's *London Labour and the London Poor* are similar texts to *The Conditions* in that they take the urban wanderer as the privileged interpreter of city life. James Buzard, in reference to Mary Louise Pratt, has called such texts "metropolitan autoethnographies" of Victorian England. Buzard argues that this discourse operates "by construing its narrator's (and many characters') desired position vis-à-vis the fictional world it depicts as that of an *insider's outsideness*—'outside enough' to apprehend the shape of the culture (and its possibilities of reform), yet insistently positioned as the outsideness of a *particular* inside, differentiating itself from the putatively unsituated outsideness of theory or cosmopolitanism as conventionally represented."[37] While Buzard identifies the realist novel as the privileged form of Victorian autoethnographies, it is hard not to also see Boz, Mayhew, and ultimately Engels as taking on similar ethnographic work. Mayhew's "outsideness" as a rational middle-class observer *for* the middle class offers him ethnographic distance toward his working-class subjects. Boz's outsideness is more complicated because it stems from his spatial and socioeconomic mobility, a characteristic the society he describes lacks in every way. For example, Boz's ethnographic work often happens when he takes the reader *across* different city spaces and social worlds. Thus in "The Streets—Morning," he moves from the road into a servant's room to her master's and then out into the street where "Mr Todd's young man" is delivering milk and flirting with the aforementioned servant.[38] While the characters depicted are contained within the spaces they are circumscribed within (and oblivious to Boz), Boz moves effortlessly between such spaces to provide a total picture of London life.

Engels's status as an outsider to England meant he was well situated to undertake similar ethnographic work. His purpose in England, ironically, was to oversee his father's business and complete his training as a businessman, an opportunity Engels pounced on in order to live amid what he understood to be the vanguard of the world's class struggles. It is well known that, when not overseeing his father's factories in Manchester, Engels spent much of his leisure time in the slums with factory workers. Steven Marcus notes that Engels "gained his intimacy [of Manchester] by taking to the streets, at all hours of the day and night, on weekends and holidays."[39] Yet such objective expertise is also compromised by the fact that Engels claims to know cities like London and Manchester "as intimately as my own native town, more intimately than most of its residents know it"—a bold statement given that Barmen (his hometown) was (and only ever was) a fraction of the size of England's major industrial cities (54). By knowing the city as a local might, the objectivity of the observer dissolves into the subjectivity of the observed. Aruna Krishnamurthy reads Engels's text in these very terms, noting how his "'readerly' text built on claims of detachment and immediacy of observation, ends up foregrounding principles of historical materialism as an a priori model for understanding the working classes of England."[40] Out of this conjuncture emerges a narrative "that is grounded in the indisputable facts of deracination, poverty and oppression . . . [as well as] the bourgeois residence and its spatial architectonics that have a necessary effect upon the narrator."[41] So while Engels assumes scientific authority about life in England's industrial metropolises, he cannot help but place himself, the narrator, at the center of its representation.[42]

Engels's flanerie produces what Michel de Certeau calls "spatial stories," a term that adapts narrative theory to think about social space.[43] Such stories consist of an interplay between the preestablished routes that the city affords (the organization of streets and the neighborhoods through which the flaneur must pass) and the perspective of the pedestrian. Engels's passages are both textual and urban, and unfold through a tension between his perspective as a pedestrian and his desire to produce an overview or map of the city's spatial design. For example, when Engels introduces the reader to Manchester, he provides an overview of the city's geographical location:

Manchester lies at the foot of the southern slope of a range of hills, which stretch hither from Oldham, their last peak, Kersall-moor, being at once the racecourse and the Mons Sacer of Manchester. Manchester proper lies on the left bank of the Irwell, between that stream and the two smaller ones, the Irk and the Medock, which here empty into the Irwell. On the right bank of the Irwell, bounded by a sharp curve of the river, lies Salford, and farther westward Pendleton; northward from the Irwell lie Upper and Lower Broughton; northward of the Irk, Cheetham Hill; south of the Medlock lies Hulme; farther east Chorlton on Medlock; still farther, pretty well to the east of Manchester, Ardwick. (57)

Such passages represent the city as a map, for phrases like "to the east" and "south of" produce a cartographic overview of the cityscape from above. These are abstractions of the city as a static *place*. Engels supplements this cartography with descriptions from the pedestrian's point of view: "So Market Street running south-east from the Exchange; at first brilliant shops of the best sort, with counting-houses or warehouses above; in the continuation, Piccadilly, immense hotels and warehouses; in the father continuation, London Road, in the neighbourhood of the Medlock, factories, beerhouses, shops for the humbler bourgeoisie and the working population; and from this point onward, large gardens and villas of the wealthier merchants and manufacturers" (59).

Engels must follow Market Street southeast over the Bridgewater Canal to London road, which takes him to the more proletarian area near Medlock.[44] Along the way, his observations give form and shape to this prescribed route. Hence the contrast between the "brilliant shops of the best sort" in Exchange square and the beer houses further south. De Certeau calls such accounts "itineraries": linear narratives of *space* constructed out of "the alphabet of spatial indication" like Engels's "on the left" and "on the right."[45] Such compositions are linear by their very nature because they log journeys on foot and therefore produce "a chain of spatializing operations" told from a pedestrian's perspective.[46] Spatial stories, de Certeau tells us, shuttle between these "two poles of experience," one characterized by a totalizing map and the other by the linear paths through predefined places.[47] Engels's passages in *The Conditions* are therefore framed by the physical space of the city he inhabits on the one hand and by his own itineraries of these neighborhoods on the other.

The challenge *The Conditions* poses to de Certeau's understanding of spatial stories is: What happens to spatial stories when the spaces they narrativize are antagonistically divided by social war? Do spatial stories presuppose the cohesiveness of the city, and if not, what kinds of spatial stories emerge out of cities rent apart in war? What does a spatial story look like when the war that saturates it is latent, everywhere but nowhere? What is Engels's poetic of social rupture?

The answer, to put it perhaps too simply, is: confusing stories. For Engels constructs neither a map of the cities he walks through nor an itinerary of his tours. Instead, his "stories" are fragmentary narratives incapable of progressing through linear sequence. In his attempt to achieve "more than abstract knowledge" of England's condition, Engels is consistently frustrated by his inability to represent what is at its center: the social war's manifestation in the city. Because the conflict he seeks to uncover hides behind the facade of everyday life, he must indirectly surmise its presence rather than see it directly. In Manchester, for example, the shops that line the streets separate middle-class districts from the working class: "They suffice to conceal from the eyes of the wealthy men and women of strong stomachs and weak nerves the misery and grime which form the complement of their wealth" (58). The segregation of urban space must be "inferred" rather than seen directly: "In this way any one who knows Manchester can infer the adjoining districts, from the appearance of the thoroughfare, but one is seldom in a position to catch from the street a glimpse of the real labouring districts" (59). The very organization of the city obscures its physical structure, for laboring districts are hidden behind the hustle and bustle of urban life.

Franco Moretti identifies similar spatial fissures in the nineteenth-century realist novel's depictions of the metropolis. Moretti argues that "different spaces are not just different landscapes . . . : they are different *narrative matrixes*. Each space determines its own kind of action, its plot—its genre."[48] Thus "a half-London in the silver-fork school; the other half there. But the two halves [of the city] don't add up to a whole. They may touch briefly and in secret . . . but it's only a moment. . . . If a novel focuses on one half of London, it simply cannot *see* the other half, nor represent the crossing of the border between them."[49] In *Oliver Twist*, for example, the two halves are the crime-ridden streets of London and the idyllic homes of Brownlow and the Maylies. But when these two worlds touch, they meet only briefly and fleetingly. So when Rose and Nancy secretly meet, they do so under darkness on a bridge that separates London. Or when Oliver catches Monks and Fagin peering at him through a window in the Maylies' home, this vision is "but an instant, a glance, a flash before his eyes."[50]

While Engels's text is far from a novel or even the realm of fiction (though is invested in and reliant on narration and, as I argue later, a sense of an ending), it does present the industrial city as a similarly fragmented topography. The only point at which Engels "knows" the city he walks within is when he *infers* adjoining districts that are otherwise "tenderly concealed" from the pedestrian or when he catches a brief "glimpse" of the poverty around the corner. Such glimpses don't offer a sustained view but are momentary lapses in the ordering of urban space. For as Engels makes clear, the bourgeois pedestrian is not meant to see the adjoining laboring districts but accidentally glimpse them instead. Consequently, Engels produces neither a mental nor textual "map" of the neighborhood because at no point can he in fact locate where the proletarian districts are and how they are positioned in relation to middle-class neighborhoods. Much like Moretti himself, Engels includes numerous maps of the city in order to better represent its segregated and partitioned structure (61, 67, 69, 70). These crude maps (some of which are typographically inserted among the words of his text) are the visual supplement to Engels's (failed) textual mappings of Manchester's internal divisions.

Even Engels's "itineraries" of London and Manchester go nowhere. Despite his claims about knowing the cities as well as local residents, he finds himself consistently lost. Reflecting on a walk he takes in the working districts of Manchester, he writes, "Of the irregular cramming together of dwellings in ways which defy all rational plan, of the tangle in which they are crowded literally upon the other, it is impossible to convey an idea" (60). And soon after, he confesses to being completely lost: "He who turns to the left here from the main street . . . is lost; he wanders from one court to another, turns countless corners, passes nothing but narrow, filthy nooks and alleys, until after a few minutes he has lost all clue, and knows not whither to turn," and soon thereafter notes how "the lanes run now in this direction, now in that, while every two minutes the wanderer gets into a blind alley, or, on turning a corner, finds himself back where he started from; certainly no one who has not lived a considerable time in this labyrinth can find his way through it" (62, 63). The hypothetical wanderer seems to be Engels himself, who admits that "I should never have discovered it [the court] myself, without the breaks made by the railway, though I thought I knew this whole region thoroughly" (63). Despite his extensive knowledge of the "region," Engels still cannot navigate within it. Tellingly, his disorientation is not because the neighborhood is especially complicated but because all the houses, buildings, and streets look identical to each other. He describes "this chaos of small one-storied, one-roomed huts" where "everywhere before the doors refuse and offal; that any sort of pavement lay underneath could not be seen but only felt, here and there, with the feet" (63). The repetitive character of these neighborhoods and the filth that they are enveloped in render them unnavigable, leading Engels to conclude the following: "This whole collection of cattle-sheds for human beings was surrounded on two sides by houses and a factory, and on the third by the river, and besides the narrow stair up the bank, a narrow doorway alone led out into another almost equally ill-built, ill-kept labyrinth of dwellings. Enough! The whole side of the Irk is built in this way, a planless, knotted chaos of houses" (63). Staggered by the "knotted chaos of houses," Engels's map of the city is equally confusing. Having pointed to the lost wanderer and admitting to his own perplexity about the terrain, Engels finds himself "surrounded" by anonymous buildings. Because the houses and paved streets all look the same, his own (otherwise perfect) vision fails, forcing him to "feel" them through the refuse and offal rather than actually "see" them. And when he finally comes to the end of one neighborhood, he is confronted with yet another that is equally labyrinthine. The endlessly repetitive quality of the slum means Engels cannot spatially orient himself when walking in it, and is immobilized for he "finds himself back where he started from." In his search for the social war that is everywhere but nowhere, Engels finds himself walking everywhere but nowhere.

Similar instances of being lost in the industrial city abound in contemporaneous texts. Their function, importantly, is closely related to the generic development of realist omniscience. In *Sketches by Boz*, a paralyzed stranger "at the entrance of seven obscure passages, uncertain which to take, will see enough around him to keep his curiosity and attention awake for no inconsiderable time. From the irregular square into which he has plunged, the streets and courts dart in all directions, until they are lost in the unwholesome vapor which hangs over the house-tops, and renders the dirty perspective uncertain and confined."[51] Unable to distinguish one street from the next, the wanderer is baffled by how each neighborhood bleeds into the next: "The peculiar character of these streets, and the close resemblance each one bears to its neighbour, by no means tends to decrease the bewilderment in which the unexperienced wayfarer through 'the Dials' finds himself involved."[52] Street, buildings, and inhabitants all seem to blend into the same undifferentiated image: "He traverses streets of dirty, straggling houses, with now and then an expected court composed of buildings as ill-proportioned and deformed as the half-naked children that wallow in the kennels."[53] In contrast to the wanderer's bafflement, Boz's narration confirms *his* expert knowledge of the city, for he can assemble its "obscure passages" and "deformed" buildings and "half-naked children" into a single heterogeneous space.[54] If Boz's sketches document the condition of England in its capital, this knowledge is premised on his movement through and assembly of different parts into a whole. When Dickens novelized such a society in *Bleak House* (1853), the anonymous narrator's Boz-like omniscience looks more like panoptic authority. In what is arguably the novel's narrative climax, Mr. Bucket and Esther Summerson search for Lady Dedlock. During the chase, Esther is flummoxed by London: "Where we drove, I neither knew then, nor have ever known since; but we appeared to seek out the narrowest and worst streets in London. Whenever I saw [Bucket] directing the driver, I was prepared for our descending into a deeper complication of such streets, and we never failed to do so."[55] Esther's bewilderment about London is sharply contrasted to Bucket's complete knowledge of it, which has the effect of making the police legible as an institution of surveillance. Esther's limited first-person narrative is thus juxtaposed to that of the anonymous narrator, who seems to know London and the lives of its inhabitants as well as Bucket. This is the novelization of the panopticon, as D. A. Miller's famous reading of the novel has argued.[56] Crucially, formalizing the Benthamite prison requires emplotment, for the search for Lady Dedlock—and by extension, the crystallization of panoptic knowledge—is closely tied to the revelation of Esther's biological origins and the final "disgrace" of the Dedlocks—both of which move the plot toward closure.

In stark contrast, Engels's first-person narrative must conjure the end it cannot find. His inability to differentiate elements of the slum around him "affront[s] the eyes and nerves" to such a degree that he exclaims: "Enough!" Enough? Enough of what? "Enough" either imposes a limit to something potentially endless or names satisfaction. But in both cases, "enough" marks the limit between the tolerable and intolerable. The exclamation signals the limit of his ability to move through and decode urban space; he is lost because he ends his walk in a place identical to where he began, at which point his spatial story of the slums too comes to a halt. Engels's spatial stories yearn for something akin to what Frank Kermode calls a "sense of an ending" to narrative, because he has had "enough" of walking.[57] But the monotony of urban space blurs the distinction between beginning and ending, thereby deferring a sense that the narrative end is near. At the beginning of *The Conditions*, Engels claims that "a man may wander [through London] for hours together without reaching the beginning of the end." And this is precisely what baffles him in Manchester, where having found no end to the slum, Engels imposes his own limit and cuts short his spatial story by interrupting the seemingly endless walk and endless narrative. It is a fit of having had "Enough!"

Recall Engels's frustration at "reading" the social war in the newspapers and his desire for "more than abstract knowledge" of it. This knowledge, as it turns out, is of a narrational variety, for his answer to the limits of journalism is the spatial story. The most visceral evidence of the social war, he claims, can be found anywhere and everywhere in the streets. But once actually walking in the midst of this war, Engels fails at creating representations of it—the very war he repeatedly claims is impossible to miss. When reflecting on these passages, Engels states that "on rereading my description, I am forced to admit that instead of being exaggerated, it is far from black enough to convey a true impression of the filth, ruin, and uninhabitableness. . . . If anyone wishes to see in how little space a human being can move, how little air—and *such* air!—he can breathe, how little of civilization he may share and yet live, it is only necessary to travel hither" (70). Isn't the reason for his narrative's shortcoming because he had "Enough!" of the urban landscape, and put a halt to his excursion, only to encourage the reader to "see it for himself" rather than read Engels's depiction? The city doesn't make sense to Engels as a pedestrian, but neither does his own narrative as a reader. Although he goes to the heart of the latent war in the streets of England's "great towns," Engels struggles to produce a narrative of the conflict. It is everywhere but nowhere. *The Conditions of the Working Class in England* may be about the condition of the working classes in England, but it is also about making visible the difficulty of perceiving and narrating this very condition.

Engels's narratorial failures are the most valuable aspect of *The Conditions* for they reveal that the hermeneutic problem of the social war doesn't lie with the viewer's ocular abilities but rather the narrator's storytelling abilities—which we know are themselves routed through the prescribed paths, streets, and alleyways of the modern city. On the one hand, spatial stories are the solution to the limits of journalism and the "abstract knowledge" of statistics and Blue books. On the other hand, these tales are forever framed by the divided and perplexing city they take place within. What Engels's text makes clear is that the social war—the awe-inspiring outcome of industrial modernity—exists as first and foremost a crisis of narration. For if *The Conditions* could in fact produce a successful spatial story, complete with a beginning and an end, then it would have to, according to its own logic, give a complete and total account of the conditions of the working classes in England. Coherent spaces would translate perfectly into coherent narratives, and by extension, coherent analyses. But as is entirely obvious in *The Conditions*, the city's obscurity to the pedestrian makes interpreting its latent war an impossible task. If one of Marxism's innovations was to bring the discourse of race war into the domain of political economy and sociological analysis, then it also reveals that essential to its own interpretive powers is an attention to narration. The burden of interpreting the social war is entirely premised on the ability to construct a narrative about it.

CHAPTER 2

A Nexus of Fratricide

No Carlylean phrase made more of an impact on the young Engels and Marx than "nexus of Cash-payment."[1] Carlyle introduces the phrase in his pamphlet *Chartism*, where he explains that in "Feudal times," it was "in many senses still as soldier and captain, as clansman and head, as loyal subject and guiding king, was the low related to the high."[2] "*Cash Payment* had not grown to be the universal sole nexus of man to man," but "with the supreme triumph of Cash, a changed time has entered" (36). Carlyle argues that capitalism supplanted religion as the unifying system of English society. While the symbol of God anchored social relations under feudalism, modernity replaced divinity with secular objects—cash—that are now the sole form of human connection. Anticipating Ferdinand Tönnies's distinction between "community" (*Gemeinschaft*) and "civil society" (*Gesellschaft*), Carlyle argues that idyllic forms of hierarchical community ("soldier and captain," "clansman and head," "subject and king") are flattened by the money relation (as between the factory owner and factory worker).[3] Capitalism displaced Christianity from its privileged place in society and created a new "Gospel of Mammonism" that transformed communal life into the secular value system of "profit and loss."[4] In *Past and Present*, Carlyle laments the "deadened soul" to whom "going to Hell is equivalent to not making money," and that "I have not heard in all Past History, and expect not to hear in all Future History, of any Society anywhere under God's Heaven supporting itself in such Philosophy" (185). What is unique to the epoch of industrialism is not the stratification of a "higher" and "lower" class but the *way* in which these groups relate to each other. That is to say, unlike Marx and Engels, Carlyle sees nothing inherently wrong with class disparity. Differences between the rich and poor are only problematic when the former claims to have no responsibility for or duty toward for the latter, as the aristocracy had to the poor during the medieval period. In the absence of such virtues, the two classes in the modern era relate to each other as "buyer and seller alone" (36).[5]

The cash-nexus does more than render England's social relations superficial. In a chapter devoted to "The Gospel of Mammonism" in *Past and Present*, Carlyle goes so far as to liken the money relation to fratricide. With characteristic disdain, he takes factory owners to task for their treatment of workers: "'My starving workers?' answers the rich Millowner: 'Did not I hire them fairly in the market? Did I not pay them, to the last sixpence, the sum covenanted for? What have I to do with them more?'" (185). Immediately after, he likens the Millowner's self-absolution to the eldest son of Adam and Eve: "When Cain, for his own behoof, had killed Abel, and was questioned, 'Where is thy brother?' he too made answer, 'Am I my brother's keeper? Did I not pay my brother *his* wages, the thing he had merited from me?'" (ibid.). What Cain did to Abel is what the factory owner does to his workers; class relations are another means of brotherly murder. Just as Cain rebels by disavowing any responsibility to his kin, so does the factory owner, who recuses himself from any implication in the worker's dire poverty. And if Cain's cunning was to lead the naive herdsman into the field away from God's gaze (for it is only after Abel's death that God confronts Cain about hearing his brother's cries from the ground), then the Millowner's duplicitousness is to commit fratricide under the protection of the law.[6] What worries Carlyle most is that the Millowner is oblivious to the fratricidal quality of his actions. The latter's justification for exploiting the worker is always the market: "Did I not hire them fairly," "Did I not pay them?" The Millowner evokes fraternity while simultaneously committing fratricide when he asks, "Did not I pay my brother *his* wages, the thing he had merited from me?" To relate as individuals via a nexus of Cash-payment is to be blind to the fratricidal violence inherent in such relations. Where Carlyle's comparison between the biblical allegory and the condition of England doesn't hold up, and precisely where his polemic is sharpest, is that there is no repercussion for the Millowner. In the secular world of capital, there is no god to exile Cain, who can now get away with murder.

Hobbes's insight centuries earlier was that "Covenants, without the Sword, are but Words."[7] In contrast, Carlyle's insight is that in industrial society, covenants *are* swords. Thus while the Millowner conducts what he sees as a fair exchange with his worker, he is, unbeknownst to him, *actually* the agent of latent fratricide against his worker. Carlyle's metaphor reimagines the role of war in society: rather than the sovereign having a monopoly over all legitimate violence, violence saturates civil society. This is precisely the shift from Clausewitz's formulation of "war is politics by other means" to "politics is war by other means" that Foucault describes as the defining feature of race war discourse.[8] Because the cash-nexus conceals the violent, fratricidal quality of money relations taking place throughout the country, Carlyle effectively argues that industrial England is saturated in a latent civil war: "We call it a Society; and go about professing openly the totallist separation: isolation. Our life is not a mutual helpfulness; but rather, cloaked under due laws of war, named 'fair-competition' and so forth, it is mutual hostility. We have profoundly forgotten everywhere that *Cash-payment* is not the sole relation of human beings; we think, nothing doubting, that *it* absolves and liquidates all engagements of man" (185). Although exterior appearances suggest England is a singular "Society" bound by "mutual helpfulness," it is in fact in a condition of "separation" and "isolation." The social, in other words, is characterized by a *lack* of connection among the populace, for the "engagements of man" have been "liquidated." Importantly, social disconnection and mass isolation are not symptoms of capitalist individualism. Rather, they are equivalent to a form of warfare, for beneath extrinsic appearances of peaceful and "fair-competition" lie "mutual hostility" and "war." Even though the cash-nexus appears to be a peaceful form of relation, it is murderous at a mass scale. Far from a state of peace, the condition-of-England is one in which a secret fratricide is "sanctioned by able computations of Profit and Loss" (177). In a word, the cash-nexus is civil warfare by other means.

Carlyle thus draws on the discourse of "race war" to present English society as divided into two antagonistic groups. The war he describes, like Engels's, is everywhere latent and conducted in times of assumed peace. But he diverges from *The Conditions* in that he casts this silent war in explicitly national terms. The actors in Engels's social war, to recall, are defined by their class and not their fraternal status. Carlyle's biblical metaphor folds the idea of class into the national question, for as the example of Cain and Abel suggests, fraternal community is what is stake in England's modern condition. Foucault's genealogy of war in *"Society Must Be Defended"* argues that race war discourse provided the blueprint for a Marxist analysis of class war. In Carlyle's description of the condition of England, race and class are completely intertwined. For while the cash-nexus might have transformed communitarian relations into associational ones, the symbolic kernel of filiation persists beneath the facade of the market. Indeed, like society's "Inner Truth," fraternity remains hidden beneath the surface of the cash-nexus/latent fratricide, waiting to be represented: "What a shallow delusion is this we have all got into, [*sic*] That any man should or can keep himself apart from men, have 'no business' with them, except a cash-account 'business!' It is the silliest tale a distressed generation of men ever took to telling one another. Men cannot live isolated: we *are* all bound together, for mutual good or else for mutual misery, as living nerves in the same body. No highest man can disunite himself from any lowest" (292–93). To relate as "buyer and seller" obscures society's true relation as "all bound together." Even worse, because the Gospel of Mammonism is fixated on individualistic gain, it means that "buyers and sellers" are antagonists in a "cloaked" civil war. Carlyle's connection between the cash-nexus and civil war is so powerful because it suggests that the bond of kinship is corrupted by capitalist exchange to such a degree that bonds turn into antagonism. In the transformation of fraternal bonds into a cash-nexus, fraternity inverts into fratricide— what previously united now actively rends apart. Hence the pathos of Cain's reply to god, "Am I my brother's keeper?" for Cain disavows any responsibility for his kin. His relation to Abel, as for the capitalist, is a relation of non-relation—he is *not* his brother's keeper. Claims to social non-relation conceal antagonistic relation, for Cain's answer is not "Abel is not my brother" but that his sociality has nothing to do with his fraternity.

What is challenging to conceptualize about Carlyle's metaphor of national rupture is the way a nexus, literally meaning "connection" or "binding together," *gives form to* English society *by un-forming it.* On the one hand, the Millowner and worker are linked by the communal bond of fraternity. On the other hand, these two are cast in an antagonistic cash-nexus—bourgeois and proletarian. Taken together, they are conjoined by, to borrow a term from Nicole Loraux (who writes of civil war in the context of classical Greece), a "bond of division."[9]

Importantly, the contradiction Carlyle speaks of concerns paradigms of sociality and community as much as it pertains to the question of historical transition. For fratricide to have the tragic meaning that it does in Carlyle's writings on the condition of England, the fraternal bond between Englishmen must persist in the time of capital—there can be no fratricides where there aren't already brothers. By virtue of being able to dissolve community, Carlyle also presupposes an original fraternity between Millowner and worker. His presentation of the historical transition from premodernity to capitalist modernity, therefore, is by definition incomplete, for otherwise Cain's murder of Abel would be meaningless in the time of capital as it would look solely like class antagonisms. The only reason the Millowner's selfish exploitation of his worker has the tragic quality it has is because both retain their filial bond to each other despite their class relation. If pre-capitalist forms of community connect and capitalist social relations disconnect, then what does it mean for these two forms of sociality to coexist? The cash-relation ties a community together to the degree that it actively rends it apart, albeit nonviolently. The cash-nexus, one might say, is a knot that unties.

Such a "bond of division" has an affinity with what Franco Moretti calls a "dialectic of fear." Moretti claims that the figure of the monster in nineteenth-century literature, specifically *Frankenstein* (1818) and *Dracula* (1897) (and, to a lesser degree, *Dr. Jekyll and Mr. Hyde* ([1886]), allegorized class divisions. Because the monster is that which cannot be integrated into society, it represents an irreconcilable split that in turn triggers the desire for a social whole: "Illiberal in a deep sense," the literature of terror "mirrors and promotes the desire for an integrated society, a capitalism that manages to be 'organic.'"[10] In Moretti's account, the fear of class war elicits the liberal desire for social unity. Perhaps not coincidentally, Carlyle also turns to the figure of the monster to describe organized working-class movements. He begins his pamphlet *Chartism* by chastising journalistic celebrations that reformism had "put down the chimera of Chartism," noting how "most readers of newspapers know withal that it is indeed the chimera of Chartism, not the reality, which has been put down. The distracted incoherent embodiment of Chartism, whereby in late months it took shape and became visible, this has been put down" (3). Like the chimera of Homer's *Iliad*—a composite of lion, goat, and snake—Chartism is "incoherently embodied." Although this "distracted" entity has been put down, the creature's true monstrosity, its "reality" as Carlyle calls it, remains intact, undisturbed, and hidden from view. For Chartism "is a new name for a thing which has had many names, which will yet have many. The matter of Chartism is weighty, deep-rooted, far extending; did not begin yesterday; will by no means end this day or to-morrow" (4). "Chartism" is only an exterior appearance that cannot fully express its inner essence. No name can fully encapsulate its latent materiality, for "it has had many names," of which "Chartism" is only the most recent. The "matter" that animates the workers' movement therefore exceeds what the name "Chartism" can represent.

What is immediately apparent in Carlyle's discussion is that the *true* danger to society lies beneath its surface, exceeding what words or political movements can fully represent. He explains that "Glasgow Thuggery, Chartist torch-meetings, Birmingham riots, Swing conflagrations, are so many symptoms on the surface; you abolish the symptom to no purpose, if the disease is left untouched. Boils on the surface are curable or incurable,—small matter which while the virulent humour festers deep within; poisoning the sources of life; and certain enough to find for itself ever new boils and sore issues; ways of announcing that it continues there, that it would fain not continue there" (4).[11] Much has been written about how debates about health informed an understand-ing of the emergent Victorian civil society, particularly as it understood class.[12] While Carlyle certainly draws on the conjuncture of biology and class, his concern is less about contamination and governance than it is about methods of diagnosis and interpretation. Chartism is symp-tomatic as a "boil" on the surface of the body politic, and the dis-ease it springs from "festers deep within." Hence "Glasgow Thuggery, Chartist torch-meetings, Birmingham riots, Swing conflagrations" are all chimeras and boils because they only *partially* represent the "real-ity," "thing," "essence," or "disease" that is otherwise hidden beneath the surface. The animating force behind "thuggery," "torch-meetings," or "riots" resists complete representation because it is infinitely more than what the sign can represent. Hence the inadequacy of "Chartism" (both the word and the political movement) to fully represent the work-ing masses. While strife might surface and become visible in the form of mass working-class movements, its discordance continues to exist by an invisible means in "secret treason" in times of assumed peace and national harmony. Riots come and go, but the discontent that animates them persists latently, always exceeding representation.

The problem of Chartism, in other words, is neither the work-ing class nor their violent protests but the difficulty of accessing the "essence" of its meaning. Chartism's *true* monstrosity lies in the invisibility of its politics. Although its intrinsic "essence" outlives its extrinsic form, the workers who embody the movement retain their access to Chartism's "reality." Carlyle's ambivalence toward Chartism is rooted in how, on the one hand, it signaled a disease and, on the other hand, it was also the only means to understand the malady itself. As John Plotz explains, "If the 'condition of England' depends on Chartism, that dependence has little to do with its words and everything to do with Carlyle's ascribing to Chartist crowds a mystical somatic access to some deeper sort of meaning."[13] As a consequence, Chartism has "the power to reveal the inner disease," but not the skill to articulate the condition-of-England question.[14] Carlyle's is a very different relation to working-class struggles than, for example, the aristocratic Sir Leicester's in Dickens's *Bleak House*, for whom the labor movement is all violence with no meaning. Hence his fears that George Rouncewell, a labor leader recently invited into Parliament, is simply "one of a body of some odd thousand conspirators, swarthy and grim, who were in the habit of turning out by torchlight, two or three nights a week, for unlawful purposes."[15] For Sir Leicester, the destructive work of class struggle goes on every day out in the open, not in secret. For Carlyle, the true danger of Chartism is not its embodiment in public protests, but its latent form during times of sociopolitical harmony. So even though Chartism might have been put down as a chimera, the true "essence" of this monster persists and continues by another means, threatening to materialize at a later date under a different name or sign. Workers' movements come and go, but the intrinsic essence behind them perseveres, waiting to be interpreted correctly. Like Engels, Carlyle transforms the entire condition-of-England question into a problem of depth-hermeneutics.[16]

PETERLOO

If the cash-nexus divides society into two antagonistic groups, then it also offers a lens for deciphering England's latent conflict. For it is no coincidence that despite his contempt for the money-relation, Carlyle turns to financial metaphors to narrativize England's social unrest. The reason, I want to argue, is because his metaphor of the cash-nexus seeks to encapsulate English society as a totality—*especially* in its divided and strife-ridden condition. This metaphor captures England's

internally divided condition, presenting both classes/citizens as paradoxically united by the link of mutual antagonism. Nowhere is this
more evident than in Carlyle's treatment of the Peterloo Massacre of
1819. Carlyle, like most historians of the massacre, saw it as a turning point in the history of Britain's class struggles.[17] Peterloo began as
a (from all accounts, peaceful) protest by Manchester weavers calling
for parliamentary reform and ended when cavalry charged the crowd,
killing over a dozen and injuring hundreds. E. P. Thompson's history
of the rise of the English working class describes the event as "without
question a formative experience in British social and political history"
that was "a clear moment of class war."[18] The massacre also had a
widespread impact on the English cultural imagination. James Chandler explains that "the effort to portray the condition of England in
the aftermath of Peterloo structures a wide variety of works in a wide
variety of ways in the final weeks of 1819: not only *Ivanhoe*, but also
Scott's *Visionary* articles, Shelley's *Ode to the West Wind* and *A Philosophical View of Reform*, the later editions of *The Political House
that Jack Built*, and works by other writers and journalists around the
country who offered their statements of the case."[19] Similarly, Nancy
Armstrong calls Peterloo a "turning point in the history of violence,"
not because of the content of the violence but because it crystalized
the "collective identity" of the working class.[20] But the riot was also a
national scandal, for "within two days of Peterloo, all England knew
of the event. Within a week every detail of the massacre was being can-
vassed in alehouses, chapels, workshops, private houses," and "in the
months which followed, political antagonism hardened. No one could
remain neutral."[21] These ripples of bias seem to have lasted for decades
because Carlyle, writing almost a quarter of a century later, exclusively
refers to the massacre as the "Manchester Insurrection," invoking a
politics of naming that shifts the agents of violence from the state to the
protestors. He transforms a peaceful protest cut down by the volunteer
Manchester Yeomanry, a "massacre," into one in which workers rose
up violently against the state, "an insurrection."

Throughout *Past and Present*, Carlyle sees Peterloo as emblem-
atic of the trouble industrial England faces. It echoes the tumult of
the French Revolution: "Yes, friends: Hero-kings, and a whole world
not unheroic,—there lies the port and happy haven, towards which,
through all these stormtost seas, French Revolutions, Chartisms, Manchester Insurrections, that make the heart sick in these bad days, the
Supreme Powers are driving us" (98). And much like the chimera of

Chartism, Carlyle recognizes that Peterloo was an isolated phenomenon that continued by another means. The massacre inaugurated a period of national history where the "essence" of strife became embedded in everyday life. Just as the "chimera of Chartism" disappears, Carlyle claims the "million-headed hydra" of Peterloo buries itself beneath the surface of the body politic in the "subterranean settlements," thereby threatening to surface again at a later date and under a different name—presumably by the name of "Chartism" in the late 1830s (82–83).[22] The victory of the Yeomanry over the weavers was therefore only of a certain type, for the "reality" of the insurrection could retreat to dormancy and revive at a later date. What distinguishes Peterloo from other such "boils" is that it represented an inaugural eruption of violence that, once disappeared, lived on in invisible form. In the case of Peterloo, the symptom *became* the disease. Symptomatic violence continues by another latent means, which Carlyle makes visible by mapping class antagonisms onto a metaphorics of debt. He laments,

> Who shall compute the waste and loss, the obstruction of
> every sort, that was produced in the Manchester region by
> Peterloo alone! Some thirteen unarmed men and women cut
> down,—the number of the slain and maimed is very count-
> able: but the treasury of rage, burning hidden or visible in all
> hearts ever since, more or less perverting the effort and aim
> of all hearts ever since, is of unknown extent. . . . In all hearts
> that witnessed Peterloo, stands written, as in fire characters, or
> smoke-characters prompt to become fire again, a legible balance
> account of grim vengeance; very unjustly balanced, much exag-
> gerated, as is the way with such accounts: but payable readily
> at sight, in full with compound interest! Such things should be
> avoided as the very pestilence! For men's hearts ought not to be
> set against one another; but set with one another, and all against
> the Evil Thing only. Men's souls ought to be left to see clearly,
> not jaundiced, blinded, twisted all awry, by revenge, mutual
> abhorrence, and the like. An Insurrection that can announce the
> disease, and then retire with no such balance-account opened
> anywhere, has attained the highest success possible for it. (83)

We learn that the Insurrection represented an original exchange of violence that has lived on in latent form. Although the "embodiment" of the violence in the number of casualties is "countable" (and can therefore be represented perfectly in statistical form), a reserve of latent rage outlived the event and has since increased over time. Carlyle's fear is that if the condition-of-England question, the "Sphinx-riddle of our time," is not answered in a timely fashion, then the vengeance that has been latently increasing in magnitude since Peterloo will continue to increase and eventually take material form, be embodied, and result in an "announcement of the disease" at a greater scale than the thirteen killed at the massacre.

The language and rationality of banking are central to Carlyle's understanding of the Insurrection and its aftermath, for he folds the language of debt into his depiction of Peterloo. Behind Englishmen's "hearts being set against one another" lie not rational political ends but sinful aggression and fratricidal vengeance. No matter how irrational and infinite this rage might be, it can nevertheless be domesticated through the rationality of finance. Waste, loss, obstruction are "computed." Casualties are "countable." "Grim vengeance" draws its "balance" from a "treasury of rage," creating an "account" that can be settled. Carlyle's metaphors measure the Insurrection and its aftermath in monetary terms, quantify its divisive sentiment, calculate its magnitude and duration with compound interest, and predict its end when the principal is paid off such that no "balance account" remains. An entire history of class struggle is monetized as a cash-nexus. That is to say, national rupture is made visible through metaphor where otherwise it lay hidden.

Carlyle's financial metaphor represents England's social condition with perfect precision.[23] For Lukács, abstraction is where "the principle of rational mechanization and calculability must embrace every aspect of life," and the factory contains "in concentrated form the whole structure of capitalist society."[24] In Carlyle's case, the "whole structure" of English society is contained within the metaphor of the bank. Both essence and its embodiment, reality and chimera, disease and symptom can be made visible by representing violence as capital.[25] He produces an anthropology of England in the language of debt, for civil society is divided into debtors and lenders—those who have money and those who don't. Those who have "debt" (the working class) have anger with no political representation, while those who have political representation and wealth (the middle class) have no rage. If "Chartism" couldn't access the magnitude, the "essence" and "reality" of the worker's movement, then Carlyle's banking metaphor can do so perfectly. Alain Desrosières identifies such a turn to financial metaphorics as a central feature of modern statistics: "On the one hand, they [metaphors] stabilize *objects*, by determining their equivalences through standardized definitions. . . . On the other hand, they provide forms for describing the *relationship* between objects thus constructed, and for testing the consistency of these links."[26] Carlyle's metaphor similarly stabilizes the heterogeneity of English society into two "objects": the debtor and lender, who are antagonistically linked by a contract—a promissory note of vengeful violence. If the economy is characterized by the exchange of capital (when money moves from one hand to another), Carlyle's imagined community is characterized by an efflorescence of strife (violence begetting more violence). Just as transactions animate capitalist society in the everyday, so does the latent violence of Peterloo's aftermath; class war is as commonplace and prevalent as debt. The cash-nexus is at once an antagonistic social relation and a field of intelligibility into the true condition of England.

Mary Poovey and more recently Audrey Jaffe have noted the centrality of abstraction in the production of a Victorian "mass culture." Jaffe tracks financial tropes in nineteenth-century writing, where "the mapping of mathematical symmetry onto unruly elements appears as the solution to a social problem, transforming anarchy into a beautiful form, wild confusion into a flowing curve."[27] In Carlyle's case, the financialization of human relations (which he claims are in fact fratricidal relations) domesticates the otherwise unruly violence of Peterloo into a similarly "beautiful form." The effect is not "a representation of actual individuals; rather, it is the projection of a 'law' of statistics that, keeping individual differences 'out of view,' yields the discovery of a regular pattern."[28] The "beauty" of Carlyle's financial metaphor is that it makes visible fratricidal violence that is otherwise "out of view" or, in Carlyle's terms, "cloaked" beneath an assumed state of peace. In contrast to Jaffe, however, Carlyle's financial anthropology of England's condition, like Engels's spatial architectonic of the industrial metropolis, doesn't make a social body as much as make its unmaking visible. He turns to the same tropes and mechanisms that Poovey and Jaffe describe as instituting social unity and homogeneity, but his tropes imagine a social body that is rent apart into two. What, by Jaffe's account, produces a social whole and dispels the inequities contained within, I find in Carlyle to articulate a deeply divided society with all the asymmetries of capital accumulation. "Social disarray" *is* the social whole.

Much like Engels, Carlyle's formalization of national rupture has a narrative element to it. For like his German counterpart, he views the confrontation between Englishmen not as a singular event but as a protracted process that saturates capitalist society. The fratricidal episode of Peterloo might have been an inaugural violent rupture, but this violence is later made manifest in the life of capital, allowing it to continue by another means. Equating the aftermath of Peterloo to a loan implies that the "Insurrection" follows the tempo of capital, because the "balance account of grim vengeance" increases with "compound interest." And more than simply a protracted affair, this conflict intensifies over time. For compound interest—what makes debt profitable—links magnitude with duration. Loans not only accrue capital, but they do so at a predetermined rate over time. In the case of interest-bearing capital, time is organized into calendrical increments, day, week, month, or year—all integral components of what E. P. Thompson describes as a capitalist "time-sense."[29] Because each unit of time simultaneously represents a unit of value, in Carlyle's case these values are representations of latent violence.

By representing the afterlife of Peterloo as an unpaid loan, Carlyle offers a crude narrative theory of internal strife. Far from an isolated episode, the civil war he describes has a linear structure. Plot, as Peter Brooks defines it, is "a structuring operation elicited by, and made necessary by, those meanings that develop through succession of time."[30] Paul Ricoeur similarly describes plot as placing "us at the crossing point of temporality and narrativity: to be historical, an event must be more than a singular occurrence, a unique happening."[31] This is exactly the effect of Carlyle's claim about Peterloo and its aftermath: a moment of rupture is untethered from its circumscription in history—1819—and allowed to continue and intensify by a different means in the following decades. This "structuring" of events, according to Ricoeur, requires the combination of two oppositional temporal dimensions, the episodic and the configurational. The episodic dimension "draws narrative time in the direction of the linear representation of time" by producing a seriality of events. It transforms the chronicle—a mere listing of events—into a story that moves from one episode to another, which "follow upon one another in accord with the irreversible order of time common to physical and human events."[32] In Carlyle's account, the "order of time" is the time of capital. And "human events," class warfare or "men's hearts being set against one another," progress and escalate in synchrony with capital's predetermined timed increments. The civic discord of August 16, 1819, is prolonged and protracted from a "unique happening" to something coterminous with the present and ongoing. As time progresses forward, the aftermath of Peterloo keeps getting worse. Carlyle's fear is that the accumulation of new principals of "grim vengeance" will not be sustained indefinitely and instead be paid in full with compound interest, meaning at a magnitude greater than the thirteen dead at Peterloo. Hence the grimness of proletarian "vengeance."

Such calculations anticipate the closure of narrative, for as Carlyle reminds us, the loan is "payable readily at sight, in full with compound interest!" Payment of grim vengeance, now accumulating for decades, is imminent. Because each temporal increment corresponds to a new principal—the amount-due to conclude the narrative—each episode points to closure. The "end-point" of any narrative is, according to Ricoeur, "the point from where the story can be seen as a whole."[33] Ricoeur calls this the "configurational dimension" of narrative, which "grasps together" episodes into a cohesive whole. It is a "reflective act" on the reader's part, thanks to which "the entire plot can be translated into one 'thought.'"[34] This dimension, it is important to note, is neither a reduction nor a negation of the episodic dimension but a paradigmatic axis simultaneous to the forward movement from one episode to the next. Carlyle's metaphor crystallizes the entire narrative of civic strife in a single unit of value: compounded principal. The metaphor makes it possible to arrange the duration of the discord into new principals at a set rate over time, and thereby make known what needs to be done to "balance the account." Unlike Engels's walks in the slums, the "sense of an ending" is always there in compound interest, for the amount due at any given point in time—past, present, or future—is calculable with complete precision.

Brooks writes that narrative is the "acting out of the implications of metaphor."[35] There could not be a more exemplary case than Carlyle's depiction of class war after Peterloo. What was a singular violent episode continues by a nonviolent means that is structured and formalized as a literary plot. Carlyle, of course, was highly critical of linear narrative form, especially when it related to history. In his early essay "On History," he argues that historical narratives are necessarily limited representations of the past: "The most gifted man can observe, still more can record, only the *series* of his own impressions: his observation . . . must be *successive*, while the things done were often *simultaneous*; the things done were not a series, but a group."[36] This limitation has less to do with man's (in)capabilities as a narrator than with narrative form itself: "all Narrative is, by its nature, of only one dimension;

only travels forward towards one, or towards successive points: Narrative is *linear*, Action is *solid*."[37] Carlyle's critique is directed toward the chronicle: a unidirectional narrative thread whose weakness lay in the fact that it was a *singular* thread.[38] Of course, he would reconcile this dislike for historical narratives in his opus, *The French Revolution: A History* (1837). John Rosenberg points out how Carlyle's decision to name this work "A History" and not "The History" "announces that the writing of history has become problematic. As Carlyle dramatizes in the course of his work, there were as many different French Revolutions as participants in the event, and its consequences are still unfolding."[39] In "On History Again," Carlyle suggests that one way of doing so is "compressing" historical representation: "History, then, before it can become Universal History, needs of all things to be compressed. Were there no epitomizing of History, one could not remember beyond a week. Nay, go to that with it, and exclude compression altogether, we could not remember an hour, or at all: for Time, like Space, is *infinitely* divisible; and an hour, with its events, with its sensations and emotions, might be diffused to such expansion as should cover the whole field of memory, and push all else over the limits."[40] An hour of historical experience exceeds what the human mind can conceive. Dividing time into abstracted increments—weeks and hours—imposes a human limit on the "boundlessness" of history, but such demarcations blot out vast swaths of historical experience. Given that the historical field is a limitless "Chaos of Being" and historical representations are always incomplete, the historian must find a way to offer the reader *a sense* of the totality of history without reducing or flattening it into a singular figure.[41] For Carlyle this means maintaining a tension between the infinite "Chaos" of history and the necessarily finite forms of representation—what Ann Rigney calls an "aesthetics of historical ignorance."[42] A salient feature of this aesthetic is "Carlylese," which J. Hillis Miller notes "is mostly metaphor or other figure which displays itself, which calls attention to itself as figure, by its hyperbolic elaboration."[43] And hyperbole is precisely what the financial metaphor affords Carlyle, for it takes Peterloo and its aftermath and condenses it into the single metaphor of the cash-nexus. Although Carlyle criticizes the cash-nexus as transforming fraternity into fratricide, for mistaking the capitalist for Cain, he also embraces the Gospel of Mammonism's defining term—the cash-nexus—as a way to compress, epitomize, and, most importantly, narrativize the totality of England's condition. What is so striking in Carlyle's metaphor is how a narrative of social unrest and division looks identical to one about social peace and unity. The capitalist time-sense—a social organism moving forward through empty homogeneous time (like the increments of balance accounts)—is the cornerstone of any account of modern national sociality. Only for Carlyle, this narrative energy doesn't institute a singular social body but produces one that is internally fractured.

Carlyle's metaphorical language diagnoses the condition of England question but also offers a solution to the problem he was contemplating. Not unlike Moretti's interpretation of what he calls the "literature of terror," Carlyle's poetic of English rupture is the occasion for the country's reconstitution. For his narrative of England's latent civil war, like all narratives, has a politics behind it. And this politics hinges on the narrative's sense of an ending. The "balance-account" Carlyle speaks of is an exact corollary to the "narrative desire" that Brooks argues "is always there at the start of a narrative, often in a state of initial arousal, often having reached a state of intensity such that movement must be created, action undertaken, change begun."[44] Rather than desiring an ongoing story, his narrative demands closure as soon as possible. Because his emplotment of a long fratricide can only ever point to ever-more violence in the future, the only logical solution to the ever-worsening condition-of-England is nullifying the balance-account, bringing the "amount-due" to zero. Indeed, Carlyle wishes workers to sustain and endure their "grim vengeance" for as long as it is necessary for the "True Aristocracy" to enact social change. Consequently, his solution is not paying off the debt via violence but debt relief: a benevolent forgiveness to those who hold "balance accounts of grim vengeance." Rather than leave social change to those who demand it, the actual transformation of society is preserved for those in power who are not asking for any transformation. Carlyle's narrative strips Peterloo of its political intervention and valence, for the only resolution to the condition-of-England question, the only end to the seemingly endless accumulation of class antagonism and "men's hearts being set against one another," is in Parliament's generous hands and not those excluded from political representation.

Carlyle's "solution" to England's class/civil war is thus radically different from that of someone like Matthew Arnold. Arnold famously opposes "anarchy"—the occasion for which was the 1866 Hyde Park riot and toward which he felt England increasingly "tended"—to "culture"—the means toward a universal human condition.[45] For Arnold, culture, especially when aligned with the state, has the potential to quell Industrial England's social and political discontent.[46] In contrast, Carlyle's solution to England's internal strife is not the cultivation of "sweetness and light" but embracing the country's divided condition to make visible the path to unity. That is to say, if Arnold opposes anarchy (social disunity) to culture (a technology of national harmony), then it is in the latter that he invests his hopes for the future. However, Carlyle's "solution" to England's internal strife lies within a narrative of this latent conflict, whose logic creates an implicit path to solving social unrest. Like a liberal jubilee, Carlyle's solution to England's divided condition is a forgiveness of "balance accounts of grim vengeance." By giving civil strife narrative form, Carlyle defangs the divisive legacy of Peterloo and the central demand of the Manchester weavers in 1819: political representation. His narration of a civil war by other means ends up being the occasion of the nation's unification, all at the cost of expanding the franchise. Far from a crisis to the nation to be avoided, narrating civic unrest in fact edifies Carlyle's idea of national unity by dispelling any agency the memory of Peterloo might have had. Cain forgives Abel—an act whose redundancy only underscores the asymmetry of Carlyle's idea of justice.

THE IRISH ABEL

Inscribed into Carlyle's poetics of national rupture is colonial difference. This difference is epitomized in the figure of the Irish worker, who recurs in Victorian treatments of the condition of England question as a barbaric interloper among the English working class. As critics have noted, representations of the Irish as savages within England helped define and edify English national identity. On the one hand, the Irish were said to bring down wages, corrupt the morality of the English working class, and worsen the sanitary conditions of industrial cities. On the other hand, representations of uncivilized Irishmen helped define the parameters of English civility. Consequently, as Mary Poovey sums up, "the Irish were available *both* as a scapegoat for national woes and as a resource to be exploited when needed."[47] Carlyle, for example, writes that "in his rags and laughing savagery, he [the Irishman] is there to undertake all work that can be done by mere strength of hand and back; for wages that will purchase him potatoes. He needs only salt for condiment; he lodges to his mind in any pighutch or doghutch, roosts in outhouses; and wears a suit of tatters. . . . The

Saxon man if he cannot work on these terms, finds no work. He too may be ignorant; but he has not sunk from decent manhood to squalid apehood" (18).

While the Englishman may be as poor as the animalistic Irishman, the former hasn't sunk into savagery because he needs more than salt, doesn't live in pig hutches, wears untattered clothes—he is a "decent" man. Civility is what separates the "Saxon man" from the Irish worker.[48] Similarly, despite Engels's unceasing sympathy for the plight of the proletariat, he too is entirely comfortable distinguishing the English worker from the Irish worker on the basis of race: "Whenever a district is distinguished for especial filth and especial ruinousness, the explorer may safely count upon meeting chiefly those Celtic faces which one recognizes at the first glance as different from Saxon physiognomy of the native, and the singing, aspirate brogue which the true Irishman never loses."[49] While evidence of the social war is consistently obscured in Engels's account of the industrial city, evidence of Irish racial alterity is self-evident from the squalor of neighborhoods and the physiognomy of "Celtic faces." Moreover, he suggests that the destitution of Irish districts is less the fault of the social war they are situated within (as it certainly is in the case of English working-class neighborhoods) and more a product of their own barbarity.

Irish barbarity was often represented by way of comparisons to other sites of the empire. Mary Jean Corbett argues that "tropes and figures typically deployed to racialize the Irish in this period were also used to describe and to denigrate a host of other groups."[50] Thus representations of "Africans, Indians, Jamaicans, Native Americans, and Jews, as well as those of native working-class people, were all constructed in terms similar to, and at some points nearly identical with," the Irish.[51] Perhaps the most famous of such examples is Carlyle's image of Jamaica as a "Black Ireland," which, as Simon Gikandi argues, enables the juxtaposition and comparison between the metropole and colony.[52] Just as the potato famine wreaked havoc in Ireland, Carlyle fears that mismanagement of the West Indies will create "a Negro Ireland, with pumpkins themselves fallen scarce like potatoes!"[53] Engels, in contrast, casts the Irish in a decidedly Eastern hue: "The Irishman loves his pig as the Arab his horse. Otherwise, he eats and sleeps with it, his children play with it, ride upon it, roll in the dirt with it, as anyone may see a thousand times repeated in all the great towns of England."[54] These behavioral differences, according to Engels, are indicative of a broader civilizational difference between the "Saxon" and the "Celt" (and implicitly also the Arab).

Engels's most jarring claim about the Irish is that they, *like the bourgeoisie*, contribute to the destitution of the English working class: "For when, in almost every great city, a fifth or a quarter of the workers are Irish, or children of Irish parents, who have grown up among Irish filth, no one can wonder if the life, habits, intelligence, moral status—in short, the whole character of the working classes assimilates a great part of the Irish characteristics. On the contrary, it is easy to understand how the degrading position of the English workers, engendered by our modern history, and its immediate consequences, has been still more degraded by the presence of Irish competition."[55] Irish competition for work brings down wages, makes dirty neighborhoods even dirtier, and, by simple proximity, seems to rub Celtic incivility onto the otherwise "decent" Saxon proletariat. Rather than fellow-workmen, the Irish compound forms of bourgeois domination that the Saxon worker must endure. Similarly, in Gaskell's *North and South*, the issue of cheaper Irish labor is at the center of the strife between Thornton, a factory owner, and his workers. When his workers go on strike (a scene in which Irish workers are distinctly absent), the narrator describes a rabid crowd: "Many in the crowd were mere boys; cruel and thoughtless,—cruel because they were thoughtless; some were men, gaunt as wolves, and mad for prey. She [Margaret] knew how it was . . .—with starving children at home—relying on ultimate success in their efforts to get higher wages, and enraged beyond measure at discovering that Irishmen were to be brought in to rob their little ones of bread."[56] The narrator implies that it is not Thornton, a factory owner, who "robs their little ones of bread" but the Irish worker. Later in the novel, we learn that even factory owners are not safe from the corrupting effects of Irish labor, whose "utter want of skill" eventually slows down Thornton's factory production, delays shipments, and leads to his business's bankruptcy.[57] Industrial modernity, we are led to believe, is doomed to fail when its workers are uncivilized.

Strangely, it is Carlyle who undermines these national demarcations by folding the Irish question into the cash-nexus. "Ireland," he writes, "now for the first time, in such a strange circuitous way, does find itself embarked in the same boat with England, to sail together, or to sink together; the wretchedness of Ireland, slowly but inevitably, has crept over to us, and become our own wretchedness" (20). The Irish question and the condition of England question become inextricably linked because of the cash-nexus. By monetizing all human relationships, the cash-nexus doesn't differentiate between English and Irish workers. Cheaper Irish immigrant labor means that "the condition of the lower multitude of English labourers approximates more and more to that of the Irish competing with them in all markets; that whatsoever labour . . . is to be done, will be done not at the English price, but at an approximation to the Irish price" (20). Englishmen do work not at an English price but at the Irish rate. If Carlyle's metaphor of fratricide—Cain's murder of Abel—characterized human relations under capitalism, then we learn that this relationship between fellow-Englishmen has been defined by the "laughing savagery" of the Irish. This is, of course, a very different notion of nationality than we find in Arnold's *On the Study of Celtic Literature* (1866), which envisions the assimilation of the Celtic and Anglo-Saxon on the basis of national culture rather than the money-relation. Implicit in Arnold's account, argues David Lloyd, is "an aesthetic conception of history as a narrative of the production of an harmonious state of culture."[58] In stark contrast, Carlyle's figuration has little to do with the institution of literature as historically progressive and everything to do with the abstraction of all social relations under capitalism. And because this abstraction makes equal workers of all, it means that the civilizational difference between the English and Irish—the very difference that according to Carlyle allows the Irish to work for less—collapses. Indeed, industrial modernity makes modern workers "gaunt as wolves, mad for prey." Colonial incivility thus defines the contours of capital relations. If the cash-nexus is for Carlyle a fratricidal act, then in the context of Irish labor, this fratricide looks more like the murder of a colonized subject.

Narratives of latent civil war are therefore tethered to the colonial question in a way that raises the issue of what exactly it is that ties a community together: fraternity/fratricide or fiscal affiliation? Formulated in this way, national rupture makes the limits of national boundaries legible. The logic is: if something is fratricidal, then it must be intranational. Narratives of fratricide are paradoxically constitutive of nationhood. What seems significant (and wholly out of character) in Carlyle's version of the Irish question is that it is rooted in the cash-nexus, which for him is a distinctly *national* problem. What is much more complicated, though equally productive, is that he makes it possible to think of national rupture *in conjunction with* extranational colonial difference.

CHAPTER 3

The Long Civil War

"The history of nations," Balibar tells us, "beginning with our own, is always already presented to us in the form of a narrative which attributes to these entities the continuity of a subject."[1] Nations come to be because they are narrated as having always been. And nationalist history makes just such a narrative possible, for it presents the nation as the culmination of a long historical project. This entails the production of a people's origins that are always, at best, precarious. As Balibar asks, "Where, for example, are we to situate the origins of France? with our ancestors the Gauls? the Capetian monarchy? the revolution of 1789?"[2] Whatever these origins or milestones might be, what matters is that such events are always already integrated into the nation's historical saga.[3] Such a schema "consists in believing that the generations which succeed one another over centuries on a reasonably stable territory, under a reasonably univocal designation, have handed down to each other an invariant substance."[4] This temporal community, narrated and reinforced everyday through institutions like the family and the school, reproduces a people as a unitary group, a "fictive ethnicity," a nation.

But what happens to the national imagination when its history concerns not one nation, but two? How might one reconcile Balibar's claim about nationalist ideology with Michel Foucault's genealogy of race war? If history is the ideological form of the nation par excellence, then what does the ideological form of race war look like? Benjamin

Disraeli's second Young England novel, *Sybil, or, The Two Nations*, raises these very questions. The polemic of the novel, evident in its second title, is that England's class divisions have become so extreme that the rich and poor appear as "two nations." Like Carlyle, Disraeli presents class divisions in a national register.[5] These "two nations," we are told, have been bound in mutual antagonism for centuries. When the virtuous (if naive) aristocrat Charles Egremont visits the working-class home of Walter Gerard and his daughter Sybil for the first time, he sees on a table Augustin Thierry's *History of the Conquest of England by the Normans* (1825)—a book Egremont confesses to have heard of but never read. To this Gerard retorts: Thierry's *History* "must interest all, and all alike . . . for we are divided between the conquerors and the conquered."[6] While the Norman invasion might be long over, "the spirit of Conquest has adapted itself to the changing circumstances of ages, and, however its results vary in form, in degree they are much the same" (171). Gerard's statement is saturated with irony. For Egremont has Norman "roots" (albeit forged by his ancestors in the sixteenth century), and the proletarian Gerards are descendants of Saxon abbots. Thierry's *History* casts a tumultuous shadow on the scene, for it folds the Norman Conquest onto Henry VIII's civil war to in turn illuminate the causes for the class divisions of the present day.[7] The only way to understand England in the present, Gerard suggests, is to look back to its history of conquest and subjugation. Just as Normans and Saxons represented conquerors and conquered within a single territory, Egremont and Sybil Gerard, possessor and dispossessed, rich and poor, stand under the same roof in apparent amity.[8]

What is so unfamiliar about Gerard's notion of conquest is that it is not a singular historical event but a modular and plastic "spirit" that "adapts" to the shifting landscape of English history, be it the Norman Conquest, Henry VIII's campaign against the monasteries, or class relations in industrial society. While Normans and Saxons might belong to one nation now, Thierry's *History*—which not coincidentally features quite prominently in Foucault's genealogy of race war— illuminates how conquest within England continues by other means and involves different antagonists. In *Sybil* these antagonists are, of course, the rich and the poor, and their antagonism is most visible when racialized into the primordial groups of English history. Hence the rich are consistently cast as "Normans" while the poor take on the characteristics of a "Saxon peasantry" dispossessed of their lands. The "condition-of-England" question presented in *Sybil* is therefore not about the destitution of the poor but about the history of one group conquering and dominating another by the other means of social warfare. Conquest to Gerard is not an event but constitutive of the entire history of England.

Gerard's conception of English history complicates the historical form of national ideology. For Gerard and *Sybil* more generally, rather than allowing the nation to forget its ancient scandals of fratricide and primordial disunity—what Anderson calls "the reassurance of fratricide"—memories of conquest and civil war constitute the symbolic core of English history. In doing so, Disraeli's novel raises an important question for the study of nationalism: If a fictive ethnicity produces a people as having "always already been," then what happens when this "genealogical scheme" is a schema of fratricide? Has civil war, like national unity, always already been?[9] To pose this question differently: If the nation's historical form is its ontology, then what happens to this ontology when the nation's history consists of a Foucauldian race war? Just as the imagined community institutes itself as an ontological presence, as a perpetual nation that remains intact across historical epochs, *Sybil* conceives of national rupture as equally perpetual. If the nation must reproduce itself as such, then Disraeli demonstrates that it can do so by locating antagonistic division at the center of its national imagination. But such a dualistic nation-form also defers any arrival at national unity, endlessly postponing the realization of a fictive ethnicity by recalling, at every step of the way, the deep fissure within the nation that has always been there. In what follows, I synthesize Balibar's argument about national ideology with Foucault's genealogy of race war, and argue that the domestic conquest and domination described by Gerard is in fact entirely complicit with national ideology. Race war, I want to suggest, can be the continuation of race, or "fictive ethnicity," or nationhood, by other means.

A COUNTERHISTORY OF ENGLAND

At the center of *Sybil*'s national saga is the contested status of historical knowledge. History is the technology that divides *Sybil*'s England into "two nations," but it is also the means by which England's condition can be diagnosed and resolved.[10] If for Engels the industrial city obscures the social war at the same time as it renders it visible, and for Carlyle the cash-nexus hides the violence of capitalism while at the same time makes England's "secret treason" visible, then for Disraeli the field of intelligibility into England's ruptured condition is historical writing. In *Sybil*'s concluding paragraphs the narrator—who almost explicitly identifies himself as Disraeli—urges his readers to "seek in a right understanding of the history of their country" because "the written history of our country for the last ten reigns has been a mere phantasma: giving to the origin and consequence of public transactions a character and colour in every respect dissimilar to their natural form and hue" (420–21).[11] "For the last ten reigns," a particular historical knowledge has given England's "public transactions" an unnatural "form and hue." "Written" representations of English history only tell half of the story, obscuring another kind of history which is a "true" rendering of English nationhood. Consequently, "all thoughts and things [in England] have assumed an aspect and title contrary to their real quality and style: Oligarchy has been called Liberty, an exclusive Priesthood has been christened a National Church, Sovereignty has been the title of something that has had no dominion, while absolute power has been wielded by those who profess themselves the servants of the People. In the selfish strife of factions, two great existences have been blotted out of the history of England, the Monarch and Multitude" (421). Disraeli's complaint is with a disjuncture between what national institutions are meant to represent and how they have been represented. This discrepancy produces "phantasmas" of a divided nation that belie the true condition of English society: a multitude unified under a single monarch. John Ulrich explains that Disraeli's "foregrounding [of the disjuncture between reality and history] serves a twofold purpose: on the one hand, the disjunction reveals the extent to which textual representation can usurp and displace historical truth, appearing to the unwary reader as an almost self-evident representation of historical truth; on the other hand, the assertion of such a disjunction opens up the possibility of restoring the relation between textual representation and historical truth, through a process of rewriting that would correct the effects of historical marginalization and dispossession."[12] Just as the industrial city for Engels and the metaphor of cash for Carlyle, historical representation in *Sybil* is both medicine and poison: it can repress England's divided condition, but it is also the means by which the country's "natural form and hue" can be made visible. At the surface of society lie false divisions, beneath which is the "natural form and hue" of England's history—a history yet to be written. Historical knowledge, we learn, is actually an instrument of latent warfare, for it creates the effect of making one race into two but is also a technology for reuniting these false divisions.

The novel's narrator thus calls for a new kind of national historiography: "If the history of England be ever written by one who has the knowledge and the courage, and both qualities are equally requisite for the undertaking, the world would be more astonished than when reading the Roman annals by Niebuhr. Generally speaking, all the great events have become distorted, most of the important causes concealed, some of the principal characters never appear, and all who figure are so misunderstood and misrepresented, that the result is a complete mystification" (14–15). All aspects of English history have been "mystified," from its "principle characters" to its salient events. These "distortions," "concealments," and omissions are so extreme that a "true" rendering of English history would "astonish" its readers more so than Barthold Georg Niebuhr's *History of Rome* (1811–32). Niebuhr's *History*, Hayden White argues, is committed to "the pious reconstruction of the past in its integrity, the spirit of which has continued to dominate nostalgic historiography down to the present."[13] Disraeli's praise for Niebuhr's *History* and Thierry's *History of the Conquest of England* situates the plot of *Sybil* "in" European history and historiography, thereby thematizing and formalizing questions of Enlightenment historicism. And like Niebuhr's and Thierry's texts, Disraeli's historical novel resurrects England's ancient conquests and civil wars in order to understand its condition in the present. Ancient fratricides illuminate the present condition. This is why, as Daniel Bivona explains, "the task of the hero in *Sybil* becomes to 'pry into the beginnings,' to apply the corrosive test of historical precedence to the social arrangements of the present, in order to determine what is in need of changing. . . . Disraeli means to establish this medievalized ideal as a centre which will ground the process of questioning: henceforth, one questions in order to measure the distance England has fallen from this 'community'; that this 'community' did once exist is not in question."[14]

Sybil's historical revisionism emplots English history as a melodrama that presents the medieval past as a "space of innocence" uncorrupted by national divisions.[15] The Marney Abbey was "a place where all rights of hospitality were practiced; where the traveller, from the proud baron to the lonely pilgrim, asked the shelter and the succour that never were denied, and at whose gate, called the Portal of the Poor, the peasants on the Abbey lands, if in want, might appeal each morn and night for raiment and for food" (57). Unlike the New Poor Law (of which Disraeli was a harsh critic) the monasteries took care of the poor without politically enfranchising them.[16] Mere philanthropy, energized by fraternal duty and the static hierarchy of feudalism, is seemingly enough to quell discontent among the peasantry during the medieval period. Just as the Norman invasion transformed England forever, *Sybil* describes Henry VIII's dissolution of the monasteries as the first in a series of events and processes that produced the country's "phantasmic divisions" into two classes/nations.[17] Walter Gerard's ancestor and namesake was raising "a new belfry for his brethren, when the stern decree arrived [from the King] that the bells should no more sound. And the hymn was no more to be chanted in the Lady's chapel; and the candles were no more to be lit on the high altar; and the fate of the poor was to be closed for ever; and the wanderer was no more to find a home" (58). This formative rupture, we are told, was fratricidal because the ruins of the Abbey

> are the children of violence, not of time. It is war that created these ruins, civil war, of all our civil wars the most inhuman, for it was waged with the unresisting. The monasteries were taken by storm, they were sacked, gutted, battered with warlike instruments, blown up with gunpowder; you may see the marks of the blast against the new tower there. Never was there such a plunder. The whole face of the country for a century was that of a land recently invaded by a ruthless enemy; it was worse that the Norman conquest; nor has England ever lost this character of ravage. (63)

Violence of a previously unknown scale and veracity "created the ruins," but its effects continued for a century after the civil war was over. Akin to the Norman Conquest, Henry VIII's "conquest" rendered the entire country into one ravaged by conflict, transforming English community into a dissociated aggregation.

Henry VIII's civil war might have been the initial blow, but it inaugurated a new era of English history configured by a dualistic schema. Disraeli's criticism of Henry VIII itself has a prehistory a decade earlier in his pamphlet *Vindication of the English Constitution* (1835), where he notes how "in the reign of Henry the Eighth, the aristocracy afforded some indications of reviving power, a new feature appeared in European, and especially in English politics, which changed the whole frame and coloured the complete aspect of our society—RELIGIOUS DISSENSION."[18] In *Sybil*, dissension created England's "two nations." Henry VIII's campaign created two groups—a new "Norman" aristocracy and a Saxon peasantry, both poised antagonistically toward each other. But rather than act on their antagonisms through outright violence, Disraeli describes a protracted and latent conflict that manifested through nonviolent means. Charles Egremont's ancestor Baldwin Greymount, for example, was the Ecclesiastical Commissioner of Henry VIII and was enlisted by the king to forcefully abolish the monasteries. Having gained the King's favor after the violent campaign, the Greymounts "planted themselves in the land" and forged their entry into the peerage as Norman aristocrats, complete with a transformation of the family name from "Greymount" to the pseudo-French "Egremont."[19] As the narrator mockingly notes, "It appeared that they were both Norman and baronial, their real name Egremont, which, in their patent of peerage, the family now resumed" (10).

Imperial conquests, the narrator tells us, offered the blueprint for such a usurpation of power. That is to say, conquest is both domestic and colonial in *Sybil*. Although the Egremonts are "Normans" (but in reality of Saxon origin) who instrumentalized the state to gain political and social power, their efforts are complimented by another family that is wholly un-English:

> In a commercial country like England, every half century develops some new and vast source of public wealth, which brings into national notice a new and powerful class. A couple of centuries ago, a Turkey Merchant was the great creator of wealth; the West India Planter followed him. In the middle of the last century appeared the Nabob. These three characters in their zenith in turn merged in the land, and became English aristocrats; while, the Levant decaying, the West Indies exhausted, and Hindostan plundered, the breeds died away. . . . The expenditure of the revolutionary was [sic] produced the Loanmonger, who succeeded the Nabob; and the application of science to industry developed the Manufacturer, who in turn aspires to be "large acred," and always will, so long as we have territorial constitution; a better security for the preponderance of the landed interest than any corn-law, fixed or fluctuating. (75)

The emergence of this "new and powerful" class relies on the "exhaustion" and "plundering" of the West and East Indies. Conquest in the Orient returns in its purest form to the metropole, ushering in the "large acred" of England. Over the course of the chapter we find out that the "Nabob," "Loanmonger," and "Manufacturer" in question is John Warren, an Irishman who forges entry into the English peerage. In contrast to the barbarity of the Irish working class in Carlyle's and Engels's accounts, Warren is "assiduous, discreet, and very civil" (67). His civility allows him to infiltrate the English aristocracy and succeed as a colonial administrator. He began his career as a waiter in London, but after ingratiating himself with "a gentleman who was just appointed to the government of Madras, and who wanted a valet."[20] Warren soon rises through the ranks to become an administrator for the East India Company. His initial wealth comes through his manipulation of famines on the native population so that "the great forestallers came to the rescue of the people over whose destinies they presided; and at the same time fed, and pocketed, millions" (76). Such "plunder" enables Warren to return to London where he moves up through the ranks of British society through political maneuvering and "loanmongering." His ambitions exceed wealth, for he is given entry into the English aristocracy by a king who, indebted to him, made him into a baron: he "figured in his patent as Lord Fitz-Warene, his Norman origin and descent from the old barons of this name having been discovered" (78).

As many have noted about *Sybil*, there is symmetry, at times perfect, between narratives of dispossession and forced possession.[21] The appropriation of wealth, land, and forging of aristocratic blood goes hand in hand with the creation and subjugation of another group.[22] The land that the Greymounts settled on, we learn, was the same land that belonged to Walter Gerard's ancestors. Similarly, Norman aristocrats are contrasted to the working class, who are cast as the "Saxon multitude" and "Saxon race" (284, 374). The narrator's descriptions of proletarian slums, drawn heavily from Blue books, don't tell the story of "pain" or poverty as much as deprivation and exile: "Before the doors of these dwellings, and often surrounding them, ran open drains full of animal and vegetable refuse, decomposing into disease, or sometimes in their imperfect course filling foul pits or spreading into stagnant pools, while a concentrated solution of every species of dissolving filth was allowed to soak through, and thoroughly impregnate, the walls and ground adjoining" (51).[23] Filth "impregnates" the walls between the inside and outside of working-class homes but also breaks through this threshold: "With the water streaming down the walls, the light distinguished through the roof, with no hearth even in winter, the virtuous mother in the sacred pangs of childbirth gives forth another victim to our thoughtless civilisation" (ibid.). As the "concentrated solution of dissolving filth" enters the home, the "victim to our thoughtless civilisation" enters the world. Both are discarded and out of place, for as the narrator points out, this "unhappy race" had "spread themselves over that land which had, as it were, rejected them" (53). The working class is not-at-home in their dwellings, but neither are they at home outside in England. Henry VIII's civil war displaced this "unhappy Saxon race" just as the Normans did centuries earlier, for with no monasteries "the people of Marney took refuge in conventicles, which abounded; little plain buildings of pale brick, with the names painted on them of Sion, Bethel, Bethesda; names of a distant land, and the language of a persecuted and ancient race; yet such is the mysterious power of their divine quality, breathing consolation in the nineteenth century to the harassed forms and the harrowed souls of a Saxon peasantry" (54). Stripped of political and economic power, the "persecuted and ancient race" "took refuge" in heretic meeting places hidden in plain sight: "in little plain buildings of pale brick." And so the "two nations" were born: a phantasmic "Norman" aristocracy and a Saxon peasantry exiled on their own land, all under the backdrop of British imperialism.

RACE WAR AND THE NORMAN YOKE

In *The Origins of Totalitarianism*, Hannah Arendt argues that "race thinking" of the kind described in *Sybil* emerged in the eighteenth and early nineteenth centuries when "race" didn't refer to a single biological group (as it would come to at the end of the nineteenth century) but to the existence of races, peoples, populations, and "historical deeds."[24] Comte de Boulainvilliers, Arendt argues, was the first to assume "the coexistence of different peoples with different origins in France" while at the same time "the first to elaborate definite class-thinking."[25] Fearing an emergent nation of equal fellow-citizens, Boulainvilliers rewrote French history in an anti-nationalist key such that its main actors were Franks and Gauls, conquerors and conquered, the peerage and the people. By insisting on France's ancient divisions between the aristocracy and the populace, and even valorizing the former's foreignness to the land, Boulainvilliers preserved a waning aristocratic class against an emergent nation of French citizen-subjects who sought to democratize political power. That is to say, he racialized the class struggles of late feudal/early modern society in an effort to preserve the aristocracy's privileged status.

When race thinking arrived in England in the late eighteenth century, the historical event at its center was the Norman Conquest.[26]
The Norman yoke was a recurrent trope in early nineteenth-century
historical discourse that nostalgically turned to the Conquest, and
medieval England more generally, to highlight the troubles of industrial society. The most famous of such histories was, in a way, not a
history at all: Walter Scott's *Ivanhoe* (1820). Scott's historical novel
is set in the aftermath of the Norman Conquest, when England was
not divided into rich and poor but Norman and Saxon, conquerors
and conquered.[27] The novel's opening passage anchors the national
saga in the land: "In that pleasant district of merry England which
is watered by the river Don. . . . Here haunted of yore the fabulous
Dragon of Wantley, here were fought many of the most desperate
battles during the Civil Wars of the Roses, and here also flourished
in ancient times those bands of gallant outlaws whose deeds have
been rendered so popular in English song."[28] Having linked history
to soil, and populated both with national myths, Scott transports the
reader to the century following the Norman Conquest, when England
was composed not of one nation but two.[29] These two nations, the
narrator tells us, were "victors" and "vanquished": "All the monarchs of the Norman race had shown the most marked predilection
for their Norman subjects; the laws of the chase, and many others,
equally unknown to the milder and more free spirit of the Saxon
constitution, had been fixed upon the necks of the subjugated inhabitants, to add weight, as it were, to the feudal chains with which they
were loaded."[30] According to Scott's narrator, the Norman Conquest
was not a singular historical incursion that took place in 1066 but a
protracted relation of force and domination between a foreign army
and indigenous population that lasted until the fourteenth century.
These struggles, the narrator explains, reproduced racial divisions of
foreigners and natives: "although no great historical events, such as
war or insurrection, mark the existence of the Anglo-Saxons as a
separate people subsequent to the right of William the Second, yet
the great national distinctions betwixt them and their conquerors . . .
continued . . . to keep open the wounds which the Conquest had
inflicted, and to maintain a line of separation betwixt the descendants of the victor Normans and the vanquished Saxons."[31] According to Scott's narrator, the Conquest usurped not only the Crown but
also Saxon institutions and property: "At court, and in the castles of
the great nobles, where the pomp and state of a court was emulated,

Norman-French was the only language employed; in courts of law, the pleadings and judgements were delivered in the same tongue."[32]

Scott's novel, which he wished to be seen as history, directly influenced Thierry's *History of the Conquest of England by the Normans* (1825) and Thomas Macaulay's *The History of England from the Accession of James II* (1848).[33] Even though Macaulay's history concerns the period after 1685 following the succession of James II, it begins with an account of the Norman yoke: "The subjugation of a nation by a nation has seldom, even in Asia, been more complete. The country was portioned out among the captains of the invaders. Strong military institutions, closely connected with the institution of property, enabled the foreign conquerors to oppress the children of the soil."[34] By fusing "strong military institutions" with "the institution of property," Macaulay suggests that conquest is actually a form of politics. Similarly, although Thierry's *History* is punctuated by wars and battles, it primarily focuses on the relations of force by which one race dominated another over four centuries. Thierry in fact outlines five epochs in this long conquest: territorial usurpation by the Norman army, the usurpation of political institutions, forcible possession of Saxon lands by Norman soldiers, internal conflicts within the Norman race, and finally the melding together of Saxon and Norman culture.[35] This historical arc reveals that the invasion was actually only a nominal part of the Conquest, which is why the vast majority of the *History* details the protracted manner in which Normans took control of Saxon institutions, a usurpation that turned out to be the building block of England's national identity. A crucial stage in Thierry's account of the Conquest is the usurpation of Saxon lands by the Normans through legal means, detailing how "king William established as a general law, that every title to property anterior to his invasion, and every act of transfer or transmission of property made by a man of the English race prior to the invasion, was null and void . . . and when the churches could not produce written proof [of to whom the land belonged] the land was seized."[36] The violence of the Conquest continues by the other means of the law. The use of juridico-political institutions for the ends of conquest, Foucault points out, is a central feature in race war discourse where "law is not pacification, for beneath the law, war continues to rage in all the mechanisms of power."[37] Because war is disguised in the institutions of everyday life, so are the agents of historical change. That is to say, this bifurcated vision of the world went hand in hand with a progressivist narrative of it. Writing of this same historical discourse, Lukács explains that historians "attempted to uncover the real driving forces of history as they objectively worked to explain history from them."[38] And Thierry's history was particularly influential because his "theory of the struggles of races was the first step towards a coherent and scientific history of progress."[39] Far from "development in reverse," as it is seen today, intranational bifurcations and struggles in fact propelled the European society forward in history.

As is already evident in these examples, inherent to race war discourse is a tension between race and class. This discourse racializes England's rich and poor into discrete populations, like Normans and Saxons, and binds them in an asymmetrical relation of force. Narratives of "race wars" therefore functioned as lenses into class difference. This is why Thierry claims present-day class divisions are "the lineal representatives of the peoples conquering and peoples conquered of an anterior epoch."[40] Social inequality, he contends, is not rooted in modes of production but historical coincidence: "The race of the invaders, when it ceased to be a separate nation, remained a privileged class. It formed a military nobility, which . . . domineered over laborious and peaceful masses below them. . . . The invaded race, despoiled of property in the soil, of command, and of liberty, not living by the sword but the compulsory labour of their hands, swelling not in castles but in towns, formed a separate society beside the military associate of the conquerors."[41] Having completely colonized sociopolitical institutions, modern-day class is simply the continuation of race by other means. Here, class difference is not a product of modes of production or even industrialization but the Norman Conquest's codification in civil society. In other words, the only way to fully illuminate class relations is through a history of race war.

Of course, neither Scott, Macaulay, nor Thierry is interested in demonstrating the falsity of English nationality. Rather, by beginning their histories in the Conquest and ending in the fusion of Norman and Saxon peoples, they chart the fusion of two foreign populations into a single nation. The arc of all their histories begins with racial foreignness and ends in national unity. While the original crime was the incursion of a foreign army followed by a brutal regime of usurpation and domination, the motor of this historical plot is the slow eradication of racial difference—the transformation of the race war into race. For Scott, the first step to the unification of these two nations into one was the formation of a "linguistic community": "The necessary intercourse between the lords of the soil, and those oppressed inferior beings by whom that soil was cultivated, occasioned the gradual formation of a dialect, compounded betwixt the French and the Anglo-Saxon, in which they could render themselves mutually intelligible to each other; and from this necessity arose by degrees the structure of our present English language, in which the speech of the victors and the vanquished have been so happily blended together."[42] England's historical arc goes from conquest to subjugation under the "Norman yoke" to the formation of a common language that eventually culminates in the unification of Norman and Saxon into a single people. And as in Scott, Macaulay suggests that the Norman yoke was integral to the mingling and eventual unification of English national identity: "Shut up by the sea with the people whom they had hitherto oppressed and despised, they gradually came to regard England as their country, and the English as their countrymen. The two races so long hostile, soon found that they had common interests and common enemies."[43] So while an ancient race war initially dispossessed and dominated the Saxon race, it is but a distant episode in England's history. That Normans and Saxons are no longer distinguishable in the present, in fact, attests to just how distant, yet formative, an event the Conquest was. Macaulay concludes (somewhat shockingly given the fact of the British empire): "In no country has the enmity of race been carried farther than in England. In no country has that enmity been more completely effaced."[44] While Thierry draws much from the tropes of race war, and Scott's historical novel in particular, his concluding pages suggest a more complicated trajectory, describing not the triumph of national unity but the selective memory of nationalist historiography. In a perfect example of what Anderson calls the "reassurance of fratricide," Thierry renders the Conquest into a quaint event in the ancient past: "Normans and Saxons exist only in history; and as the latter fill the less brilliant part, the mass of English readers, little versed in the national antiquities, willingly deceive themselves as to their origin, and regard the sixty thousand companions of William the Conqueror as the common ancestors of all the people of England. Thus a London shopkeeper and a Yorkshire farmer say: 'our Norman ancestors.'"[45] Although divisions between the classes or city and country may persist in the present day, and may indeed have their roots in the Conquest, the English people remain one.

Sybil inverts the narrative arc of all of these histories. Rather than begin with the division between two foreign groups, its counterhistory begins in unity, transitions to disunity during and after Henry VIII's reign, and reverts again to unity during the peak of the industrial revolution. In the novel's climax, a riot breaks out that recalls imagery of England's birth, for it "announced to the startled country that in a short hour the splendid mimickry of Norman rule would cease to exist" (416).[46] It is noteworthy that in this scene, the working class, who have until now been likened to "Saxons," are equated to Normans. All of a sudden, the dominated become the dominant. By inverting the relation of power, the scene underscores how the category of "race" in *Sybil* doesn't refer to a particular ethnological unit but describes a relation of power. This is precisely what makes the positions of the conquerors and conquered so easily reversible. Gallagher argues that the riot "reverses the original violence of [Sybil's] displacement from history. Instead of being another displacement, it is the reversal of a displacement, the undoing of history."[47] Sybil regains her rightful place in the aristocracy, thereby dispossessing "new" aristocrats like Lord Marney, righting centuries of domination. Much as in Carlyle, Disraeli's narrative of national rupture concludes, as Chris R. Vanden Bossche puts it, with "a working class that ultimately relinquishes its claims for a role in governance and accepts the benign rule of a single aristocrat."[48] The "splendid mimickry of Norman rule" by rebellious workers undoes centuries of repression and recuperates England to its medieval ideal.[49] Rather than a repetition of an ancient fratricide, the riot pulls the veil off the two nations, showing them to be the same, thereby reverting England to its "natural form and hue" as one nation. The novel's denouement is therefore premised on the retrospective recognition that English history from the sixteenth century onward is not saturated with a war between two nations but within one nation.

As though to drive home this fact, the final scene of the novel symbolizes the unification of England's two nations in the marriage of Sybil and Egremont. Early in the novel, Sybil is a staunch supporter of the People's Charter and refuses Egremont as a husband because she is "one of those who believe the gulf [between rich and poor] is impassable." The novel's conclusion disproves this impassibility when Egremont, following a long courtship with Sybil, saves her from a mob of workers in the midst of a riot.[50] As Egremont tells Sybil in the penultimate chapter of the novel (the last conversation between them before the novel ends): "We will never part again," to which she responds: "never" (417). Their union is not a reconciliation but the recognition that the gulf between the two nations, between Sybil and Egremont, was never really there. Bivona has described the takeaway from this conclusion succinctly: "*Sybil* sets out initially to demonstrate that

England is two nations, only to awaken the reader finally to the same realization as Sybil and Egremont at the end: that the two nations are really one."[51] In other words, the novel's claim is that there is no need to "surpass" the gulf between the classes because it is an imagined chasm—everyone belongs to the same nation. *Sybil* perfectly dramatizes the novel's classic function within nationalist discourse, which, as Jonathan Culler explains, doesn't imagine the nation as much as represent national unity as a condition of possibility of imagining the nation. *Sybil* doesn't create England's national unity but emplots its unity as a story—it makes the idea of a single English nation legible by calling attention to its distinctively *English* internal divisions over the course of its history. While the novel's polemic might be that England is divided into two antagonistic nations, its intervention is to actually demonstrate the falsity of this divide. By the novel's end, we learn that the gulf between the two nations was never really there; at its core, *Sybil* never truly believes its second title.

One could, as many have, understand *Sybil* to instrumentalize the concept of the nation to flatten and neutralize class difference and antagonism. No matter how wide the gap, how sharp the mutual antagonism between the classes, England's underlying fraternity dispels dangers of class war. Such readings follow a tradition as old as *The Communist Manifesto* that views the "nation" as a hindrance to and obfuscation of class struggle. Balibar explains that nationalist discourse "dissolves social inequalities in an even more ambivalent 'similarity'; it ethnicizes social difference which is an expression of irreconcilable antagonisms by lending it the form of a division between the 'genuinely' and 'falsely' national."[52] The institution of the novel, Raymond Williams has famously argued, is implicated in this ideological maneuver. The Victorian industrial novel in particular, while invested in a realist rendering of the poor and their struggle, pulls back out of fear of an irreconcilably divided society, turning instead to plots that resolve in marriage, inheritance, and national unity: "Sympathy was transformed, not into action, but into withdrawal," such as inheritance, marriage, and travel to the colonies.[53] Hence *Sybil* does away with the problem of class divisions without actually alleviating the structures that create class as such.

However, because *Sybil*, and English race war discourse more generally, understands civil war as a hybridization of nation, race, and class, it means that the flattening of social difference by nationality doesn't work in the same way as it is typically understood to. While critics have been correct to understand *Sybil* to institute English unity by utilizing history as a technique of the national imagination, they have mis-recognized the implications of this "unification." For what is up for debate in Disraeli's novel is *the foreignness* of the two nations from each other, *not the war* they have been intertwined in for centuries. Very simply, we begin the novel aware that there are two Englands and end the novel by realizing that there is only one. *But what doesn't change* is the history of war and conquest that has bound these two groups for centuries. The logical consequence of retrospectively collapsing two nations (who are actually two classes) into one nation is that a history of class antagonism is recast as a history of intra*national* conflict; a history of class war becomes a history of civil war. All along, it is not "bourgeois and proletariat, oppressor and oppressed" who have been engaged in latent war but fellow-countrymen. Thus it is not quite correct to say that the novel turns to the category of the nation to unify English society, for the community it imagines is constituted by centuries of civil war. *Sybil*'s response to the "two nations" thesis seems to be: because the history of England is really a long civil war, it can't be "two nations" but one. Paradoxically, the fratricidal quality of England's internal conflicts retrospectively "proves" the nation's racial unity. Fraternity might shift the reader's attention away from class difference, but not without also undermining fraternal harmony by narrating a history of fratricide. *The fact of fratricide institutes English unity.* Rather than a crisis to be avoided, the internality of the war between the "new" aristocracy and the "natural" peerage, Normans and Saxons, rich and poor, resurrects the underlying bond between Englishmen. *Sybil* thus produces England's fictive ethnicity counterintuitively: it undermines the "two nation" theory by showing the falsity of this divide, and in effect narrates a fictive ethnicity *as* fratricide. The function of Disraeli's poetics of national rupture, much like Carlyle's, is to at once reveal the crisis that lies beneath the surface of English society and at the same time present its solution. Only in Disraeli's case, the "solution" to the "two nations" is simply recognizing the falsity of this divide.

Herein lies one of the novel's most suggestive observations about nationalism: because the plot shifts from the axis of class to nation, it places a protracted civil war at the center of the national saga. The category of the "nation" in *Sybil* is not implicated in the embourgeoisement of English society, supplanting class with kinship, but maps class antagonisms onto civic conflict. The problem Disraeli's poetics of national rupture therefore raises for theories of nationalism and historians of the nation is that it places civil war at the center of the historiography of England. Attending to *Sybil*'s narration of civil war thus requires reevaluating some of the basic assumptions about national historiography: Why is the historical signifier of the nation fraternity and not (also) fratricide? Instead of race, can't "race war" be the symbolic kernel of the national imagination? If the nation's historical form is its ontology, then what happens to this ontology when history's focal point is national rupture? One of Benedict Anderson's most influential claims about nationalism is that the novel was central to consolidating the national imagination of Europe's emergent civil societies. But if the novel, and specifically the historical novel, creates "the conditions of possibility" for imagining political community as nation, then *Sybil*'s narration of a long civil war makes it possible to conceive of national *disunity* as the symbolic kernel of political community. *Sybil* imagines English community by, as it were, demonstrating that it has been un-imagined over centuries. If the nation is *the* ideological form of societies divided by class because it denies the very possibility of thinking about real divisions, then *Sybil* teaches us how the novel can be an ideological form by denying the possibility of thinking about real union. For if novels make national unity legible, then they must necessarily make national rupture equally conceivable.

PART II

Civilizing Mission

Lord Acton's 1862 essay "Nationality" argues that imperialism is essential to the lifeblood of the nation. The premise of his essay is that "where political and national boundaries coincide, society ceases to advance, and nations relapse into a condition corresponding to that of men who renounce intercourse with their fellow-men."[1] Progress falters and social bonds weaken when the state is in territorial synchrony with the nation. The antidote to this condition of degeneracy (when "political and national boundaries coincide") is imperialism. In fact, the expansion of the state outside of the nation benefits colonizer and colonized alike: "Inferior races are raised by living in political union with races intellectually superior. Exhausted and decaying nations are revived by the contact of a younger vitality."[2] If it were not for imperialism, Europe's great empires would have lost "elements of organizations and the capacity for government" and "relapsed" into a lower stage of civilization. By Acton's account, English nationalism without British imperialism would result in something akin to what the World Bank today calls "development in reverse"—regressing progress made by capitalist modernity. For England to avoid sociopolitical degeneracy, it would have to endlessly expand outward, eventually encompassing the entire globe and all its peoples. One day, Acton suggests, all of humanity will be English.

Acton's essay anticipates the late Victorian dream of an imperial nation-state. In 1869, Charles Dilke published *Greater Britain*, a travelogue about England's colonies—current and old—in which he proclaimed that places as diverse as America and India were in fact "Englands planted across the seas."[3] Some years later, J. R. Seeley argued in *The Expansion of England* that England's settler colonies, Canada, Australia, New Zealand, and (most problematically) South Africa, were in fact satellite Englands.[4] For Acton, Dilke, and Seeley, the civilizing mission goes hand in hand with the expansion of national identity.[5] Even non-settler colonies like India were en route to becoming English. Echoing Macaulay's call for the education of a class "Indian in blood" but "English in taste," Dilke maintains that Englishness can in fact be taught.[6] His civilizing mission centers on reproducing English culture and society overseas: "All that is necessary at the moment [for British rule in India] is that we should concede the principle by appointing, year by year, more natives to high posts, and that, by holding civil service examinations in India as well as in England, and by establishing throughout India well-regulated schools, we should place the competent native youths upon an equal footing with the English."[7] By making Indian subjects in the image of the English, Dilke suggests that perhaps one day Indians will be fellow-subjects, as proclaimed by the queen, as well as "fellow-men."[8] In this "waiting room of history," the defining feature of historical progress is the making-English of the uncivilized outside through cultural education.[9]

But Acton's essay also contains within it the collapse of this imperial dream. For according to the logic of his essay, the highest stage of civilization—when the English nation is global—is also the moment of its decline. With nowhere left to conquer, this future global England would eventually crave "contact with a younger vitality," grow old, "exhausted," and "decay" into something less developed and civilized. Lacking the "younger vitality" of places like India to nourish itself, England would have nothing to consume but itself.[10] The civilized nation's insatiable appetite for conquest and regeneration means that its imperial *telos* is always toward self-starvation; the civilizing mission sounds its own death knell. It is no coincidence that late Victorian writers were fixated on the fall of the British empire and nation. Richard Marsh's *The Beetle* (1897) and H. G. Wells's *War of the Worlds* (1898), for example, narrate fears of "reverse imperialism," be it Egyptian loot that wreaks supernatural havoc in London or the invasion of a technologically superior but biologically inferior Martian race. Lesser-known fiction like Horace Frank Lester's *The Taking of Dover* (1888) and Louis Tracy's *The Final War* (1896) narrate the conquest of Britain by

European armies.[11] Jurists like James Bryce contemplated the future of the British empire in conjunction with the ancient Roman empire, paying especially close attention to the causes for the latter's decline.[12] Even Dilke would question the tenability of "Saxondom" when he published a sequel to Greater Britain in 1890 under the much humbler title, The Problems of Greater Britain.

At the heart of this transformation is a crisis in the narrative of progress. In the mid-nineteenth century, a writer like Dickens had complete faith in modernity's natural expansion from the center to the periphery. Bleak House excoriates Mrs. Jellyby's "telescopic philanthropy" toward the Borrioboola-Gha of the Niger delta because she is blind to the lack of cultivation among the English working class.[13] In his reflection on the failed Niger Expedition of 1841, arguably the inspiration for his rendering of Mrs. Jellyby, Dickens argues that it is better to wait for modernity to globalize itself over time rather than for England to undertake directed efforts to civilize Africa: "The stone that is dropped into the ocean of ignorance at Exeter Hall, must make its widening circles, one beyond another, until they reach the negro's country in their natural expansion."[14] The shock wave of modernity sounds in the center and must be allowed to expand outward of its own accord. Historically postponed though it may be, the waves of British modernity, having originated in the metropole, will one day arrive at the shores of "the negro's country." But when these ripples finally arrived on the coasts of Africa at the turn of the century, British writers were confronted by the contradictions of the civilizing mission, leading to a historical sensibility of stalled progress and uneven development in the peripheries. And no generic mode was better equipped to narrate this crisis in the story of modernity and progress than literary modernism. When Marlow reaches the African coast in Heart of Darkness (1899), the waves of modernity Dickens spoke of are as irrational as they are impotent: "The edge of a colossal jungle, so dark-green as to be almost black, fringed with white surf, ran straight, like a ruled line, far, far along a blue sea whose glitter was blurred by a creeping mist. . . . Settlements—settlements, some centuries old, and still no bigger than pin-heads on the untouched expanse of their background."[15] Marlow then lays bare the violence at the heart of the civilizing mission: "We came upon a man-of-war anchored off the coast. There wasn't even a shed there, and she was shelling the bush. . . . In the empty immensity of earth, sky, and water, there she was, incomprehensible, firing into a continent. Pop, would go one of the eight-inch guns; a small flame would dart and vanish, a little white smoke would disappear, a tiny projectile would give a feeble screech—and nothing happened. Nothing could happen."[16] For a realist like Dickens, nothing needed to happen to civilize Africa; modernity would come in due time through its own natural expansion. For Marlow, and arguably Conrad himself, "nothing could happen."

Such a sensibility, as many critics have noted, was central to the aesthetic of early modernism.[17] In what follows, I argue that integral to the historical imagination of early modernism was a poetics of national rupture that no longer indexed the force of history but instead the failures of modernization in the colonial world. I find that narratives of civil war were essential to the way in which late imperial discourse could, on the one hand, celebrate the zenith of its civilizing mission for successfully creating a world in its own image and, on the other hand, lament this very empire's downfall. If the poetics of national rupture acted as a field of intelligibility into the national condition in the early Victorian period, then at the turn of the century this very literary discourse exposed the contradictions of colonial modernity. Hence Cecil Rhodes's famous declaration to his countrymen: "If you want to avoid civil war, you must become imperialists."[18] This line was made famous by V. I. Lenin, who saw imperialism not as the savior of metropolitan political unity but as a "moribund capitalism," "a shell which must of necessity begin to decay if its destruction be postponed by artificial means."[19] Imperialism, the zenith of capitalism, was also the natural tipping point toward its downfall. The chapters that follow revise Lenin's thesis so that the axis of modernity is not capitalist development but civil war, which I argue was at the turn of the century in transition from representing the highest to the lowest stage of civilization.

CHAPTER 4

Civil War, the Highest Stage of Civilization

Prior to writing *Imperialism* (1902), arguably one of the most influential critiques of empire of the twentieth century, J. A. Hobson traveled to South Africa to report on the Second Anglo-Boer War. Hobson was most struck by what he called "the 'civil' nature of this war" because the conflict pitted members of the same settler community against each other. "Dutch and British are at each other's throats in Africa," Hobson comments, "but there is scarcely a single family where the races in some way do not meet. Everywhere men of British descent have married Boer girls, and many of them have taken burghership and have grown sons who are by upbringing and by sympathy full Boers. Enter any of these farms, and you would find that there are relatives living in the Colony or in Natal, British subjects, divided in feeling between loyalty to the Empire and affection for their Republican kin."[1] Although the war was ostensibly between foreign armies, British and Boer integration at the Cape meant that the war had a civil quality to it. Because Boers were British subjects rebelling against their own queen and fighting fellow-British subjects, they were effectively also at war with their own "Republican kin" whom they married and with whom they shared homes and had children.[2] Hobson doesn't characterize the war in South Africa as an offshore European conflict like the Crimean War or a colonial war like the Indian Mutiny or the Morant Bay Rebellion but likens it to a war fought between fellow-citizens.[3]

Hobson was not alone in his summation of the Boer War as a civil war. Amid the jingoistic fervor that accompanied the outbreak the conflict, Arthur Conan Doyle, despite his mother's concerns about his "height and breadth," rushed to enlist in the British army. Mary Doyle's trepidations were, as it turned out, validated by a colonel who rejected her son's application to join the army.[4] Undeterred, Doyle reached the war front by resurrecting his dormant qualifications as a physician and served as a surgeon for a British hospital in Bloemfontein. While in South Africa, Doyle undertook his most jingoistic piece of writing, an extended report titled *The Great Boer War* (1901), which celebrated the war in the Cape because it brought together Britons from all over the globe. He writes that "the [settler] colonies appreciated the fact that the contention was no affair of the mother country alone, but that she was upholding the rights of the empire as a whole."[5] Doyle romanticizes the British army in the South African war effort as an amalgam of "Cowboys from the vast plains of the North-West, gentleman who ride hard with the Quorn or the Belvoir, gillies from the Sutherland deer forests, bushmen from the back blocks of Australia, exquisites of the Raleigh Club or the Bachelor's, hard men from Ontario, dandy sportsmen from India and Ceylon, the horsemen of New Zealand, the wiry South African irregulars. . . . On the plains of South Africa, in common danger and in common privation, the blood brotherhood of the Empire was sealed."[6] Doyle's imperial vision is that the "hard men from Ontario" belong to the same imperial nation as the "horsemen of New Zealand." In other words, the geographic realities of the empire no longer impeded British national feeling, thereby allowing the joint war effort to congeal the "blood brotherhood of the Empire." That the Boer War brought all these peoples together proved what was at stake for nationalists like Doyle: a national kinship that had been globalized yet which remained anchored in race.

Animating Hobson's and Doyle's response to the war is the sense that the British nation-state had expanded beyond the British Isles.[7] But the moment Greater Britain seemed to become a reality is also the moment of its dissolution. Doyle contemplates, "Had we really founded a series of disconnected nations with no common sentiment or interest, or was the empire an organic whole, as ready to thrill with one emotion or to harden into one resolve as are the several States of the Union?"[8] In Doyle's mind, there were only two possible outcomes of the war: the solidification of the empire into a single nation-state, as "several States of the Union," or the "dissolution" of the entire *imperium*. And

Doyle, like Hobson, turns to the figure of civil war to characterize this moment of contradiction:

> It was pitiable that it should come to this. These people [the Boers] were as near akin to us as any race which is not our own. They were of the same Frisian stock which peopled our own shores. In habit of mind, in religion, in respect for law, they were as ourselves. Brave, too, they were, and hospitable, with those sporting instincts which are dear to the Anglo-Celtic race. There was no people in the world who had more qualities which we might admire, and not the least of them was that love of independence which it is our proudest boast that we have encouraged in others as well as exercised ourselves. And yet it has come to this pass, that there was no room in all vast South Africa for both of us.[9]

Victorians were notoriously vague about the distinctions between race and nation, invariably using the terms interchangeably, and Doyle was no exception.[10] In *The Great Boer War*, Boers are described as racially proximate to the British and culturally identical to the "Anglo-Celtic race." They share the same sense of "hospitality," "sporting instincts," and "love of independence" that defines British culture. In doing so, Doyle gives the Boer War an internal quality for although it took place in the colonies, it effectively amounted to a war between "equal fellow-citizens."[11] Hence the Second Anglo-Boer War was romanticized as "The Last of the Gentleman's Wars," or as Kipling would call it, a "sahibs' war" because "gentlemanly" combat was (supposedly) reserved for those who were civilized, Britons and Boers, and excluded those who were uncivilized, non-European colonial subjects.[12] Once foreigners, the imperial experience had rendered Briton and Boer into fellow-citizens at war.

Of course, the idea of an imperial civil war was nothing new in British history. The American War of Independence was frequently characterized by its early historians in precisely these terms.[13] For Britons (and tellingly, *not* American settlers), the "imperial civil war of 1776" represented a constitutional problem that emerged in the years prior to the War of Independence: by defining themselves a separate state, American settler colonies declared themselves to be wholly outside of the British constitutional purview. To put it plainly, civil war was a scandal of statehood, not nationhood. But this juridical schema for understanding colonial rebellion vanishes in the mid-nineteenth century when the defining feature of political community shifted from the state and its legal reach to national culture. If the juridical paradigm of imperial civil war had remained intact in the nineteenth century, then uprisings and revolutions like the Indian Mutiny and the Morant Bay Rebellion, despite being wars of independence, would have also been seen by metropolitans as civil wars and not irrational acts of colonial treachery. The possibility of Britain's colonies being in a civil war with the metropole, however, returns at the end of the nineteenth century when Britain's national imagination expanded into a global entity, and furthermore sought to crystalize "Saxondom" into a single imperial nation-state.

Why is it that the most ambitious moment of the British empire, when it seemed to have become a global nation-state, coincides with one of its most destabilizing moments, when its citizens were at war with each other? Why is the highest stage of civilization—of having successfully "planted Englands across the sea"—also the moment of its internal rupture? This conjuncture of national unity and disunity represents perhaps the most vivid historical instance of the Victorian "bond of division" I have been tracking in this book so far. For while the "civil nature" of the Boer War proves that Briton and Boer had evolved from fellow-Europeans into "equal fellow-citizens," the very nature of this antagonism as "civic" undermines their political union. Thus while the Boer War is to a writer like Doyle (and, as I will argue in this chapter, Kipling) the occasion for crystallizing a British imperial nation-state, it also calls Britain's transcontinental national bonds into question. Although a "bond of division" continues to characterize Hobson's and Doyle's national thinking as it did in the early Victorian years, it is now geographically untethered from the British Isles. So while writers like Engels, Carlyle, Disraeli, and Gaskell turned to narratives of national rupture to differentiate the condition of England question from the Irish question, the intranational from the extranational, by the end of the nineteenth century civic conflict was increasingly enmeshed in the imperial milieu within which it could now take place. As I argue toward the end of this chapter, this had the added effect of confusing distinctions between anticolonial wars and "white men's wars" as in the case of the Boer War, "civil" civil wars and uncivil anticolonial uprisings. At stake in this historical moment is not only the possible unity or disunity of a nation but the boundaries between the national and the extranational, between civility and incivility, progress and stasis. In what follows, I discuss how one of the reasons for the conjuncture of national unity and disunity in the colonies is the idea that Greater Britain did not so much expand England, as some of its proponents claimed, but shuttled between the registers of the national and colonial, metropolitan and peripheral, intranational and extranational. This oscillation created the very instabilities of the imperial domain that would eventually be fundamental to the confusions between imperial civil wars and anticolonial rebellions.

SAXONDOM

Dilke begins *Greater Britain* by reflecting on his travels throughout the empire and the Americas: "I followed England round the world, everywhere I was in English-speaking, or in English-governed lands."[14] Seeing settler colonies as "greater Englands planted across the seas," Dilke reinvents the imagined community of England at a global scale.[15] He envisions an empire-form that sees no distinctions between London and Sydney—both are equally and evenly English. Dilke removes England from its territorial casing in the British Isles and redistributes to its settler colonies around the world. What globalizes this nation-form is neither its size nor reach but what John Plotz has called the "portability" of Englishness.[16] England's settler colonies were "Rooted in Alfred's laws and Chaucer's tongue," enabling them to replicate the metropole in complete fidelity, thereby valorizing the universality of English culture.[17]

Culture, as it turns out, is all that is needed to unify Greater Britain. Despite America's war of independence in the previous century, the United States in Dilke's view is an integral part of Greater Britain. "After all," he explains, "there is not in America a greater wonder than the Englishman himself, for it is to this continent that you must come to find him in full possession of his powers."[18] America is the fullest expression of English national identity and thrives in isolation of formal political unity with Britain.[19] Using the term "Saxondom" synonymously with "Greater Britain," Dilke goes so far as to call for the political and economic *untethering* of settler colonies from the metropole, because "the strongest of the arguments in favour of separation is the somewhat paradoxical one that would bring us a step nearer to the virtual confederation of the English race."[20] Greater Britain doesn't need political or juridical unification because the unity of the Anglo-Saxon race and culture persists despite America and

England inhabiting different political frameworks, which Dilke calls a "virtual confederation."[21] Hence America directly contributes to British imperial expansion: "America is becoming, not English merely, but world-embracing in a variety of its type; and, as the English element has given language and history to that land, America offers the English race the moral directorship of the globe, by ruling mankind through Saxon institutions and the English tongue. Through America England is speaking to the world."[22] What is key here is that "Saxon institutions and the English tongue" allow England to permeate the world by way of America, which acts not of its own accord but as a proxy for English hegemony around the world. The project of Greater Britain involves a "mental miscegenation" that produces national homogeneity throughout the empire.[23]

But if Greater Britain is rooted in language and institutions, then why must it be disseminated throughout the world via offshore sites like America? If England is uniquely portable so as to retain its core identity overseas, why can't it speak to the world? Why must America do all the talking?

Dilke's answer has to do with England's innate provincialism. He argues that settler colonies are essential to the project of a Greater Britain because they "preserve us from the curse of small island countries, the dwarfing of mind which would otherwise make us Guernsey a little magnified. . . . That which raises us above the provincialism of citizenship of little England is our citizenship of the greater Saxondom which includes all that is best and wisest in the world."[24] England's geographic condition—a "small island country"—has a natural tendency toward a "dwarfed mind." By privileging territory as the defining characteristic of national identity, Dilke implies that England cannot imagine a transcontinental empire like Greater Britain because it is naturally inclined toward Guernseyian provincialism. English nationality is "dwarfed" by territorial limitations and boundedness. But if this is the case, then how can it extend beyond these borders while retaining its Englishness? How can England be globalized if provincialism is congenital to it?

Settler colonialism thus emerges as a decidedly *un-English* means by which to undo England's a priori insularity. The civilizing mission of Greater Britain had to retain some incivility within its domain, or else it would, as Acton suggested, degenerate into incivility. This is why Dilke's ambivalence about English national identity is so important to his idea of Greater Britain, because for nationality to be removed from its territorial casing, to be portable, to be plantable across the seas, it relies on something foreign to itself. Like supplements to Saxondom, settler colonies are racial, linguistic, and cultural replicas of England while at the same time foreign to it.[25] To speak to the world, America must have an identity of its own different from an England "planted across the sea." Inversely, although America, New Zealand, and Canada are replicas of England, they don't inherit its innate provincialism. If New Zealand is "the Britain of the South" by virtue of its "situation, size, and climate," then why doesn't it suffer from the same debilitating provincialism that England does? In all these cases, it is impossible for Saxondom to be merely English or merely global, as evident in the contradiction announced in the opening sentence of *Greater Britain*: "I followed England round the world." My point here is that the idea of Greater Britain doesn't describe a homogeneous, static place but a *dynamic* that shuttles between England and "Englands planted across the seas." To speak of Greater Britain, Dilke teaches us, is to speak of the intranational and extranational, the metropolitan and the colonial simultaneously.

The imperial project described in *Greater Britain* was institutionalized in the decades after its publication. The Colonial Society (founded in 1868) and the Imperial Federation League (1884–1983), for example, represented different offshoots of the project of a British imperial nation-state. But of all the mouthpieces of a British imperial nationhood, J. R. Seeley was and continues to be the most central figure concerning Greater Britain. Seeley's contribution was to present Greater Britain less of a project and more of a concrete geographical reality. His best-known work, a series of lectures titled *The Expansion of England*, was one of the best-sellers of the late Victorian period, read routinely by schoolchildren, and remained in print until 1956. His achievement in *The Expansion of England* was to historicize Britain's expansion into a global polity. Seen as the founding father of British imperial history, Seeley was the first to bring together Britain's national and imperial history, narrating Cromwell's rise alongside the conquest of the New World.[26] Seeley's goal in the lectures, David Armitage explains, was "to effect an expansion of the English historical imagination, particularly as it remembered the eighteenth century."[27] Central to Seeley's history was the elimination of geographic distances by technological advancement. The extranational space of empire was absorbed into the national domain as their distances were reduced. Hence Seeley states that the late Victorian empire is "not an Empire at all. . . . It does not consist of a congeries of nations held together by force, but in the main of one nation, as much as if it were no Empire but an ordinary state."[28] Seeley's England, rather than being naturally "Guernseyian," has an innate "tendency towards expansion."[29]

But where Seeley diverged most was in his understanding of Greater Britain as a state *in addition to* a nation.[30] Although Britain had "conquered and peopled half the world in a fit of absence of mind," this accidental expansion was accompanied by "a real enlargement of the English State," for Greater Britain "carries across the seas not merely the English race, but the authority of the English Government."[31] Seeley's nation and state always correspond, and consequently, his idea of Greater Britain, despite its transoceanic form, is imagined as a contiguous entity. He accomplishes this by distancing himself from a Greek conception of sovereignty and bases his notion of empire on the conflation of the English nation (understood in entirely racial terms) and the state: "The Greek mind identifies the State and the City so completely that the language, as you know, has but one word for both. . . . If the State is a City, it follows that he who goes outside of the City goes out of the State. . . . But if the State is the Nation . . . then we see a sufficient ground for the universal usage of modern states, which has been to regard their emigrants not as going out of the state but as carrying the State with them. . . . Where Englishman are there is England."[32] Colonial territories are blank slates with no national imprint. The implication is that all soil is potentially English soil, as long as English bodies can settle on it. Seeley assumes "Englishmen" retain their Englishness in foreign lands.[33] And by linking the state to its subjects, he renders England as portable as its people. Seeley inherits this statist conception of the empire from Lord Palmerston, who in his famous speech in 1850 on the Don Pacifico affair argued that Britain was justified in militarily intervening in foreign countries because "as the Roman, in days of old, held himself free from indignity, when he could say *Civis Romanus sum*; so also a British subject, in whatever land he may be, shall feel confident that the watchful eye and strong arm of England will protect him against injustice and wrong."[34] Because the "strong arm of England" follows British subjects wherever they set foot, Palmerston envisions the British *imperium* to be potentially everywhere.[35] Such a vision for the empire is statist through and through, relying on the state to create civilizing contact-zones between the metropole and its ever-widening circle of colonies.

The conflation of English bodies and English soil—the classical registers of citizenship, *jus sanguini* and *jus soli*—transforms what national territory looks like. Seeley makes the point that until the nineteenth century, "the Ocean had been a limit, a boundary, not a pathway."[36] What had been a geographic frontier to imperial expansion—the ocean—is transformed into a means of connection. He crystallizes what this means by calling Greater Britain a "world-Venice, with the sea for streets," an illuminating characterization that transforms homogeneous and amorphous oceanic space into regulated networks of canals and waterways.[37] But rather than Venetian *canaletti*, Seeley has submarine telegraphs and transcontinental railways in mind. He explains that in the eighteenth century, "there could be no Greater Britain in the true sense of the word, because of the distance between the mother-country and its colonies and between the colonies themselves. This impediment exists no longer. Science has given to the political organism a new circulation, which is steam, and a new nervous system, which is electricity."[38] In a vitalist key, Seeley suggests that geographic distance sapped the vitality of Greater Britain in the eighteenth century, and it took the efflorescence of the railway and telegraph lines to breathe life back into the "political organism."[39] The rise of steam and electricity does not connect disparate territories to each other but "dissolves the distance" between them. In other words, the expansionist logic of the English nation-state goes hand in hand with the contraction of geographic space. As Seeley contemplates, "Canada and Australia would be to us as Kent and Cornwall."[40] To be connected is to be contiguous.

Although Seeley's historicization of territorial contiguity can be read as a corrective to Dilke's oscillations between racial and territorial national registers, *The Expansion of England* actually inverts *Greater Britain*'s model while retaining its core logic of a global nation. After having argued for the close homology between nation and state, Seeley claims that English provincialism perseveres despite imperial expansion by way of a peculiar metaphor: "When the boy expands into the man, the boy disappears. He does not increase by an accretion visibly different from the original boy and attached to him so as to be easily peeled off. But it *is* in such a way that England seems to have increased. For the original England remains distinctly visible at the heart of Greater Britain, she still forms a distinct organism complete in herself, and she has not even formed the habit of thinking of her colonies and her Indian Empire along with herself."[41] The colonies are external appendages that can be "peeled off" from the metropole painlessly because there remains at the point of origin an England numb to its connections around the globe. Although England took part in a "natural overflow" into the New World, there remains at the *geographical* point of origin something that could not be transported overseas. In Seeley's case, English culture is eminently portable around the world, but some element of it remains provincial, rooted in the land. English provincialism remains at the heart of Britain's globalized identity.

Such a framework stands in sharp contrast to how recent historiography has approached the late nineteenth-century British empire. In an effort to move away from classical colonial tropes of center and periphery, critics have borrowed from scholarship on contemporary globalization and increasingly understood nineteenth-century British imperialism through metaphors of "networks," "webs," and "connectivity."[42] Telegraphs, railroads, and an increasingly efficient postal service integrated provincial or distant places within the national imagination. While certainly helpful in understanding British imperial relations as fluid and decentered, these approaches are less useful when thinking about what a civil war means in the context of empire.[43] For if civil wars always come from within the bounds of the nation-state, then where does one locate the frontiers of civic interiority within the networked milieu and web of empire? In the case of Hobson and Doyle, would the no-man's-land of the Boer War be limited to the Cape— thereby relegating it to a peripheral territory and forfeiting the imperial nation-state? Or would the war extend to other parts of the empire, such as London or Christchurch, thereby preserving the integrity of Greater Britain at the cost of a global civil war? How might one think about the "internal borders" of the nation-state while attending to the mobility that imperial networks afford?

No settler colony revealed the contradictions of late Victorian imperial thought more clearly than South Africa. Because of the significant native population and the legacies of Dutch rule, the Cape colony straddled the line between a strategic colonial holding like India and an equal member of Saxondom. When reflecting on the political instability of the Cape colony in *The Problems of Greater Britain*, Dilke explains that "the only possible policy is the conciliation of the Dutch party in the Cape and the Free State, and the conversion of the term 'Afrikander,' from an epithet virtually meaning Boers, to that wider signification in which it will embrace all the inhabitants of the white race. It must be understood, however, that . . . we cannot abandon our half-way house to India and Australia."[44] The Cape has a double role both as a potential member of

Greater Britain and as a territory that holds strategic importance for the rest of the empire.[45] On the one hand, South Africa is a possible extension of England because of racial filiation. On the other hand, the Cape is a territory that must be forcibly retained for the empire at large. At once home *and* an annexed territory, the Cape is crucial to the future of British imperial interests in the Subcontinent and Australia. Echoing Dilke's concerns with racial homogeneity, Seeley is skeptical about the Cape's inclusion within Greater Britain because it was initially settled by the Dutch and is not a reflection of English society. As he explains, "No rapid English immigration has come to give a new character to the community."[46] Moreover, the indigenous population, "instead of disappearing and dwindling before the whites, greatly outnumber them."[47] According to Seeley, because of a lack of Englishmen and the presence (rather than expulsion and extermination) of natives, British rule in South Africa is especially precarious. Colonial violence and settlement were incomplete in that they were unable to render the Cape racially or culturally homogeneous with the metropole.

Thus it is no coincidence that when the Boer War broke out, it was seen by Britons as simultaneously an intranational and extranational conflict. On the one hand, because the British empire was a single nation-state, the war in the Cape colony represented a civil war between England and an "England planted across the seas," not a colonial uprising. The fact that this was a war between, as Doyle put it, "equal fellow-citizens" meant that what was at stake in the conflict was not Britain's sovereignty but the sovereignty of Greater Britain. On the other hand, South Africa's place on the margins of Greater Britain meant that such notions of civic discord often coincided with representations of colonial conflict—those that are decidedly uncivil. At once a civil war and a colonial war, the conflict in South Africa exposed the fault lines of Britain's civilizing mission. In what follows, I look at how Rudyard Kipling worked through many of these contradictions in his responses to the war in the Cape. Kipling gives the geopolitical dynamics and oscillations of Greater Britain a literary form, specifically through his play between national languages (English, Afrikaans, Urdu/Hindi) and via the instrumental use of translation and mistranslation.

CIVILIZING COLONIAL WAR

In a letter written less than a week after his return to England from South Africa in May 1900, Kipling likens art to the art of war. The letter coordinates a sitting with his friend John Collier, who is to paint a portrait of him. Kipling writes, "I am hideously in arrears of my work on account of frivoling in S. Africa wherefore, taking me as a Kopje, if you will detail your general plan of attack with dates and estimate of time necessary to complete the operations I will do my best to meet you on my base."[48] While in the Cape, Kipling had witnessed the early months of the Boer War, and his letter jokes that sitting for a painting at his home in Sussex would be like battling on a South African "kopje" (meaning "a small hillock" in Afrikaans). Kipling's metaphor brings the geographies of the English coast and the South African *veldt* into the same imagined space, while also characterizing aesthetic practice as imperial warfare. Hence Kipling's home in Sussex is militarized into a "base" at the South African war front, and Collier must conduct his artistry as he would a military "operation" complete with "plans of attack" and "dates and estimate of time necessary to complete" the maneuver.

Animating Kipling's geopolitical play is the conversion of text into sound, written language into foreign words. Thus when Kipling asks Collier to "take me as a Kopje," he means the Afrikaans word for a small hillock. But for Collier to understand the joke he must hear "copy," which in the context of the letter refers to Kipling as the subject of a painterly reproduction. In other words, to inhabit the Cape and Sussex simultaneously, "kopje" must be read while "copy" heard. In doing so, Kipling's pun animates what Garrett Stewart characterizes as the "friction" between the "'air/ink' difference" of a text, whose "effect is registered as a semantic dissonance. . . . A 'dyslocutionary' tension between phonemic and graphemic signification."[49] The resistance between the written and aural registers of a text is akin to what Derrida calls the "movement of *différance* . . . between two differences," for while textual difference is maintained, the muteness of phonetic difference defers knowing precisely what is being signified.[50] Kipling's jest functions similarly, for in its written form "kopje" transports the reader to the war front in the colonies, but its phoneticized form "copy" locates him in The Elms in Rottingdean, Sussex—Kipling's home at the time.

Contextualizing the hermeneutic play of Kipling's jest is the foreignness of the word "kopje," an introjection from Afrikaans that calls attention to the Englishness of the word "copy." As Theodor Adorno notes, the use of foreign words requires the author to "do his formulating from the inside and the outside at the same time."[51] Kipling's "inside and outside" have imperial coordinates: England and the Cape colony, English and Afrikaans, and his pun transports a colonial lexicon into metropolitan discourse. His letter dramatizes the frictions of air/ink and renders places like England and South Africa audibly identical but textually and linguistically different. Crucially, Kipling's imagined space does not seamlessly collapse metropole and colony into a hybridized terrain, nor does it envision the empire as a cosmopolis, for although the phonetic and accentual difference between "copy" and "kopje" is mute, their linguistic distinctness is maintained materially and textually.[52] It is perhaps no coincidence that what we are meant to hear in "kopje" is the signifier of mimetic representation, "copy." If kopje is a geographic marker by virtue of its linguistic foreignness, then at stake in the letter is the representation of a place that is metropolitan and colonial, national and imperial simultaneously.

Kipling's phonic *imperium* gives literary form to the late Victorian dream of a Greater Britain by rendering South Africa proximate to England—a sensibility, if we recall, that was integral to the idea of "Saxondom." If Seeley contemplated that "Canada and Australia would be to us as Kent and Cornwall," then South Africa was to Kipling as Sussex. But by transcribing this territorial homophony, Kipling's letter also retains the distinctions between these two locales and languages. The homophony between the two national languages conflates Adorno's "inside and outside"—or perhaps more precisely, makes it impossible to decipher where the "inside" ends and the "outside" begins. If Kipling's metaphor brings the antipodes of empire into "semantic proximity," then his homophone "silences" the line separating metropole and colony.[53] Sussex and South Africa, English and Afrikaans seem indistinguishable to the ear, while remaining textually distinct. To the ear, art is not only *like* but *is* the art of war. But to the eye, art and war remain discrete.

Similar "frictions" between text and sound, English and the foreign word saturate Kipling's writings on the Boer War. Because his puns are across languages they are contrapuntal, they require a "simultaneous awareness" of point (metropole/"copy") and counterpoint (colony/"kopje").[54] While Edward Said's notion of contrapuntal interpretation is readerly, perspectival, and historical, one might say that Kipling's homophony is contrapuntal in the original sense of the term—as an auditory experience.[55] However, the challenge Kipling's homophonic play poses to contrapuntal interpretation is: What happens when point and counterpoint are indistinguishable? How can one interpret the discrepant experiences of empire when the threshold between these places is inaudible? What if the apogee of civilizational achievement looks identical to its other, barbarism? What does a comparative or contrapuntal approach to the late Victorian empire look like if the sites of comparison are seemingly indistinguishable?

These tensions are most visible and audible in Kipling's short story "A Sahibs' War" (1902). Written while he was revising *Kim*, "A Sahibs' War" is one of a handful of stories about the conflict that Kipling wrote during the war, none of which has received much critical attention.[56] Thus a brief synopsis is in order. The story concerns Umr Singh, a Sikh from Punjab who is an Indian officer in the British army, and Kurban, a British officer born, raised, and stationed in India. The two know each other because their fathers fought on opposite sides of the Indian Mutiny, resulting in their families being linked by what Umr calls a "blood-tie." The irony of such a bond is underscored by how Umr has known Kurban since he was a boy and affectionately refers to him as "his child." At the outbreak of the Boer War, both travel to South Africa to help in the war effort. The falsity of their "blood-tie" is highlighted when, after the two join an Australian platoon at the war front, Umr is disallowed from participating in the conflict because it is said to be a "sahibs' war." Umr instead serves as Kurban's servant until the latter is killed in battle.

The story is premised on a disjuncture between text and sound. The narrative begins three months after Kurban's death and we find Umr struggling to communicate with a British solider about how to find his way back from South Africa to India. "The Lieutenant-Sahib does not understand my talk?" asks Umr, at which point an anonymous British officer (who remains unnamed throughout the story) intervenes and interprets for him.[57] In gratitude, Umr offers his services as a servant for the day and then proceeds to narrate his experiences in the war. Ivan Kreilkamp argues that Victorian culture understood the storyteller to be the native other of print-culture. Both are nostalgic back-formations, "an idealized agent deployed to anchor a regretful story of origins for a modern culture seen as oppressive."[58] In "A Sahibs' War," one might say, print is the realm of the "sahib" while orality belongs to the native—that imagined other upon which a dominant discourse is realized. Although "A Sahibs' War" makes Kreilkamp's analogy between the native and the storyteller literal, their unity is complicated by the fact that there is a great degree of mediation in the story between direct and reported speech. For the officer's speech and responses are entirely omitted from the text, implying that what we read is a transcription of Umr's storytelling, and presumably one that the British officer has translated and composed (it is unclear if it is done so during or after their encounter). In other words, the story is less about Umr's storytelling and more about the anonymous narrator's listening and ability to translate; rather than story*telling*, Kipling's tale is about story*listening*.

Listening, in fact, is the reason Umr's narrative exists in the first place, because an aural pun makes his journey to the Boer War possible. When it becomes clear to Kurban that war in South Africa is imminent, he takes sick leave to travel to the Cape to help with the war effort. Umr does so too, but doing so requires him to pun between being "sick" and a "Sikh." Umr explains, "I went to my Colonel, and sitting in the chair . . . I said, 'My child goes sick. Give me leave, for I am old and sick also.' And the Colonel, making the word double between English and our tongue, said, 'Yes, thou art truly *Sikh*'; and he called me an old devil—jestingly, as one soldier may jest with another" (75). Homophonic play enables Umr to travel to South Africa and experience the war—the content of the very story we *read*. Given that Kipling's story is ambiguous about who its author is as well as the meaning of many of its key words, one might understand the entire framing of the text to be that of a similar friction between the "air/ink" difference of grapheme and phoneme.

"A Sahibs' War" adds to this friction the added dimension of translation. Umr and the officer's discourse is ostensibly in Urdu/Hindi, what he calls "our tongue," because as we know from the opening scene, Umr's English is limited (71). But the narrative is not purely a translation of what Umr says, for it is written in the Anglo-Indian vernacular, one that is largely in English but which slips into the Indian vernacular from time to time. Hence words like "permit" appear as *purwana*, the post office as *dâk*, and, most bizarrely, Johannesburg becomes "Yunasbagh"—a mistranslated phoneticization, for while Yunas is the Urdu equivalent of Johann, *baġ* means garden, not fort or city as the "burg" in Johannesburg suggests (80, 76, 73). But the phoneticized translations are inconsistent in the story, as Umr says *rêl* for trains, at other times correctly says "train," and elsewhere mispronounces train as *terain*—all within the same page (71). He refers to the Australians as

Durro Muts, a translation of the Australian platoon's slogan "no fear," which itself is phoneticized in the text to capture an Australian accent: "No fee-ah" (79). More puzzlingly, Urdu/Hindi explicatives appear in literal translation in English, such as "fathers of owls," an insult that makes sense only in the Indian vernacular as *ullū ka paṭha*, which actually means "*son* of an owl" (76). Such linguistic awkwardness has been seen as a trope in much of Kipling's writings where, as Gayatri Spivak explains, "the Hindusthani speech of the Indian servants is painstakingly translated into archaic and awkward English. The servants' occasional forays into English are mocked in phonetic transcription."[59] In "A Sahibs' War," however, the question is more about the interpreter's translations and transliterations, for what we read is not necessarily Umr's clumsy language but the officer's approximations of the former's narrative in the scene of writing—we are made aware of the centrality of listening in the composition of the story. By calling the fidelity of the transcription/translation into question, the entire framing of the story makes it impossible to decide with any precision who the narrator is and what the original elocutions were. Consequently, the story reminds the reader that Umr's "storytelling" is not merely from the mouth of a native, or only the pen of an officer, but is both text and sound, inside and outside of metropolitan discourse.

As one critic has noted about the language of *Kim*, Kipling "transcribed English that was under the stress of an alien environment."[60] In "A Sahibs' War," this "stress" manifests in the transcriptions/translations of Umr's speech. John Marx argues that in the increasingly networked world system at the turn of the century, English language and literature transformed into something that was "not *not* English." This transformation was essential to the aesthetic of modernism: "What was no longer indispensable for modernism, as it turned out, was English's status as a standardized imperial language. The English vernaculars that appear in the pages of early twentieth-century fiction can best be understood as not *not* English, languages shaped by British imperialism that nevertheless represent clear attempts to reject the inside/outside alternatives that organized the peoples, cultures, and idioms of the British empire in previous centuries."[61] Kipling's "not *not* English" in "A Sahibs' War" is essential to making visible a crisis in the civilizing mission and its narrative of progress. Indeed, the very imperial infrastructures that, according to Marx, make it possible for modernism to denaturalize English are also essential to the rise of anticolonial nationalism. When discussing the impact of Boer uprisings on anticolonial rebellions in the Subcontinent, Umr links the representational "frictions" between text and sound to the status of imperial sovereignty. He explains that the Boer rebellions prior to the outbreak of war in 1899 led to the Tirah Campaign—a British war against the Afridi tribe in present-day Afghanistan. Indians in the Cape communicated news of Anglo-Boer conflict back to the Subcontinent through the post office:

> There were many box-wallahs, pedlars, with Pathans a few, in
> this country, notably at the city of Yunasbagh [Johannesburg],
> and they sent news in every week how the Sahibs lay without
> weapons under the heel of the Boer-log. . . . The Sahib knows
> how we of Hind hear all that passes over the earth? There was
> not a gun cocked in Yunasbagh that the echo did not come into
> Hind in a month. The Sahibs are very clever, but they forget
> their own cleverness has created the *dâk* [the post], and . . .
> all things become known. We of Hind listened and heard, and
> wondered; and when it was a sure thing . . . certain among us
> asked questions and waited for signs. Others of us mistook the
> meaning of those signs. *Wherefore, Sahib, came the long war in
> the Tirah!* (74)

Umr claims that a "sahibs' war" in settler colonies elicited a colonial war in the Subcontinent; a "gentleman's war" unleashes frontier wars elsewhere. In Kipling's story, we see how imperial networks like the postal service not only were instruments of imperialism but could be co-opted as technologies of emergent anticolonial nationalisms. Umr's description of Indians spreading rebellious sentiment from South Africa to the Subcontinent is identical to the "networks of resistance" of the late nineteenth and early twentieth centuries, where anticolonial movements in one part of the empire energized those elsewhere. Elleke Boehmer argues that political relationships between British colonies (such as between Irish and Boer nationalists, or Gandhi's activism in South Africa) were not necessarily routed through the metropole but were "positioned *between* peripheries."[62] What made such decentered relations possible were the material forms of colonial exchange, which "took the form of newspapers, the telegraph, new road and railway links, and faster shipboard journeys."[63] Similarly, Pradip Kumar Datta describes the Boer War as an "international event" because of how the postal service and telegraph created "near simultaneity" of its effects between South Africa and other colonies.[64] If the post office dissolved geographic distance between the colonies, and the difference between

English and the colonial tongue, then it also aided in the efflorescence of anticolonial sentiment at the end of the nineteenth century. Much as the British empire's global reach destabilized English as a national language by introjecting foreign words and accents, such ambitions also unsettled the sovereignty of the British *imperium* by making rifts within one part of the empire resonate throughout.[65] By "dissolving the distance" between metropole and colony, imperial infrastructures actually threatened to break apart the entire *imperium*.

In contrast to how Benedict Anderson sees simultaneity as an effect of national print culture, the "near simultaneity" of anticolonial nationalism in Kipling's story spreads through transnational circuits that transmit writing (letters) rather than print.[66] Importantly, these letters are listened to rather than read. Umr states that "Gunshots" from South Africa are transcribed by "box-wallahs" and "pedlars" in Johannesburg and mailed as letters to the Subcontinent where they are heard as "echoes." These in turn energize anticolonial conflicts like "the long war in the Tirah." In other words, the transcription of a "gentleman's war" in letter form is phonetically interpreted in the colonies as anticolonial strife. Echoes also have a close relationship to colonial mimicry, for as Homi Bhabha explains, "What emerges between mimesis and mimicry is a *writing*, a mode of representation, that marginalizes the monumentality of history, quite simply mocks its power to be a model, that power which supposedly makes it imitable."[67] Hence the "menace of mimicry," wherein the echo mimics but in the process alters the original.[68] In contrast, the scene of writing Umr speaks of concerns listening and transcription. Umr makes clear that the letters are misinterpreted and not mis-transcribed, for those who started the Tirah war "mistook those signs" from South Africa. Afridis "misinterpreted" textual representations to be aural repetitions (echoes are always copies of an original) and therefore "mistakenly" questioned British rule. The story suggests that transcription is not the problem to imperial rule but the tendency for texts to be (mis)read phonetically. Anticolonial interpretation, it would seem for Kipling, is having an ear for a text.

The danger misinterpretation poses to imperial rule looms large elsewhere in the story. As its title makes clear, the story's concern with the Boer War centers on non-European participation in the war effort. Despite Umr's bellicosity, he is disallowed to take up arms against the Boers. The possessive "sahibs'" in the story's title registers this exclusion but also differentiates a European mode of war from a colonial one. Umr distinguishes a sahibs' war from what he refers to as a "war at the border," meaning a war at the frontiers of the empire against a native army. He insists that the actions of the Boer army belie their designation as sahibs because, "as I understand it, when a Sahib goes to war, he puts on the cloth of war, and only those who wear that cloth may take part in the war. . . . But these people [the Boers] were as they were in Burma, or as the Afridis are. They shot at their pleasure, and when pressed hid the gun and exhibited *purwanas* [permits], or lay in a house and said they were farmers" (80). Umr likens the Boers' actions to those of the Afridis and Burmese, who led anticolonial revolts against the British during the 1880s and 1890s. He cannot understand the confluence of Europeans and anticolonial forms of war—why are civilized white men fighting like colonial natives? The *purwanas* were official documents given to Boers during the war that functioned as oaths of allegiance to the British. Umr is baffled by the Boers' instrumental use of *purwanas* because "he who fights should be hung if he fights with a gun in one hand and a *purwana* in the other, as did all these people" (80–81). The symbols of war (the gun) and legal amity (the *purwana*) can never coincide in the hands of the same individual. For Umr, the Boers' disregard for protocols of civilized warfare (such as wearing "the cloth of war," meaning uniforms) means that they are comparable to the Afridis and Burmese: those non-Europeans who only know how to fight anticolonial wars at the border. A sahibs' war, then, is supposed to be "civil" in the sense that it is not only fought between "equal fellow-citizens" of the empire but also civilized in that it is fought between fellow-gentlemen.

Before proceeding any further, I want to make clear that while Kipling's text might be understood to be giving voice to anticolonial rebellions in the Subcontinent, it does so by foreclosing the possibility of native resistance to Boer and British settlement within South Africa. Kipling's equation of the Boer War to an anticolonial war hides the fact that the Boers were rebelling against the British *in order to solidify their own colonization of Southern Africa*. Although Kipling makes visible the ambiguities between British imperial warfare and anticolonial rebellion, Briton and Boer, he implicitly sanctions the Boers' own settler-colonial project. While Kipling disapproves of the Boer rebellion, their violence against the British is in his mind more politically meaningful than the anticolonial violence of the natives. Kaori Nagai has argued something quite similar in his discussion of the peculiar prevalence of Irish heroes in Kipling's fiction.[69] He notes that Kipling's use of these figures was a way of willing away Irish anticolonial nationalism at the time. One might add to this erasure indigenous anticolonial resistance to Boer and British settlement within South Africa.

Kurban's death is the climax of the story, the reason for which is his ethnologic misinterpretation of the Boers as "sahibs." His platoon comes upon a Boer village whose inhabitants demonstrate their allegiance to the British by showing their *purwanas*. Umr explains: "One night when we lay on top of a ridge in the cold, I saw far away a light in a house that appeared for the sixth part of an hour and was obscured. Anon, it appeared again thrice for the twelfth part of an hour. . . . I said to Kurban Sahib 'Send half a troop, Child, and finish that house. They signal to their brethren'" (82). Umr speaks from experience, claiming, "I have been on the Border in eight wars, not counting Burma. . . . *I know when house signals to house*" (82). But Kurban disregards Umr's observation, assuming that the Boers will act as sahibs do and not, as Umr would put it, "fight with a gun in one hand and a *purwana* in the other." The oversight proves fatal. The Boer occupants of the house—a priest and his son—attack the platoon and kill Kurban. The latter's mistake, in other words, comes because of interpreting Boer actions as those of "sahibs" like himself rather than natives at the peripheries— something Umr cannot miss.

Kipling picks up an identical theme in his poem "Two Kopjes," which was written in 1903 after the end of the war in South Africa and published in *The Five Nations* (1905). The poem's title draws attention to the tensions between text and sound, for "two kopjes" can refer to two kopjes (the topographic features) as well as the two "kopjes/copies" (meaning textual and aural signifiers, graphemes and phonemes). Kipling alerts his readers that kopjes are never what they seem, for they are often sites of ambush by the Boer army: "Oh, mock not the African kopje, / Not even when peace has been signed— / The kopje that isn't a kopje— / the kopje that copies its kind."[70] The warning recalls Kurban's fatal error, which mistook Boer actions as those of the British (who we find out by the end of the story copy the British, who themselves copy the Boers in their ungentlemanly tactics). If the lesson of Kurban's death was that Boers are never what they seem (they hold a *purwana* in one hand and a gun in the other), the poem dramatizes something similar about the South African landscape (one might also recall that Kurban dies on a "hill of rocks," presumably a kopje). Deciphering kopjes for what they really are requires the reader to pay attention to the silences embedded within the text: "The silent and simmering kopje, / the kopje beloved by the guide. You can never be sure of your kopje, / But of this be you blooming well sure, / A kopje is always a kopje, and a Boojer is always a Boer!"[71] Kipling warns against the "silent and simmering kopje," a seemingly harmless topographic feature "beloved" by the traitorous Boer guide who leads British soldiers into ambush. If "the kopje that copies its kind" is the kopje that the soldier needs to be wary of, interpreting this requires him to read and listen for the "silent kopje" simultaneously. The "silent kopje" is, of course, also "copy," a word that the poem textually has already alerted the reader to. By making the friction between text and sound its central interpretive practice, the poem suggests that the art of the war in the *veldt* requires the soldier to shuttle between textual and aural representation, reading and listening. To interpret in only one of these registers runs the risk of becoming a casualty in war: "Only a Kensington draper / Only pretending to scout . . . / Only bad news for the paper, / Only another knock-out."[72]

A similar "frictive" interpretation is at the center of the meaning of "A Sahibs' War." After Kurban's burial, the Australian platoon he fought with leaves an engraving on his grave and gives Umr a copy of the epitaph to keep. But because Umr can't read English, he hands the copy to the British officer to read. The inscription is separated from the rest of the story's text typographically, so as to signal a shift from a transcription/translation/transliteration of oral language to a reading of written language. Because what the reader reads is presumably what the unnamed British officer reads, it is unclear if the "copy" is read silently or aloud in the story. Either way, by including written text within translated and transcribed speech, the story recalls our attention to the very friction between "air" and "ink" that caused such tumult in Afghanistan. The inscription states: "In Memory of / WALTER DECIES CORBYN / Late Captain 141st Punjab Cavalry . . . / Treacherously shot near this place by / The connivence of the late / Henrik Dirk Uys / A Minister / of God / Who thrice took the oath of neutrality / And Piet his son, / This little work. . . . / Was accomplished in partial / And inadequate recognition of their loss / By some men who loved him— / *Si monumentum requiris circumspice*" (91–92). Umr claims the Latin inscription translates to "those who would desire to behold a proper memorial to Kurban Sahib must look out at the house" (92). He calls this a jest because "the house is not there, nor the well, nor the big tank which they call dams, nor the little fruit-trees, nor the cattle. There is nothing at all, Sahib, except the two trees withered by the fire. The rest is like the desert here—or my hand—or my heart. Empty, Sahib—all empty!" (92). Neither Umr's loss nor the house that belonged to Kurban's assailants can be located, for all he sees is emptiness. The perverseness of the humor lies in celebrating the total destruction of the Boer home.

But the joke is also on Umr, who was presumably told an incorrect translation of the Latin by the Australian platoon. Although he has a written copy of the inscription, his lack of English means his knowledge of what it says is entirely dependent on what the Australians verbally told him what it said. What it should read is: "If you wish to see his monument, then look about you." The inscription is taken from the memorial to Christopher Wren, which is housed within St. Paul's Cathedral in London. Wren was the cathedral's architect, and the dedication instructs viewers to look around at the building if they wish to see how he has been memorialized. Umr is therefore misguided in looking for the destroyed Boer house to mourn Kurban, for he must simultaneously look at St. Paul's. But because he cannot read English, let alone correct the mis-translated Latin he was told, Umr's gaze fails to achieve the contrapuntal perspective required to fully mourn "his son." In fact, to only see the *veldt* and not the metropole has the effect of blindness, as Umr cannot make any meaning out of the inscription: "There is nothing at all . . . like the desert here—or my hand—or my heart. Empty, Sahib—all empty!"

The emptiness Umr sees, ironically, is proof of the incivility of the platoon's actions. For it refers to the razed Boer home, evidence of the "scorched earth" tactics that the British army used during the war—a kind of tactic deemed ungentlemanly in Kipling's story. Malvern Van Wyk Smith has argued that the narrative device of a Sikh storyteller serves to "validate the arguments for genocide at the same time as it exonerates the British from holding them."[73] For example, Umr quotes Kurban saying that the British army "will foolishly show mercy to these Boer-*log* because it is believed that they are white . . . the Government have not employed [the Indian army], but have made it altogether a Sahibs' war. Very many men will be killed, and no vengeance will be taken" (76). Although "A Sahibs' War" is transparent about its racism toward Boers and Indians alike, it also seems invested in showing the tactics of the British army to be as violent as those of their colonized subjects. After Kurban is killed by the Boer priest, Umr intends to hang his assailant as revenge—and therefore transgress the decree that the Boer War be a "white man's war." Before the hanging can take place Kurban's ghost appears, stating, "No. It is a Sahibs' war." Umr obeys the command and instead waits for an Australian troop to arrive to whom he hands over the prisoners, explaining that "an order has reached us here from the dead that this is a Sahibs' war. I take the soul of my Kurban Sahib to witness that I give over to the justice of the Sahibs these Sahibs who have made me childless" (90). Kipling inverts the episode of the ghost of King Hamlet; rather than the ghost of the father telling his son to seek revenge, the son tells his "father" to *not* kill his assailant. Although the Boers use violence akin to the "frontier violence" that Umr is inclined to use, the former remain protected from such violence only if it is perpetrated by colonial subjects like Umr. The text preserves uncivilized vengeance for sahibs who properly belong to the metropole. We find out at the end of the story that the "justice" Umr mentions refers in fact to the killing of the priest and leveling of his home by Australian soldiers. The racial schematics that the "sahibs' war" is premised on fall apart, for not only do Britons and Boers fight alike, their actions seem to be indistinguishable from those of the Burmese and Afridis. The "sahibness" of the conflict is unveiled as a complete fantasy—civil war is identical to colonial war. What once seemed to be the most civilized type of war is shown to in fact be nothing but savage conflict. Once again, the border between the geographic and linguistic is indecipherable—if South Africa is inaudibly different from Sussex in Kipling's letter, his story cannot clearly locate the border between a "sahibs' war" and a "war at the border," civil war and anticolonial rebellion.

It is easy to see Umr as a mouthpiece for Kipling's imperialism. His bellicosity and commitment to the empire make him a close mirror of Kipling's own jingoism. But he is also the mouthpiece for a radical critique of empire. For the most striking aspect of the Australians' inscription is that Umr has been either mispronouncing "his son's" name all along or that the unnamed officer who transcribed/translates Umr's story mishears him, for we learn that Kurban's name is actually "Corbyn." The juxtaposition of Kurban (phonemic) to Corbyn (graphemic) animates an "air/ink" friction identical to that in Kipling's letter to John Collier. In much the same way as kopje/copy required shuttling between two named historical languages and geographies, the same tensions are at work in the story's most salient pun. Umr's mispronunciation of Corbyn's name, and the officer's transcription of it as such, translates Corbyn into the Urdu/Hindi vernacular, for "Kurban" is a close phoneticism of *qurban*, which means sacrifice—perhaps meaning that Corbyn was tragically sacrificed by the British empire. *Qurban* in fact names what is at stake in the closeness between Corbyn and Kurban, for its root comes from the Arabic word *qurb*, related to *quarov* in Hebrew, meaning proximity and one's kin. Hence what is sacrificed is always close to you, and why Umr (unlike Abraham) needs to mourn the death of his "son" Kurban. The linguistic "inside and outside" that is transcribed collapses as a result of the homophony between the two words Corbyn/Kurban.

More importantly, the pun raises issues of filial proximity, recalling the "blood-tie" between Umr (the father) and Corbyn (the son). The pun, like British and Boer tactics in the conflict, undermines the entire premise of the sahibs' war, for it obscures the racial border between sahib and servant, father and son, civilized and uncivilized. Just as the aural border between the two phonetic forms "Corbyn" and "Kurban" is (almost) mute, so is the racial/geopolitical divide between sahib and native. If a distinction was to be made between a "sahibs' war" and a "war at the border," between a gentleman's war and a colonial war, then the racial difference that underlies these distinctions collapses because of homophony across national languages. In Umr we can see how a mere "mouthpiece" can nevertheless sound a critique of the foundational categories of empire—in this case, racial and national difference. And while the only site of decipherable imperial difference is the text itself, this form of representation must inherently reproduce the aural tumult mentioned above by virtue of linguistic coincidence.

Finally, it is no insignificant fact that the sahib Umr mourns for (or rather yearns to mourn for) is Irish. That a "blood-tie" exists between Corbyn and Umr highlights their peripheral status in the empire. Of course, Irish protagonists loom especially large in Kipling's fiction during this period—most notably in *Kim* but also in short stories like "The Mutiny of Mavericks." Kim O'Hara, for example, can "think in Hindustani," "lie like an Oriental" (itself a pun between being untruthful and lying horizontally because of opiates), and "learn whole chapters of the Koran by heart, till he could deliver them with the very roll and cadence of a mullah."[74] But what makes Kim so valuable to Colonel Creighton (and the British empire more generally) is that he also masters mathematics and mapmaking—the work of imperial cartography.[75] If the Irish constituted the border between the intranational and extranational in early Victorian England, they retain this status in Kipling's fiction at the end of the century. Hence Corbyn's "sahibness" means he adheres to the protocols of civilized warfare, so much so that even his ghost ensures Umr takes no part in combat. And yet his death is also the occasion to reveal the barbaric quality of the Boer War—how neither the Boer nor the Briton abides by the rules of gentlemanly warfare. Standing on the thresholds of civility and incivility, the figure of the Irishman offers Kipling a way to stage the geopolitical and ethnic crisis that the idea of Greater Britain faced amid the Boer War. If a sahibs' war is identical to a "war at the border," then the entire premise of the civilizing mission—bringing civility to the uncivilized—is moot.

Kipling's writings on and around the Boer War describe an empire in which the boundaries between metropole and colony, sahib and native, civility and incivility, were crumbling. Importantly, the outcome of this dissolution is neither a hybrid nor cosmopolitan world but an imperial milieu in which the politics of the intranational and extranational are increasingly bound up with one another. At the beginning of Queen Victoria's reign, civil war was something exclusive to the metropole—the "birthplace" of civility and modern civilization. But at the turn of the century we find in Kipling the moment it became possible for Britons to see civil war as possible at the peripheries of the empire. It is no coincidence that in the very years nationalist movements in the peripheries were galvanizing the colonized under the banner of nationhood, "civil war" becomes possible beyond the shores of Britain, all in the name of decolonization. And yet this is not an untroubled apprehension, for as I have tracked throughout this chapter, the distinction between sahibs and natives was intensely unstable and fragile at the time Kipling was writing. Kipling's own language absorbs and dramatizes these geopolitical tensions, exposing the contradictions at the heart of the civilizing mission. Modernity in the colonies, Kipling teaches us, has a troubling likeness to the incivility that it seeks to eradicate. Despite his jingoism, "A Sahibs' War" dramatizes how the highest stage of civilization, a gentlemanly contest between the "blood-brotherhood of the Empire," is also its lowest when these very sahibs act as savages.

CHAPTER 5

Civil War, the Lowest Stage of Civilization

It is money that saves a country.

—JOSEPH CONRAD, *Nostromo*

Two years after Kipling considered what civil war meant in Greater Britain, Joseph Conrad contemplated its meaning in the furthest reaches of the British imperial imagination. *Nostromo*, Conrad's most labored novel, is set on the Pacific coast of Costaguana, a fictional ex-Spanish colony in South America. Rooted in the Spanish imperial experience, Costaguana is an outgrowth of Simón Bolívar's revolutions in the early nineteenth century, and later influenced by Garibaldi's campaigns in Uruguay. In addition to belonging to a different imperial legacy, the country's politics appear to its British visitors and residents a perversion of familiar liberal ideals. Even Charles Gould, an Englishman born and raised in Costaguana and ever-proud of his South American home, describes his country as making a mockery of the Enlightenment's most treasured concepts: "The words one knows so well have a nightmarish meaning in this country. Liberty—democracy—patriotism—government. All of them have a flavour of folly and murder."[1] The dream of the Enlightenment is a perverse "nightmare" in Costaguana because "liberty—democracy—patriotism—government" all look uncannily sanguinary.[2]

Costaguana has had a tumultuous existence since independence from Spanish rule in the early 1800s, sliding from one dictatorship to the next. The narrator sums this history up as a "tale of civil wars" (106). Each new regime arrives with the promise of stability and security, only to reproduce old methods of terror and disorder, thereby giving way to newer rebellions, coups and revolutions, and so on. When Gould's wife, Emilia—the closest the novel has to an unflawed perspective—learns about Costaguana's tumultuous past, she is horrified by the "stories of political outrage; friends, relatives ruined, imprisoned, killed in the battles of senseless civil wars, barbarously executed in ferocious proscriptions, as though the government of the country had been a struggle of lust between bands of absurd devils let loose upon the land with sabres and uniforms and grandiloquent phrases" (66). Adorned in the costumes of world history, Costaguana's political leaders repeat the past rather than give birth to new regimes. Ignoble movements lacking vision, politics in Costaguana seem a barbarous game played by "absurd devils." The violence they perpetrate is neither history-making nor a necessary evil in the name of progress.

Nostromo is about the attempt to jolt Costaguana out of its endless cycles of revolution and counterrevolution, and bring it into the fold of Western modernity. If the ex-colony's civil wars have encumbered its development into a modern nation-state, then the burden of the novel's plot is to narrate a historical transition out of the stifling condition of endless strife. Charles Gould is this very angel of history. Coming from a family of "liberators, explorers, coffee-planters, merchants, revolutionists," Gould sees in the San Tomé mine—a silver mine rich in resources—Costaguana's "ray of hope" (37): "What is wanted here," Gould proclaims, "is law, good faith, order, security. Any one can declaim about these things, but I pin my faith to material interests. Only let the material interests once get a firm footing, and they are bound to impose the conditions on which alone they can continue to exist. That's how your money-making is justified here in the face of lawlessness and disorder. It is justified because the security which it demands must be shared with an oppressed people. A better justice will come afterwards. That's your ray of hope" (63). No passage in *Nostromo* better sums up what is at stake in the political world of Costaguana. Faced with the "endlessness of civil strife" that has given Costaguana's modernity a "murderous" hue, Gould's solution to the interminable "game of revolutions" lies in "material interests," the novel's euphemism for industrial and finance capitalism.[3] To Gould, "money-making" is coextensive to peace-making because it provides the "firm footing" for the establishment of liberal ideals like security, law, and justice—all of which follow capitalism's arrival ("a better justice will come afterwards"). Economic development thus becomes the antidote to civil war and the harbinger of the very Enlightenment ideals Costaguana lacks (or rather mocks).

It has become routine to see *Nostromo* as a novel about imperialism.[4] But critics have overlooked how civil war is the entire premise for Gould's civilizing mission, and the novel's plot more generally. Civil war, I would go so far as to say, is the plot's very condition of possibility. For if Costaguana were a peaceful place, Gould's thesis that "moneymaking" brings progress, prosperity, and justice would be redundant. His revival of the San Tomé mine, the central act of the novel, is meaningful *because* its purpose is to save Costaguana from the "endlessness of civil strife" and civilize the country so that the "words one knows so well" don't have the "flavor of folly and murder." Framed in this way, the narrative desire of *Nostromo* is to bring Costaguana's "tale of civil wars" to an end. Put differently, the novel's "sense of an ending" constitutes an end to the "tale of civil wars," an end reachable through Gould's civilizing mission.[5]

But this end is never reached. Even before the novel's conclusion, it becomes clear that Costaguana's "ray of hope" has failed at enlightening the country: the mine doesn't eradicate political turmoil but instead installs a regime committed more to the "material interests" of foreign nations than to those of Costaguana.[6] By the end of the novel Costaguana (or the Occidental Republic as it comes to be known) is in financial ruins and internal strife looms on the horizon once again, promising yet another chapter in its "tale of civil wars." In other words, the desire for an end to civil war, the very motor of *Nostromo*'s plot, cannot be satisfied, and so the "tale of civil wars" continues, as it were, entrapped within its own narrative of development and historical progressivism with no historical transformation. *Nostromo*'s narrative structure makes visible how the civilizing mission, with civil war as its alibi, ends up reinscribing its own necessity. If the premise of the plot is to modernize Costaguana by eradicating its civic discord, then this plot doesn't have a narratable end in *Nostromo*—the plot becomes entrapped within its own structure. By so thoroughly linking Gould's attempt at modernization to the narrative arc of the novel, Conrad frames the desire for an end to the "tale of civil wars" as at its core an imperial desire.

The question remains: Why locate this "tale of civil war" and development in Costaguana, the least British place imaginable? Why does Conrad, the British novelist of empire par excellence, choose a fictional ex-Spanish colony in South America as the venue for "A Tale of the

Seaboard"? Far from an aberration, Nostromo's imperialism in fact pivots on Costaguana's foreignness to the British imperial mission and imagination. Latin America was an infrequent setting for Victorian and Edwardian fiction. And when novels did take place in Latin American countries, they shuttled between depicting the continent as an untouched landscape and dysfunctional and violent sites of internal strife. William Henry Hudson's *Green Mansions* (1904) and Arthur Conan Doyle's *The Lost World* (1912), for example, depict the landscape as wholly wild, home only to primitive societies and lost tribes. However, Hudson's earlier novel *The Purple Land* (1885) characterizes the Banda Oriental of Uruguay as both idyllic and a site of constant political turmoil. On the one hand, the novel's narrator Richard Lamb sees before him "one of the fairest habitations God has made for man."[7] On the other hand, the constant civil wars and revolutions leave the country "in a complete state of paralysis."[8] The novel is in many ways a meditation on whether to "save" the Banda Oriental from internal tumult by making it a part of the British empire, if not also Greater Britain. The narrator laments, "Oh, for a thousand young men of Devon and Somerset here with me, every one of them with a brain on fire with thoughts like mine! What a glorious deed would be done for humanity! . . . For never was there a holier crusade undertaken, never a nobler conquest planned, than that which had for its object the wresting this fair country from unworthy hands, to make it for all time part of the mighty English kingdom."[9] Yet if this dream were to become a reality, the "distinctive flavour" of the Banda Oriental would be lost. Lamb learns over the course of the novel that the constant turmoil that befalls the country is in fact a part of its natural landscape. In the novel's conclusion, he admits that "I cannot believe that if this country had been conquered and re-colonised by England, and all that is crooked in it made straight according to our notions, my intercourse with the people would have had the wild, delightful flavour I have found in it. And if that distinctive flavour cannot be had along with the material prosperity resulting from Anglo-Saxon energy, I must breathe the wish that this land may never know such prosperity."[10] The civil wars and revolutions that befall Uruguay are devoid of their own history and exist as background elements of the exotic landscape. This "wildness" would be lost if "Anglo-Saxon energy" were infused into it.

In what follows, I want to argue that the "wildness" of Costaguana in Conrad's *Nostromo* was the occasion to rethink the parameters of the New Imperial mission. For by having a country wholly foreign to the British empire be the venue for this novel, Conrad transforms civil war from a crisis of English nationhood (as in the case of early Victorian Britain) and British imperial nationhood (as in the case of Greater Britain) into a crisis of development at the peripheries. In doing so, Conrad deterritorializes Britain's civilizing mission.[11] No longer directed toward its actual colonies—India, South Africa, Australia, New Zealand, Canada, and Jamaica, for example—Conrad conceives of imperial interventionism as taking place *anywhere* in the peripheries, even those sites previously untouched by Britain, like Costaguana. Importantly, these interventions are not undertaken out of a duty to protect subjects within the British *imperium* but to expand the international influence of global capital. And at the center of this new influence, as many critics of *Nostromo* have noted, is the United States, which fulfills the Greater British dream of a global British *imperium* by funding industrial development in Costaguana and militarily intervening in its civil wars to protect its investments. In *Nostromo*, Britain indeed speaks to the world through America as Dilke intended it to and, in the process, relocates the British sphere of influence to the United States.

At the heart of this new kind of empire is also a new kind of colonizer. Writing toward the end of his career in the midst of anticolonial uprisings in many of the British colonies, Lord Cromer argued that the future success of the British empire lay in the transformation of imperial policy from annexation and domination to decentralized governance—what he called the "spirit of decentralisation."[12] While acknowledging the importance of the "sword" in the imperial mission, the key to the British empire's longevity, he argued, was in a "race of officials" characterized by their independence from strict administrative hierarchies.[13] Rooted in a distinctly English individualism, Cromer argues that the British official would never lose his national identity or his commitment to the empire, and yet at the same time, he would never be constrained by it. "This kind of informal influence," Hannah Arendt explains, "was preferable to a well-defined policy because it could be altered at a moment's notice and did not necessarily involve a home government in case of difficulties. It required a highly trained, highly reliable stage whose loyalty and patriotism was not connected with personal ambition or vanity and who would even be required to renounce the human aspiration of having their names connected with their achievements. Their greatest passion would have to be for secrecy . . . for a role behind the scenes."[14] The figures who best embodied such a policy, Arendt continues, were the bureaucrat and the secret agent, who, she claims, were realized most fully in the eponymous hero of Kipling's *Kim*.[15]

Nostromo tells us about a third such figure: the industrialist. Despite his thoroughly English manners and dress, Charles Gould's civilizing mission has no allegiance to the British flag, operates independently of the colonial state, and is funded by an American. Yet it remains committed to making the Enlightenment ideals of "law, security, justice" a reality in Costaguana. Rather than utilize the colonial state, administrative offices, or imperial infrastructures as the bureaucrat or spy might, his civilizing mission invests money and hope in the San Tomé mine to transform the country into a modern nation-state. As Hobson himself noted, the ones pulling the strings in the New Imperialism were "cliques of businessmen—investors, contractors, export manufacturers, and certain professional classes."[16] In the same way as Cromer and Rhodes sought to create a "secret society" of rulers who "pull the strings of history" outside of the visible domain of politics, Gould does so by creating the conditions for modernization. By recasting decentralization as deterritorialization, Gould finds a way to continue Britain's civilizing mission by the other means of development. He, in the words of Cromer, is not "possessed with any secret desire to see the whole of Africa or of Asia [or in his case, South America] painted red on the maps" but instead in bringing to Costaguana "material interests."[17]

AN EPOCH OF UNCIVIL WAR

Costaguana's nineteenth century, we are told at one point, is an "epoch of civil wars" (86). What does an "epoch of civil wars" look like? Mid-nineteenth-century discourses of race wars—encompassing writers as diverse as Marx, Engels, Disraeli, Thierry, Guizot, and Michelet—saw politics as the other means of warfare. Consequently, civil war was not a singular event but understood to be a relation of power that suffused social and political life.[18] *Nostromo* shares with this discourse the understanding that civil war is not a rupture but an extended affair that can characterize a large block of historical time. Thus ever since its independence in the early nineteenth century, Costaguana has been plagued by numerous civil wars, none of which has a proper name. However, rather than being fought nonviolently through institutions (as in the case of urban development for Engels, the commodification of labor for Marx, banking for Carlyle, industrial labor for Gaskell, and historiography for Disraeli), the civil wars that populate Costaguana's history are brutally violent. Instead of taking place latently beneath the surface of a peaceful society, civil wars are *the* fixture of political life. Furthermore, Costaguana's "epoch of civil wars" departs from race war discourse in its depiction of civic strife as a decidedly demodernizing event. Instead of being the motor of history as it was for early Victorians, civil war in *Nostromo* is an obstacle to historical progress; the "endlessness of civil strife" stalls Costaguana's transition into modernity. The constant revolutions and counterrevolutions keep it from fully embracing industrial development and integration into the world market.

Nostromo narrates Costaguana's stalled history by weaving the country's fictional history into the world-historical events of the nineteenth century. As Claire Rosenfield puts it, in *Nostromo* "historical fact reinforces fictional fact, which itself pretends to history."[19] In this "novel history," Bolívar's campaigns in South America liberate fictional countries like Costaguana alongside many other "real" Latin American nation-states from the Spanish empire.[20] Costaguana exists as a federation for some years after these revolutions until the dictator Guzman Bento, with the support of the aristocratic Blanco class, wages a war to unify Costaguana into a single nation-state. Looming in the background of such peripheral republicanism are the revolutions of Europe and the Americas, most pronounced of which are the 1848 revolutions in France, Garibaldi's campaigns in Uruguay, and the Italian Risorgimento. After Bento's death in the 1860s, Costaguana experiences a quick succession of civil wars resulting in the rise and fall of numerous regimes. Much as in the "real" Latin America, the following decades see a slow increase in international investment in the continent.[21] British and foreign investments, for example, funded the opening of silver and tin mines as well as the export of guano (to which the name "Costaguana" is a reference). In *Nostromo*, Charles Gould's project to revive the San Tomé silver mine is funded by the American tycoon Holroyd in the mid-1880s, which the former hopes will bring stability to the country. Like the situation in many other Latin American countries during the period, international investment integrates Costaguana's economy into the world market such that it becomes heavily reliant on a single industry. For Costaguana the commodity in question is, of course, silver. Eventually, with the continued financial support of Holroyd, Gould successfully installs a reformist government led by Don Vincente Ribiera to better serve the country's "material interests." Within a year, however, Gould's political experiment comes to an end. In the process, Costaguana is increasingly left to the mercy of finance capital. The Panic of 1890 made British finance capitalists more and more aware of the reciprocal relationship between British banks and Latin America and beyond. As Hobson notes in *Imperialism*, "The public debts which ripen in our colonies, and in foreign countries that come under our protectorate or influence, are largely loaned in the shape of rails, engines, guns, and other materials of civilization made and sent by British firms."[22] Frustrated with Ribiera's capitulation to foreign debt, General Montero topples his leader in a nationalist coup. One of the main instigators of this conflict is Montero's brother, Pedro, whose "ambition seemed to become a sort of Duc de Morny to a sort of Napoleon" (172). Inspired by the revolutions of 1848, Montero's propaganda machine disseminates nationalist rhetoric about "the atrocious calumnies, the appeals to the people calling upon them to rise with their knives in their hands and put an end once for all to the Blancos, to these Gothic remnants, to these sinister mummies, these impotent paralíticos, who plotted with foreigners for the surrender of the lands and the slavery of the people" (116). In doing so, Montero starts a civil war between Sulaco's "material interests" and the mainland of Costaguana, which comes to an end after the United States militarily intervenes in the conflict. In order to preserve Sulaco's mining industry, it and the province to which it belongs are partitioned into sovereign nation-states. Although a prosperous period follows the partition, by the end of the novel war once again looms on the horizon of Sulaco's history, which is now gearing up to annex Costaguana in yet another war.

The formal effect of translating this "epoch of civil wars" into a "tale of civil wars" is a historical novel that has a decidedly unstable narrative structure.[23] *Nostromo*, Edward Said explains, is obsessed "with rapid change, with inaugurations of new states, with a cascade of beginnings that intimate novel visions, actions, and protagonists. There are constant changes from one political status to the next, from one emotional mood to another, from one personal confrontation to another."[24] The novel's restless narrative style reflects the oscillatory nature of Costaguana's politics. Aaron Fogel similarly notes that the "rhythmic obstacles force the reader to share a feeling of historical disproportion with the characters."[25] The effect is a fragmented tale told out of order—one that has been notoriously difficult for readers of *Nostromo* to reassemble.[26] Pamela Demory argues that "the sheer volume of work that has gone into finding the 'real' sources [of *Nostromo*] illustrates the desire the novel creates in its readers to know 'what really happened' and where and when (which seems to me an indication of its successful depiction of history in the making), and that the tendency in some cases to ignore or downplay the distinction between the novel and its sources can be detrimental to our understanding of the novel."[27] Unlike, for example, Disraeli's *Sybil* where England's history is told through explicit narrative digressions with the implicit understanding that the narrator's history is the authorized version, *Nostromo* weaves Costaguana's history into the musings, meditations, and faulty perceptions of the main characters and narrator.

Nostromo therefore revises the classical historical novel of the nineteenth century, which narrated the emergence of the modern nation-state by constructing a linear arc across a series of historical crises (*Waverley, War and Peace, Vanity Fair, Sybil*). Instead, the arc of Costaguana's history is all crisis with no moment of arrival; its "endlessness of civil strife" is an endless state of transition. National-historical *telos* is further complicated by the proliferation of historians and histories within the world of the novel. Don José Avellanos's written history of Costaguana, "Fifty Years of Misrule," offers an official history of the country, whose title, as Said notes, "reminds us that for all those fifty years of misrule there could have been a rule right."[28] *Misrule*, according to Avellanos's worldview, is the cause of civil war; "Fifty Years of Proper Rule," we are led to believe, could in fact be "Fifty Years of Prosperity." Martin Decoud's understanding of Costaguana is indebted to Avellanos's book and told in an extended letter to his sister who lives in Europe.[29] In contrast, Captain Mitchell's oral history of Costaguana is sensationalist, aimed at tourists, and narrated in reductively epochal terms: "Almost every event out of the usual daily course 'marked an epoch' for him or else was 'history'" (84). Dr. Monygham's pessimistic account of Sulaco's future is expressed largely in the final chapters of the novel. Emilia Gould's preservationist version exists through her paintings of the San Tomé mountain before Gould revives its mine.[30] And perhaps most significantly, *Nostromo*'s narrator is not omniscient but situated within the world of the novel, for he refers to his own visit to Sulaco:

> Those of us whom business or curiosity took to Sulaco in these years before the first advent of the railway can remember the steadying effect of the San Tomé mine upon the life of that

remote province. The outward appearances had not changed
then as they have changed since, as I am told, with cable cars
running along the Street of the Constitution, and carriage roads
far into the country, to Rincón and other villages, where the
foreign merchants and the Ricos generally have their modern villas, and a vast railway goods yard by the harbour, which has a
quay-side, a long range of warehouse, and quite serious, organised labour troubles of its own. (72)

It is clear that the narrator visited Sulaco at a certain point, but also
that other parts of his narrative rely on secondary accounts because he
clarifies "I am told."

The proliferation of historians and histories represents *Nostromo*'s
most significant departure from the conventions of the classical historical novel. Seamus O'Malley argues that nascent modernism revised the
classical structure of the historical novel so that it features "historians
as characters, signaling a self-interrogation of history (shifting the focus
from history as referent to history as narrative); or, conversely, they
have characters suffering from faulty memory or amnesia, employing
the absence of memories to signal the presence of the past, thus questioning the very foundations of the historical discipline."[31] If Lukács's
historical novel depicts the past as the prehistory of the present, then
the modernist historical novel depicts the past as *prehistories* of the
present. Moreover, historical events that befall Costaguana (an industrial revolution, a coup, international intervention, a partition) are
never directly narrated, and must instead be inferred through ellipses
in the story. As O'Malley notes, in *Nostromo* "plot time has continued but there is no narrative time dedicated to describing those events.
Events 'occur' in the white space between chapters."[32] The effect is a
text where the force of history is thoroughly palpable and yet is entirely
absent from the events narrated in the text; history is everywhere but
nowhere.

Such an unstable narrative structure is precisely why critics have
avoided reading *Nostromo* as a historical novel. This is because, as
Perry Anderson sums up, modernism lacks the historical novel's "total-
ising retrospect."[33] Hayden White goes further to say that literary and
filmic modernism "marks the end of storytelling."[34] Such "antinarrative
nonstories" resist "the temptation to employ events and the actions of
the characters so as to produce the meaning-effect derived by demonstrating how one's end may be contained in one's beginning."[35] But in

the context of a novel like *Nostromo*, the resistance to a "totalizing retrospect" is inseparable from how modernism was shaped by the colonial experience. The unevenness of colonial modernity inflected the
plots and generic forms of colonial fiction, and in turn the itineraries
of progressivist historicism necessary to the kind of retrospect Anderson and White speak of. As Jed Esty shows with regard to another
nineteenth-century genre, the bildungsroman, modernism revised the
narrative of growth so that it told tales of stalled youth, endless ado-
lescence, and untimely deaths in order to allegorize the crisis of modernity in the colonial world. In much the same way, nascent modernism
revised the classical form of the historical novel to dramatize the crisis
of colonial modernity.

Difficult and heterogeneous though it may be, a consistent theme runs
through *Nostromo*'s many versions of Costaguana's past: the country's
civil wars have been symptoms of barbarity. Indeed, there is consensus
between the Costaguaneros and Europeans that the "crises" that befall
Costaguana are collectively crises of uncivilized political violence. The
narrator explains that Costaguana's politics are "rooted in political
immaturity of the people, in the indolence of the upper classes and
the mental darkness of the lower" (277). Led by a lazy intelligentsia
and unintelligent populace, Costaguana's political sphere is depicted
as impulsive, crude, and childish. In an especially cynical moment, Dr.
Monygham—who was tortured during the especially brutal regime of
Guzman Bento—evacuates the entire nation of rational politics: "It is a
fine country, and they have raised a fine crop of hates, vengeance, murder and rapine—those sons of the country" (223). Echoing Monygham,
Emilia Gould describes the "continuous political changes, the constant
saving of the country," as "a puerile and blood-thirsty game of murder
and rapine played with terrible earnestness by depraved children" (38).
Reform seems to have no place in Costaguana, which must instead be
violently "saved" from brutal regimes by partisans waging ever more
civil war. Giorgio Viola, a Genoese revolutionary who once fought for
Giuseppe Garibaldi's campaigns in Uruguay and Italy's Risorgimento,
is an "Idealist of the old, humanitarian revolutions" (409). And to him
too, Costaguana's political movements are "non-political" because at
their helms are "not a people striving for justice, but thieves" (14, 17).
Far from the latent strife of early Victorian England or the gentlemanly
conflicts of the late Victorian imagination, civil wars in Costaguana
are "blood-thirsty," "murderous," "vengeful," and "barbaric." Consequently, the country's revolutionary energy can never enact a regime

change that pushes the country forward in history. At stake, in other words, is the crisis of modernity in the non-West—a crisis whose defining feature is civil war, and whose literary form torques the realist conventions of the historical novel. Thinking in the progressivist terms of historicism, Irvine Howe reads *Nostromo* as a retelling of Marx's *Eighteenth Brumaire* in the colonial peripheries. Howe explains that "in Europe Bonapartism arises from a fairly equal balance of antagonistic classes: the rulers cannot rule, the ruled cannot displace them. Into this crisis of the nation there leaps the military man raising the banner of social order and harmony." But in Costaguana, Bonapartism emerges "from the mutual lassitude of exploiters and exploited . . . such a country can reach neither stability nor democracy."[36] If Marx saw in the revolutions and counterrevolutions of 1848 a world-historical transition, the endlessness of civil strife in Costaguana is a local affair that stalls historical transformation into paralysis: an extended state of failed transition and arrested development—what I later call an "interregnum."

Far from the "murderous follies" of a select few, Costaguana's entire populace plays "blood-thirsty games of murder and rapine." Nicholas Visser observes that in *Nostromo* even the popular "crowds are fickle, anarchic, irrational, given to random violence, subject to 'mob psychology.'"[37] Costaguana's political elites routinely instrumentalize the lower classes for personal gain, and consequently, the country's masses seem incapable of "saving" the country from itself. After the fall of the dictator Guzman Bento, workers at the foreign-owned San Tomé mine are mobilized by their political leaders in the far-off capital to destroy the mine: "the native miners, incited to revolt by the emissaries sent out from the capital, had risen upon their English chiefs and murdered them to a man" (41). The working class in Conrad's *Nostromo* has none of the agency that Carlyle feared in Chartism (the "million-headed hydra") and is instead closer to what Marx, referring to the *lumpenproletariat*, called a "sack of potatoes."[38] Captain Mitchell, who "prided himself on his profound knowledge of men and things in the country—cosas de Costaguana," describes the rioting crowds as behaving "with regrettable barbarity to the inhabitants [of Sulaco] during their civil commotions" (10, 233). The anonymous narrator describes this "revolutionary rabble" as a rabid animal, which after "pouring out of the town, had spread itself all along the shore, howled and foamed at the foot of the building in front" (11). In the minds of bourgeois republicans like Gould, Viola, Mitchell, and even the anonymous narrator, Costaguanero politics are entirely devoid of political content, motivated instead by barbarity, greed, and vengeance.

Such uncivil tumult incessantly disrupts economic and industrial development. During its decades of turmoil, personal fortunes are obliterated while infrastructural projects are left abandoned: "There was no saying what would happen to the railway if the revolution got the upperhand. Perhaps it would have to be abandoned. It would not be the first railway gone to pot in Costaguana" (123). Even the Oceanic Steam Navigation Company—Sulaco's only maritime link to world trade and renowned for its uninterrupted service—struggles to conduct business during "the frequent changes of government brought about by revolutions of the military type" (10). The San Tomé mine— what will become Costaguana's "ray of hope," economic development and modernity—was abandoned and destroyed in the revolutions that followed independence. Its "buildings had been burnt down, the mining plant had been destroyed, the mining population had disappeared from the neighborhood years and years ago; the very road had vanished under a flood of tropical vegetation as effectually as if swallowed by the sea. . . . It was no longer a mine; it was a wild, inaccessible and rocky gorge of the Sierra" (42). Whatever ruins are left behind by the revolting miners the natural landscape "swallows" up like a swell in the sea, drowning this beacon of modernity in the tidal rhythms of civil war.

Costaguana's epoch of civil wars, it turns out, is really an epoch of uncivil wars. Benita Parry sums up that "the composite picture constructed [in *Nostromo*] is of a continent ravished by persistent barbarism, where fatuous imbecility and blindly ferocious fanaticism characterise political life, and the succession of civil wars, conspiracies, revolutions and counter-revolutions, *pronunciamentos* and plebiscites manifest the absence of a solid foundation for stability."[39] No longer "civil" as it was in early Victorian England, civil war in *Nostromo* is symptomatic of lawless political dysfunction. And because Conrad, like his Victorian predecessors, understands civil war to be a category tied to the historical forces of modernity, it becomes a tool to present a decidedly Orientalist vision of the world. Hence the novel's double standard for revolutions, for all revolutionary action in *Nostromo* is not bad revolutionary action. Visser correctly points out that while insurrectionists in Sulaco seem "non-political," Viola's revolutionism is depicted as virtuous because at its heart it is republican idealism and nationalism.[40] His involvement in Garibaldi's campaigns in Italy and Uruguay is championed because he was fighting for the "sake of universal love and brotherhood, instead of a more or less large share of booty" of Sulaco's riotous crowds (225). This contrast throws the difference between "good" and "bad" revolutionary action into sharp relief: the former is justified because its ends are republican national unity—"universal love and brotherhood"—while the latter is dismissed as solely motivated by greed rather than the common good. So while *Nostromo* presents civil war as taking place in the global periphery— something early Victorians could not do—it nevertheless preserves the classical coordinates of imperialism: of a modernized metropolitan center and a backward colonial periphery. By so thoroughly linking the problem of civil war with civilizational depravity, *Nostromo* inverts Victorian narratives of civil war from being the driving force of history to the agent of history's obstruction.

CIVILITY BY OTHER MEANS

Woven into such an Orientalist vision of the world, of course, is the civilizing mission. But as I pointed out earlier, the agents of this mission no longer represent the British government but the civilizing effects of "material interests," meaning industrial and economic development. And so Costaguana's civility, like its liberators, like its leaders, like its businessmen, like its philanthropists, like its skilled labor, must come from beyond its own shores. The need for international development in the face of historical stagnancy is crystallized when Emilia Gould travels through the country for the first time: "Mrs. Gould, with each day's journey, seemed to come nearer to the soul of the land in the tremendous disclosure of this interior unaffected by the slight European veneer of the coast towns, a great land of plain and mountain and people, suffering and mute, waiting for the future in a pathetic immobility of patience" (66). This "soul" of Costaguana, dumb though it may be, speaks a resounding message: "And on all the lips she found a weary desire for peace, the dread of officialdom with its nightmarish parody of administration without law, without security, and without justice" (66). Although Costaguana "desires peace," law, security, and justice, its pitiful resilience and muteness needs those who are in fact impatient for the future, who can speak and therefore realize civility. Conrad reduces the civilizing mission to a mere speech act.

And so it is Westerners—the English Goulds, the O.S.N. company, the railway company, the Italian workers and intellectuals, American tycoons—who bring Sulaco and Costaguana out of the "nightmare" of backwardness and its "blood-thirsty games of murder and rapine." These agents of modernity are "the great body of strong-limbed foreigners who dug the earth, blasted the rocks, drove the engines for the 'progressive and patriotic undertaking'" (28). When the plans for a railway line connecting Sulaco to the rest of the country are put into place, the narrator metaphorizes the train as a vehicle of historical progress: "there was generated a power for the world's service; a subtle force that could set in motion mighty machines, men's muscles, and awaken also in human breasts an unbounded devotion to the task" (33). Sulaco, shielded from modernity for centuries, begins to inch forward in history, powered mechanistically by the "subtle force" of "progressivism" and "patriotism"—the very liberal ideals Gould initially found missing (or rather, perverted) in Costaguana. While these ideals motor Costaguana's progress, they also emplot its future by laying the tracks, as it were, for the town's journey through history. That is to say, Europeans animate Sulaco's modernization, but they also chart its historical itinerary into a singular modernity.[41]

Charles Gould is most impatient to conduct this train of progress. He is especially well suited to the task of engineering Sulaco's (and later Costaguana's) future because the history of his family is intertwined with that of the country's. His grandfather was a "revolutionary swashbuckler" who fought for Bolívar's revolutions. His uncle is the martyred president of Sulaco, assassinated by the Guzman Bento—Costaguana's most brutal dictator. "With such a family record," the narrator comments, "no one could be more of a Costaguanero than Don Carlos Gould; but his aspect was so characteristic that in the talk of common people he was just the Ingléz—the Englishman of Sulaco" (37). Despite growing up in Costaguana, Gould retains his Englishness across geographies and generations, an important trait of which is the need to "save" the country from its own political depravity.[42]

The epicenter of Gould's mission is Sulaco, a small coastal town that has historically "never been commercially anything more important than a coasting port with a fairly large local trade in ox-hides and indigo" (5). The reason for the town's detachment from global commerce is the landscape that surrounds it: "Sulaco had found an inviolable sanctuary from the temptations of a trading world in the solemn hush of the deep Golfo Plácido as if within an enormous semi-circular unroofed temple open to the ocean, with its walls of lofty mountains hung with the mourning draperies of cloud" (ibid.). Precipices to the east, a lifeless gulf to the west, and clouds above, the natural topography has historically shielded the town from integration into the world economy. Sulaco is further protected by the snowy peak of Higuerota that soars 18,000 feet high, so supreme that even Sir John, chairman of a railway company seeking to build a railway connecting Sulaco to the rest of Costaguana, concedes: "We can't move mountains!" (33). The town's topographic dislocation from the world is almost excessive, for while it is situated in a placid gulf, the "Golfo Plácido" that leads to the Pacific Ocean, the town's harbor is in fact nestled within a second, even smaller gulf, "as if chopped with an axe out of the regular sweep of the coast" (8). So absolute and vast is this serenity that "your ship floats unseen under your feet, her sails flutter invisible above your head. The eye of God himself . . . could not find out what work a man's hand is doing in there" (7). The winds of Spanish conquest themselves had a hard time reaching the shores of Sulaco: "The clumsy, deep-sea galleons of the [Spanish] conquerors, that, needing a brisk gale to move at all would lie becalmed" (5). As though respecting their highest authority, Spanish conquistadores abide by God's own limitations by failing to penetrate the natural barriers in which the town takes refuge.

Charles Gould undermines this historico-theological truth by supplanting an older form of imperial conquest with a new kind. The most powerful characterization of Gould as Costaguana's conquering savior comes from his comparison to an old equestrian statue of Charles IV of Spain. The statue, located within Sulaco, "was only known to the folk from the country and to the beggars of the town that slept on the steps around the pedestal as the Horse of Stone. The other Carlos . . . looked as incongruous, but much more at home, than the kingly cavalier reining in his steed on the pedestal above the sleeping leperos, with his marble arm raised towards the heavy rim of a plumed hat" (38). The narrator's comparison dramatizes a twofold interregnum. First, it depicts a transition from Spanish colonialism to late nineteenth-century British imperialism. Second, we see a shift in authority from royal decree to bourgeois leadership. Now in decay and home to the homeless, the statue of the Spanish king is replaced by a new regime: a living "Carlos" who is entirely at home in Costaguana (despite being English). Instead of ruling from afar, the new English "King of Sulaco," as Gould comes to be known, is "the visible sign of stability that could be achieved on the shifting ground of revolutions" (139). Rather than the king's sword, Gould's "weapon was the wealth of the mine, more far-reaching and subtle than an honest blade of steel fitted into a simple brass guard" (261). And yet, because of his innate English dignity, this new bourgeois king retains all the dignity and stoicism of the statue: "The weather-stained effigy of the mounted king, with its vague suggestion of a saluting gesture, seemed to present an inscrutable breast to the political changes which had robbed it of its very name; but neither did the other horseman, well known to the people, keen and alive on his well-shaped, slate-coloured beast with a white eye, wear his heart on the sleeve of his English coat" (38). Old forms of regnal domination give way to a newer kind whose political authority derives not from divine right and telescopic benevolence but its modern equivalent: capital. In this regard, Gould is unique from other leaders of Sulaco and Costaguana because his politics are not national liberation as in the case of his own grandfather (the president of Sulaco when it belonged to a federation) but the introduction of industrial capitalism: "Just as years ago . . . Henry Gould had drawn the sword, so now, the times being changed, Charles Gould had flung the silver of the San Tomé mine into the fray" (104). History necessitates a new revolutionism that does not rely on the violence of the sword but the exchange value of silver.[43] Armed with the commodity form, Gould's mine is the "subtle force" of history that can power the engines of Costaguana's singular modernity.

In Charles Gould we find a reinvention of the civilizing mission that is undertaken neither by Spanish conquistadores nor by a British imperial state but through investment and development. It is closest to, as I discussed in the previous chapter, the partnership between England and America that Charles Dilke pictured as the future of British imperialism. For Gould's silver mine is funded by Holroyd, an American tycoon as interested in maximizing profits as he is in spreading Protestantism throughout the world. Holroyd assures the young Charles Gould: "We shall be giving the word for everything; industry, trade, law, journalism, art, politics, and religion. . . . We shall run the world's business whether the world likes it or not. The world can't help it—and neither can we, I guess" (58). "Running the world's business" amounts to influencing all aspects of life, from industry to law and art at a global scale. In the minds of Gould and Holroyd alike, Sulaco's economic development—meaning its integration into the world market— will naturally create the conditions for peace and cultivate liberalism. But crucially, Gould is unable to undertake this mission on his own and relies on the American Holroyd to fund his politico-economic project. If "England is speaking to the world" through America in Dilke's

Greater Britain, then Gould speaks through Holroyd in Costaguana; Holroyd's money does the talking.

No longer "suffering and mute" in the company of its new king, Sulaco's modernity resounds. When Gould resurrects the silver mine Sulaco, placid for a century, becomes enveloped in the constant sound of silver extraction from the San Tomé mine and enmeshed in the political life of the country. The mine's rebirth makes the natural landscape unrecognizable: "the clearing of the wilderness, the making of the road, the cutting of new paths up the cliff face of San Tomé" transform the region. Its characteristic feature, a waterfall, "existed no longer. The tree-ferns that had luxuriated in its spray had dried around the dried-up pool, and the high ravine was only a big trench half filled up with the refuse of excavations and tailings" (79).[44] Instead of resisting modernity, the landscape becomes a symbol of industrial triumph. And far from a "subtle force," the mine propels Sulaco forward with unceasing energy. The quaint waterfall is replaced by the "great clattering, shuffling noise, gathering speed and weight" of the mine. Its operations "would be caught up by the walls of the gorge, and sent upon the plain in a growl of thunder" (78–79). To Charles Gould, the mine's resonance becomes a metaphor for Sulaco and Costaguana's modernization more generally: "it seemed that the sound must reach the uttermost limits of the province. . . . There was no mistaking the growling of the mountain pouring its stream of treasure under the stamps, and it came to his heart with the peculiar force of a proclamation thundered forth over the land and the marvelousness of an accomplished fact fulfilling an audacious desire" (79). No longer paralyzed by the "pathetic immobility of patience" and silence, the landscape of the Occidental province (of which Sulaco is the capital) "growls" and "thunders" notes of progress, stability, and peace.

Gould's plan does indeed work for some years. "Business," Captain Mitchell boasts, "was booming all along this seaboard" in the years following the mine's reopening (351). The corresponding effect of prosperity, as Gould and Holroyd hypothesized, has a "steadying effect" on Sulaco (72). More than a node of resource extraction, this subterranean "fountain of honour, of prosperity, and peace" becomes a sociopolitical institution: "For the San Tomé mine was to become an institution, a rallying point for everything in the province that needed order and stability to live. Security seemed to flow upon this land from the mountain-gorge" (284, 82). Just as the mountain "pours its stream of treasure," a torrent of capital brings with it a paradoxical torrent of security and stability. As though waging a peaceful war on war, "each passing of the [silver] escort under the balconies of the Casa Gould was like another victory gained in the conquest for peace in Sulaco" (86).[45] To a writer like Disraeli, narrating conquest by other means made visible the relations of force and domination that permeated English society. Hence his comparison of the Norman Conquest to the rise of England's "new aristocracy" highlights the secret war between the upper and lower classes of England. Conrad's metaphor revises the formulation of politics as war by other means as: *development is conquest by other means.* Conquest no longer relies on the sword but rather on the other means of subterranean resource extraction. Hence the name of the mine, "Tomé," meaning "to take"; Gould's mining operation "takes" Sulaco's wealth in exchange for peace.

Though the success of the San Tomé mine is aided by Gould's bribery of political leaders and administrators, the "King of Sulaco" eventually becomes powerful enough to influence the installation of a reformist government favorable to him and the world market. With the continued financial backing of Holroyd, the Ribiera party, led by "men of education and integrity," takes power in Costaguana (105). But the alignment of Gould's "material interests" with Costaguana's political interests is short-lived. Largely unpopular, the Ribiera regime falls prey to Montero's coup, which creates yet another civil war. What becomes entirely clear in the period that follows is that money alone cannot preserve the material interests of Costaguana—which are, in fact, the material interests of foreigners like Holroyd. In yet another example of the partnership between Britain's imperial ambitions and America's civilizing missions, the United States government intervenes in Costaguana's conflict, sending a military cruiser to aid the secessionist movement and put a stop to the civil war. Once Montero is defeated, Sulaco becomes the capital of a new state, the Occidental Republic. And when its flag is raised, the "United States cruiser, *Powhattan*, was the first to salute the Occidental flag" (349). The cruiser's name, "Powhattan," announces a new epoch of conquest that conscripts previous epochs of colonization into a new imperial arrangement. For Powhattan is the name of a Native American chief of an Algonquin tribe exiled to Virginia by the Spanish empire. Powhattan's daughter, Pocahontas, was later married to John Smith, symbolizing a supposed union between British settler colonials and the native population in Jamestown. And finally in *Nostromo*, Powhattan is the name given to the American vessel that militarily intervenes in South American politics. Thus three epochs of colonial domination are folded into a single name: Spanish conquest, American settler rule, and American imperial interventionism—Powhattan. Having aligned the material interests of the United States and Occidental Republic, and by extension, secured the military backing of Washington, D.C., Sulaco prospers for a decade thereafter, gaining the nickname "Treasure House of the World" (344). For a time at least, Holroyd and Gould succeed in securing "the world's business whether the world likes it or not," but with the lesson that such economic development necessitates military intervention by foreign powers.

The historical transformation at the heart of *Nostromo* is the arrival of capitalism in Costaguana. As Fredric Jameson puts it: "So the act happens—capitalism arrives in Sulaco."[46] But capitalism doesn't just arrive. It *needs* to arrive in order to save Costaguana from the "endlessness of civil war." Because civil war is the alibi for capitalism's arrival, *Nostromo* inverts the relationship between these two categories that predominated in the nineteenth century. For while capitalism had brought civil war to the doorstep of early Victorian society, civil war brings capitalism to the doorstep of Costaguana, a long-neglected corner of the world. And crucially, the civil war that ushers in capitalism is orchestrated by San Franciscan tycoons and concluded by the USS *Powhattan*, the name for New Imperialism.

AN IMPERIAL SENSE OF AN ENDING

But perhaps Conrad's most significant achievement in *Nostromo*—one that remains important for postcolonial writers of the late twentieth century and for our own times—is that the novel undermines the very historical transition it initially sets out to narrate. For once "the act" does indeed happen and capitalism arrives in Sulaco, we learn that in a world of increasingly globalized capital, the problem of civil war doesn't go away; the "tale of civil wars" goes on. Far from triumphalist about the successes of international intervention, *Nostromo* narrates the utter failure of Gould and Holroyd's project. Gould's "gift" of modernity brings with it class consciousness and "organised labour troubles" specifically directed at the foreign interests of the mine (72). Even the Goulds' most influential allies begin questioning the motives of the San Tomé mine. Nostromo, the novel's eponymous flawed hero, grows bitter and greedy. And Antonia Avellanos—daughter of

Sulaco's most prominent intellectual and the Goulds' closest ally, José Avellanos—makes the case for the Occidental Republic's reabsorption of Costaguana on the basis of common national identity: "How can we abandon, groaning under oppression, those who have been our countrymen only a few years ago, who *are* our countrymen now? How can we remain blind, and deaf, and without pity to the cruel wrongs suffered by our brothers?" (364). Echoing the "bond of division" of the early Victorian imagination, Sulaco, once feeling nothing but antagonism toward Costaguana, now finds its separation from its former fellow-countrymen intolerable. Somewhere between civil war and international intervention, the Occidental Republic's annexation of Costaguana remains on the horizon at the end of the novel.

Also looming in the distance is a domestic rebellion against the "material interests" of foreigners like Gould and Holroyd. Cardinal Archbishop Corbelan—a longtime friend and supporter of the Goulds who vowed to protect the mine during the Sulaco-Costaguana war—begins to question the foreign influence of the mine: "We have worked for them; we have made them; these material interests of the foreigners," elaborating that "let them beware, then, lest the people, prevented from their aspirations, should rise and claim their share of the wealth and their share of the power" (365). Corbelan no longer sees the mine as the "rallying point" for peace and prosperity but yet another institution subjugating the indigenous population. What was a "conquest of peace" during the heyday of Gould's reign now increasingly looks like foreign domination. Corbelan's anticolonial rhetoric reveals Gould's project of peace and prosperity to simply be the continuation of colonial rule by other means. Even the mobs no longer act "non-politically" but form a group consciousness, directing their anger toward foreign interests, chanting cries for the "death of foreigners" (221).

By the end of the novel the San Tomé mine, once the ex-colony's "ray of hope," begins to look like the very dictatorships it sought to depose. Reflecting on the country's future, Dr. Monygham declares to Emilia Gould in an often-quoted passage: "There is no peace and rest in the development of material interests. They have their law and their justice. But it is founded on expediency, and is inhuman; it is without rectitude, without the continuity and force that can be found only in a moral principle. Mrs. Gould, the time approaches when all that the Gould Concession stands for shall weigh as heavily upon the people as the barbarism, cruelty, and misrule of a few years back" (366). Monygham's moralistic critique is about the irreconcilability of capitalism and the ideals of liberal humanism. Despite its transformations of the political sphere of the country, the mine is reduced to another chapter in Costaguana's "tale of civil wars." Indeed, his comment suggests that Avellanos's "Fifty Years of Misrule" might be revised as "A Century of Misrule." Even Emilia Gould is convinced of the matter: "She saw the San Tomé mountain hanging over the Campo, over the whole land, feared, hated, wealthy, more soulless than any tyrant, more pitiless and autocratic than the worst Government, ready to crush innumerable lives in the expansion of its greatness" (373). Rather than saving the country from the conflict trap, Gould and Holroyd's mission, like the "absurd devilish children" of Costaguana's past, reproduces the very dictatorships it seeks to put an end to. Sulaco may now be integrated into the world system, but the "endlessness of civil strife" remains. The civilizing mission looks uncannily like the incivility it set out to cure; "Liberty—democracy—patriotism—government" take on nightmarish meanings. If in Kipling a sahibs' war slipped into a war at the border, in Conrad the civilizing mission slips into a dictatorship.

Herein lies *Nostromo*'s most important intervention into the story of empire. The novel ends, in a sense, where it began. It begins "In the time of Spanish rule" and ends in a time of international rule. History may have moved forward, and even transformed Costaguana in fundamental ways (the silver mine, the railway, the telegraph, an industrial proletariat), but the symbolic kernel of civil war that was at the heart of the country's history—*a kernel that defined its backwardness and incivility*—remains unchanged. The final passage finds Sulaco just as it has always been, "from the deep head of the gulf, full of black vapour, and walled by immense mountains . . . out upon the ocean with a bright line marking the illusory edge of the world, where a great white cloud hung brighter than a mass of silver in the moonlight, in that cry of a longing heart sending its never-ceasing vibration into a sky empty of stars, the genius of the magnificent Capataz de Cargadores dominated the place" (422). Despite Sulaco's integration into the world system and becoming the "Treasure House of the World," the coastal town remains at the "edge of the world," as far off from Europe's modernity as it had always been. Said interprets this passage as signaling a stalled future: "The immobility that ends *Nostromo* is a sterile calm, as sterile as the future life of the childless Goulds, in which all action is finally concentrated into a cry of motionless despair."[47] If the novel seeks to narrate an exit from a "tale of civil wars," then this is a tale that cannot in fact come to an end. Incapable of imagining an ending, the "tale of civil war" remains completely intact—the entire plot of the novel goes seemingly nowhere. Actors change, regimes change, but the chapters keep getting written. Indeed, it is perhaps no coincidence that Conrad had such a hard time finishing writing *Nostromo*. Said, Jameson, and Ian Watt, among others, have all offered extensive accounts of how Conrad's difficulties in bringing the book to a close impacted the novel itself. The anguish Conrad experienced in finishing the novel is arguably an anguish of being unable to imagine an ending to the "endlessness of civil strife." So while *Nostromo*'s thematics suggest that the civilizing mission can indeed save Costaguana from its uncivil wars, its plot, or more specifically, its *emplotment*, suggests a much bleaker picture—one with no end, no conclusion, no escape from the "bloodthirsty games of murder and rapine."

Conrad is unable to point to a future other than imperialism because he saw the civilizing mission as an inherently limited project. In *Heart of Darkness* the "cry of motionless despair" belonged to Kurtz and sounded like "The horror! The horror!"[48] It was through this cry that Conrad voiced his critique of imperialism. The "darkness" that Kurtz and eventually Marlow find in Africa is, of course, the horrors of empire and the rise of anticolonial nationalism—the figure for what Conrad cannot give representational form, but whose horrific presence he is nevertheless aware of. As Said explains, Kurtz, Marlow, and ultimately Conrad "are ahead of their time in understanding that what they call 'the darkness' has an autonomy of its own, and can reinvade and reclaim what imperialism has taken for *its* own. But Marlow and Kurtz are also creatures of their own time and cannot take the next step, which would be to recognize that what they saw, disablingly and disparagingly, as a non-European 'darkness' was in fact a non-European world *resisting* imperialism so as one day to regain sovereignty and independence."[49] In *Nostromo* it is neither darkness, nor horror, nor even anticolonial nationalism that looms but silence and immobility.[50] This is at the heart of Emilia Gould's final realization that the San Tomé mine has been just another brutal dictatorship in Costaguana's history of civil strife. Costaguana's future is but a "solemn hush," still and silent, in stark contrast to the "growls" and "thunders" of progress that Gould temporarily brought to Costaguana with the San Tomé mine (6). Instead, the country returns to being "suffering and mute, waiting for the future in a pathetic immobility of patience." To have a sense of an ending to this "tale of civil war," to be impatient for the novel's end, would be to share Gould's impatience for imperial triumph—a sensibility the text systematically keeps out of reach. The "cry of a longing heart sending its never-ceasing vibration into a sky empty of stars" is a cry for the novel to narrate a historical transition— one that falls on deaf ears.

SULACO: AN ARCHETYPE

Writing in 1958, literary critic Albert Guerard praised *Nostromo* for being an archetypical text about Third World modernity: "*Nostromo* is without question Conrad's greatest creative achievement: successful creation (from a few books read and a 'short glance' at Central and South America a quarter of a century before) of a city, a country, a history. In its absurd rhythm of exploitation and misrule, of revolution and counterrevolution, Costaguana may evoke almost any South or Central American republic; its tales are as contemporary as yesterday's *coup d'état* in Honduras or Haiti or the Guatemalan intervention of a few years ago. The forces of deception and self-deception are the same as those at work anywhere."[51] *Nostromo*'s "completeness" of city, country, and history is effective not because of its mimetic quality but because of what it anticipates. Conrad's achievement in *Nostromo*, according to Guerard, was to have created in the fictional country of Costaguana an allegory of postcoloniality. And the story it tells is the "absurd rhythm of exploitation and misrule, of revolution and counterrevolution" that plagues "almost any South or Central American republic," like Honduras, Haiti, Guatemala, and (some pages later) even the Middle East, "anywhere."[52]

What is startling about Guerard's statement is not so much that Costaguana is a blueprint for *a particular* country but that it is a blueprint for seemingly every country in Latin America, the Middle East, "anywhere." Having visited Latin America through a "short glance" a quarter of a century earlier and reading a handful of books, Conrad's "genius" is to have created a thoroughly realistic picture of the peripheries with so little attention to the particular histories of such places. For Guerard, Costaguana is an approximation of any tumultuous country at the periphery and comes to stand for all dysfunctional countries and their respective civil wars and dictatorships.[53] Guerard, who extensively attends to the problem of class in *Nostromo*, is entirely unable to see the *international* division of labor both at the heart of the novel and at the heart of his national allegorization. *Nostromo* makes clear that civilizing missions take as their starting point the assumption that "the words one knows so well" like "Liberty—democracy—patriotism—government" translate perfectly in places other than Europe.[54] This is Gould's mistake. What *Nostromo* takes to be a *relation* between metropole and colony, Europe and Latin America, Guerard takes to be about a *place* that is as singular and homogeneous as it is a stand-in for the entire developing world. Guerard therefore fails to see how *Nostromo*'s world is as much a reflection of the Orient as it is of Europe. To recall Aijaz Ahmed's critique of Jameson's essay "Third World Literature in the Era of Multinational Capital," "we live not in three worlds but one; that this world includes the experience of colonialism and imperialism on both sides of Jameson's global divide . . . that the different parts of the capitalist system are to be known not in terms of a binary opposition but as a contradictory unity—with differences, yes, but also with profound overlaps."[55] What is plainly obvious in *Nostromo* is that the "problem" of incivility in the peripheries is integral to Europe's civilizing missions. And while Conrad could not articulate the limits of such an endeavor explicitly, his art could nevertheless formalize it in the novel's plot. So while the opposition between civility and barbarism remains intact in *Nostromo*, the novel also makes clear that the attempt to erase this difference—ending civil war through development—is profoundly limited in what it can achieve, reproducing the very difference it seeks to eradicate.

What is most telling about Guerard's interpretation, however, is not his interpretation as much as the period in which it was articulated. That he reads *Nostromo* as a Third World allegory in 1958, *the heart of the age of decolonization and the birth of the Bandung movement*, is indicative of how civil war and international interventionism would continue to haunt the postcolonial world after the fall of official empires. Even in the midst of several anticolonial revolutions throughout the world, Guerard is unable to see how the "tale of civil war" in the Orient is woven into the West's tale of the civilizing mission—what I have been arguing is at the center of *Nostromo*'s vision of the world. The following chapters look at how in the aftermath of Bandung and the shortcomings of the project of decolonization, narratives of civil war continued to offer a way to think the nation and empire—only now in a postcolonial key against its geographical other, Europe, as well as against its historical other, the colonial past. And here too, as in Conrad, it is in resisting a sense of an ending to tales of civil war that novels formalize the stakes of postcolonial nationhood and futurity.

PART III

Incivility

Published three years before the World Bank's report on civil war and developmental policy, Michael Ondaatje's *Anil's Ghost* (2000) takes us to the front lines of the conflict trap. Set amid the Sri Lankan civil war during the late 1980s, Ondaatje's novel thematizes the Bank's account of civic conflict in the Global South, focusing less on the particular complexities and history of Sri Lanka (very little is said about the actual content of the conflict between Tamil insurgents and the Sri Lankan government) and far more on the tensions between international human rights groups and perpetrators of civil unrest.[1] "This is an unofficial war," we are told at one point, "no one wants to alienate the foreign powers. So it's secret gangs and squads. Not like Central America. The government was not the only one doing the killing. You had, and still have, three camps of enemies . . . using weapons, propaganda, fear, sophisticated posters, censorship. . . . There's no hope of affixing blame. And no one can tell who the victims are."[2] And yet the entire premise of the novel's plot is identifying victims and affixing blame for human rights abuses. The novel follows Anil Tissera, a forensic pathologist on assignment in Sri Lanka for an international human rights organization, and Sarath Diyasena, a local archaeologist who accompanies Anil in her search for evidence of wartime atrocities.

Anil and Sarath's work of identifying victims, it turns out, looks identical to the act of historicizing. The narrator explains, "Tectonic slips and brutal human violence provided random time-capsules of

135

unhistorical lives. . . . But in the midst of such events, she [Anil] realized, there could never be any logic to the human violence without the
distance of time. For now it would be reported, filed in Geneva, but
no one could ever give meaning to it. She used to believe that meaning
allowed a person a door to escape grief and fear. But she saw that those
who were slammed and stained by violence lost the power of language
and logic."[3] Backed by organizations in places like Geneva, Anil sees
her human rights work as bringing victims of civil war, the "unhistorical lives," into the fold of history.[4] So while narratives of national
rupture in the nineteenth century depicted civil war as a latent conflict
that motored the history of the West (which I discussed in the first part
of this book), in Anil's world civil war evacuates historical content by
burying the victims of its violence. Because all parties in Sri Lanka's
civil war are involved in the "unofficial war," it is up to human rights
organizations like the kind Anil works for to exhume these histories, so
that the victims of war might regain "the power of language and logic."
The narrator sums this up in a striking metaphor: "A good archeologist
can read a bucket of soil as if it were a complex historical novel."[5] If the
Lukácsian historical novel "makes history live," then Anil and Sarath's
archaeological work brings the "unhistorical dead" to life.[6] Unlike the
novels of Walter Scott or Benjamin Disraeli that narrativize England's
national-historical consciousness, the "historical novels" Anil reads
make the dynamics of international human rights watchdogs visible.
For while "buckets of soil" contain important data about the slaughter
of civilians during the civil war, they also contain the seeds for international intervention. Microscopic details like pollen grains or hairline
bone fractures carry political meaning, whose interpretation is essential to Anil in her historical reconstruction of the Sri Lankan war. That
is to say, the minutiae of Anil's forensic analysis carry with them the
weight of a world-historical drama in which a benevolent West gives
back to the East what it has lost in civil war: its own history.

Anil valiantly confronts the Sri Lankan government in Colombo in
the climax of the novel. She declares: "I'm not hired by you. I work
for an international authority. . . . We are an independent organization. We make independent reports. . . . What I wish to report is that
some government forces have possibly murdered innocent people."[7]
Her defiance makes the world-historical stakes of forensic work done
in the name of human rights explicit: an "independent international
authority" holding civil war–mongering governments accountable for
war crimes. But Anil's attempt to speak on behalf of "buckets of soil"

reproduces clichés of Western interventionism. Her report on extrajudicial killings implicates Sarath in the investigation into government killings, triggering his own assassination at the hands of the state, ironically making him, an archaeologist, into a unit of forensic evidence and interpretation—a "bucket of soil." In contrast, Anil escapes to her home in the United States on her UN passport, reinscribing the international division of labor that brought her to Sri Lanka in the first place. To drive home the discrepancy of Anil's and Sarath's trajectories, Ondaatje interjects between their respective "departures" a past conversation they have with Gamini (Sarath's brother) about Western interventionism. Gamini sardonically notes how in American movies and English literature, the hero always returns from war-torn peripheries back to the metropole: "The American or Englishman gets on a plane and leaves. That's it. The camera leaves with him. He looks out of the window at Mombasa or Vietnam or Jakarta, someplace now he can look at through clouds. . . . So that war, to all purposes, is over. That's enough reality for the West. . . . Go home. Write a book. Hit the circuit."[8] Gamini's commentary on cultural depictions of heroism is unmistakably a critique of Anil's "reality." And although Anil is no Hollywood heroine, she is afforded the luxury of escape, while Sarath's death simply reproduces the necessity of "international authorities" like the kind Anil works for.

By showing the international division of labor to be intertwined with human rights work in civil war–torn countries, Ondaatje folds the genre of the historical novel into the politics of liberal-humanitarian interventionism. For of course, *Anil's Ghost* is itself a historical novel. Which is to say that the reader interprets Ondaatje's text as an archaeologist might read a bucket of soil, or as a human rights worker like Anil reads bones, identifies victims, implicates perpetrators, and sows the seeds of international intervention. By bringing "buckets of soil" and the "historical novel" into semantic proximity, Ondaatje makes us sense how the act of reading literature, and specifically interpreting "a complex historical novel," is entirely implicated in the "conflict trap." Ondaatje makes it impossible to interpret civil war as a local affair emanating out of the peripheries, showing instead how civil war must be interpreted in the international milieu of interventionism.

Ondaatje's framing of the historical novel registers how civil war has been a persistent theme in postcolonial historical fiction.[9] Ngũgĩ wa Thiong'o's early novels *Weep Not, Child* (1964) and *A Grain of Wheat* (1967) are set against the backdrop of the Mau Mau Rebellion and narrate the relationship between the anticolonial struggle against British settlers and conflicts within the Gikuyu community. Published on the eve of Nigeria's coup d'état, Chinua Achebe expresses his dismay at postcolonial independence in *Man of the People* (1966), a prescient tale set in a fictional African postcolony about the corruption of populist leaders into military dictators that culminates in the declaration of a state of emergency. Naipaul's writing in the 1970s is entirely preoccupied with the failures of Bandung-era Third Worldism, especially in sub-Saharan Africa. *In a Free State* (1970), *A Bend in the River* (1979), and *A Congo Diary* (1980) all thematize civic unrest as a symptom of contradictions inherent to postcolonial modernity. Civil war was somewhat of a leitmotif in white South African writing during the late apartheid years. Rather than a crisis to modernity, Gordimer's *July's People* (1981), Coetzee's *The Life and Times of Michael K* (1983), and Andre Brink's *State of Emergency* (1988) place civil war as the backdrop to narratives about the fall of the apartheid regime. As I have already suggested, Ondaatje's *Anil's Ghost* reads like a rebuttal of the World Bank's report on civil war, detailing the limits of social scientific knowledge about victims and perpetrators in civic conflict and the contradictions of international interventionism. More recently, Chimamanda Adichie's *Half of a Yellow Sun* (2006) is the most famous of the extensive archive of literature on the Nigerian Civil War, which charts how the optimism in Nigeria's postcolonial modernity is shattered by the outbreak and conclusion of the Biafran War. Maaza Mengiste's *Beneath a Lion's Gaze* (2011) is set amid the early years of the Ethiopian revolution and its transformation into the counterrevolutionary Derg regime.[10] In much the same way as writers of the nineteenth century turned to the poetics of national rupture as a field of intelligibility into the crisis of industrial modernity, or how late colonial writers told tales of civil war to make the exhaustion of empire legible at the turn of the century, postcolonial authors have turned to narratives of civic conflict as a way to reveal the contradictions and limits of postcolonial modernity.

While civil war has been a recurrent theme in postcolonial historical fiction through to the present, my interest in the final two chapters of this book is in a set of texts that, on the one hand, offer a critique of postcolonial nationalism by showing the limits, contradictions, and violence inherent to it and, on the other hand, make visible the parameters of international interventionism into civil wars in the developing world. Consequently, these texts disavow postcolonial nationalism's claims to unity as well as the West's attempts to "save" such polities from internal strife. Caught between failed states and the modern-day civilizing mission, novels like Naipaul's *A Bend in the River*, Coetzee's *The Life and Times of Michael K*, and Gordimer's *July's People* narrate impasses, dead ends, and repetitions. That is to say, they refuse to narrate exits out of the "conflict trap." In doing so, these texts displace and revise the historical novel's emplotment toward an accomplished future. In Lukács's foundational account of the genre, historical novels like Walter Scott's *Waverley* and *Ivanhoe* created the condition of possibility of imagining the nation because they succeed in "bringing the past to life as the prehistory of the present, in giving poetic life to those historical, social and human forces which, in the course of a long evolution, have made our present-day life what it is and as we experience it."[11] Staying ever close to Hegel's historicism, what matters for Lukács is that the historical novel narrate the "course of a long evolution" of "social and human forces" in such a way that it illuminates our experience of the present day.[12] In doing so, the historical novel creates the conditions of possibility of imagining the nation, to recall Balibar's formulation, as a "continuous subject" progressing through history. The progress narrated by these novels always culminates in an arrival of some kind. *Ivanhoe* arrives at the fusion of Norman and Saxon. *Waverley* (1814) arrives at a cohesive political community of England. *Sybil* ends by resurrecting "one nation" out of two. Leo Tolstoy's *War and Peace* (1869) arrives at the Decembrist revolt. William Thackeray's *The History of Henry Esmond* (1852) concludes with the consolidation of English Protestantism. Dickens's *A Tale of Two Cities* (1859) follows the rise of the bourgeoisie. And Chinua Achebe's *Arrow of God* (1864) concludes with the rise of an anticolonial bourgeoisie.

But what does the historical novel look like in the age of the "conflict trap"? In my discussion of Disraeli's *Sybil, or, The Two Nations*, I argued that the historical narration of a race war within England in fact reconstituted its national unity. Essential to this logic of the nation was the historicism of the modern nation-state, of a social organism "moving through empty homogenous time." But what happens to the national imagination when national history doesn't progress forward but is "entrapped" by civic conflict? How can such a genre, which is by definition committed to dramatizing the "past as the prehistory of the present," narrate historical regression? If civil wars are said to reverse the course of history, then what do they do to the plot of the historical novel whose narrative desire is to make legible the norms of historicism?[13] If civil war paralyzes the developing world at the thresholds of modernity, as the World Bank suggests it does, then how is such stasis narrativized in the form of a novel?

The premise of these questions is that the postcolonial historical novel acts as a counterdiscourse to knowledges of civil war and development produced within the social sciences. John Marx makes precisely this argument in *Geopolitics and the Anglophone Novel*: "Through stories about civil war and collapsing government, novels give voice to multiple positions and leave room for multiple interpretations of what caused and what might resolve a given crisis. When fiction imagines competing authorities and authorizes competing readings of state failure, it suggests the mentors and trustees endorsed by the United Nations and by international relations scholars may not always know best."[14] The experts Marx has in mind are the novel's characters, who produce accounts of civil war, failed states, and insufficient development from a range of perspectives that raise sets of questions quite different from those conjured in metropolitan think tanks.[15] Adichie's *Half of a Yellow Sun* is a case in point. The novel is organized around five central characters who live through Nigeria's civil war: Odenigbo, a professor of mathematics at the University of Nsukka; Ugwu, Odenigbo's adolescent houseboy who is later abducted and forcefully conscripted into the Biafran war effort; Olanna and Kainene, twin sisters and daughters of a wealthy businessman; and Richard Churchill, an Englishman visiting Nigeria to study pottery who undertakes reportage on the civil war. The novel's narration of their discrepant experiences during the war (from the upper classes to intelligentsia to the uneducated poor to foreign observers) is supplemented by excerpts from a history of Nigeria and its civil war presumably written and published in the novel's imagined present, titled *The World Was Silent When We Died*. While the reader is led to believe that the history is composed by one of the many intellectuals featured in the novel—Odenigbo, Olanna, Richard, Dr. Patel or Professor Ezeka—the final page of the novel reveals it to actually have been authored by Ugwu.[16] The revelation is significant because it recasts Ugwu from houseboy to expert on Nigerian history and politics. Not only is he a victim in the civil war (he is abducted and forced into the Biafran army as a child soldier), but he is also a perpetrator of its violence (he participates in the civil war and the gang rape of a "bar girl"). That he later publishes *The World Was Silent When We Died* suggests that his expertise also extends to a more formal academic study of the conflict. In his summation of the characters of Adichie's novel, Marx writes, "These heroes are the unaccredited analysts, unwilling participants in civil wars, and flawed government flacks. Fiction strives to make their expertise intelligible as specialized knowledge every bit as consequential as that of development economists and political theorists."[17]

Marx's argument is immensely helpful in considering the novel's "usefulness" as a form of knowledge, especially in our times when the use-value of literature and the humanities more generally is routinely called into question. The following two chapters argue that the counterdiscursive work undertaken in the postcolonial historical novel can equally rely on the *limits* of what the characters immersed in failed states and civil wars can know. In novels like *A Bend in the River*, *July's People*, and *The Life and Times of Michael K*, the main characters all qualify as literature's "experts" in civil war exactly the way Marx describes. Yet the knowledge characters like Salim, Maureen Smales, July, and K have concerns the limits of comprehending their own historicity, particularly in a time of regime change. The burden of this poetic of national rupture is a politics of transition that doesn't valorize or claim to know where historical transitions lead to or if they are even possible. Consequently, none of the novels I discuss at length offers a "satisfying" ending or perspective; the information provided by their native informants is of little use to international developmental discourse, nor is it an especially "usable" alternative. In a word, the "specialized knowledge" that these novels make intelligible is unique in that it is uninterested in escaping the conflict trap, and instead learning to live within its confines.

CHAPTER 6

A Bend in the Historical Novel

Business never dies in Africa; it is only interrupted.

—v. s. NAIPAUL, *A Bend in the River*

In what is perhaps his clearest statement on the postcolonial novel, which is not coincidentally an homage to Joseph Conrad, V. S. Naipaul reflects on the "curse of derivativeness" for the postcolonial writer.[1] "The great novelists," he explains, "wrote about highly organized societies. I had no such society; I couldn't share the assumptions of the writers; I didn't see my world reflected in theirs. My colonial world was more mixed and secondhand, and more restricted."[2] Conrad is the exception because he "meditated on my world, a world I recognize today. I feel this way about no other writer of the century."[3] Conrad's fiction is omnipresent to Naipaul, whose world is prefigured by its colonial past, one that is most thoroughly captured by his predecessor. Naipaul explains this "derivative discourse" by way of a passage from *Nostromo*: "Conrad had been everywhere before me. Not as a man with a cause, but a man offering, as in *Nostromo*, a vision of the world's half-made societies as places which continuously made and unmade themselves, where there was no goal, and where always 'something inherent in the necessities of successful action . . . carried with it the moral degradation of the idea.' Dismal, but deeply felt: a kind of truth and half a consolation."[4] Naipaul admits that his imaginative capacities are restricted by Conrad's imperial vision. The secondhand world into which Naipaul was born is prefigured by the experience of colonialism, a derivation that persists for the post-colonial author in the 1970s—a far cry from the promises of Third

143

Worldism and Bandung-era postcolonial nationalism of the period Naipaul is writing in.

Naipaul anticipates a claim Edward Said (for whom Conrad was equally formative) makes a handful of years later about Orientalism's representational scope and authority: "What gave the Oriental's world its intelligibility and identity was not the result of his own efforts but rather the whole complex series of knowledgeable manipulations by which the Orient was identified by the West. . . . Knowledge of the Orient, because generated out of strength, in a sense *creates* the Orient, the Oriental, and his world. . . . The Oriental is *contained* and *represented* by dominating frameworks."[5] Having been "contained" and "restricted" by the colonial experience, an experience Conrad "meditated on" in his fiction, Naipaul concludes that his predecessor's "darkness" is his own.[6] As Naipaul's quote from *Nostromo* suggests, Conrad's particular vision of the imperial project was that it was fundamentally flawed. Not coincidentally, the passage quoted directly precedes Emilia Gould's recognition of the failures of her husband's project to civilize an ex-colony out of its cycles of civic unrest. Gould, once so confident in the imperial ambitions of her husband for bringing "security, law and justice" to Costaguana, realizes in the end, just as Conrad himself realized, that inherent to Europe's civilizing mission was its own "moral degradation." As I argued in the previous chapter, *Nostromo* narrates this degradation through the story of the San Tomé mine, whose role transforms from savior to dictatorship, "more soulless than any tyrant, more pitiless and autocratic than the worst government, ready to crush innumerable lives in the expansion of its greatness."[7] In trying to "make a half-made society" whole, in trying to rid such a society of barbaric civil war, Gould unwittingly unmade it, extending the "tale of civil wars" indefinitely. Conrad's dismal vision about the limits of the "civilizing mission" most frames Naipaul's world—the very limits Emilia Gould comes to realize at the end of *Nostromo* when she despairingly "stammers out aimlessly the words—'Material interests.'"[8]

Importantly, Naipaul understands such dismal truths to be the starting point of Conrad's fiction as well as his own. He explains that "with writers like Ibsen and Hardy, fantasy answers impulses and needs they might not have been able to state. The truths of that fantasy we have to work out, or translate, for ourselves. With Conrad the process is reversed. We almost begin with the truths . . . and work through to their demonstration."[9] The meaning of Conrad's tales—what Ricoeur would call the "configurational" dimension of narrative visible at the "end point" when the plot is "grasped together"—is evident as an aphorism at the beginning of Conrad's fiction rather than at its conclusion. Or to put it in Peter Brooks's terms, if the motor of all plots is "narrative desire," then in Conrad this desire is fulfilled at the outset of the plot. Conrad begins where others traditionally end—hence *Nostromo*'s "tale of civil wars" ends where it began, leaving Sulaco at the cusp of civil war, away from the thresholds of modernity where it has always resided. With no room for "fantasy," Conrad's fiction simply "demonstrates" truths of the colonial experience. Fictions from the periphery, Naipaul suggests, must therefore completely rethink, indeed invert, the classical structure of plot and narration to fully grasp their historicity. Hence Naipaul's own representations of the "half-made" and "secondhand" postcolonial societies are channeled through Conrad's civilizing vision of making these very worlds "whole."[10] All he can do is "demonstrate" despairing truths about the "making and un-making" of "half-made" colonial societies.[11]

If *Nostromo*'s poetics of national rupture allows Conrad to expose the limits of imperialism, then Naipaul narrativizes the conflict trap in *A Bend in the River* to expose the limits of postcolonial nationalism. Naipaul's novel is the culmination of his decade-long meditation on the failures of postcolonial modernity in Africa—*A Free State*, the essays on Zaire in the *New York Review of Books*—whose echoes reverberate throughout *A Bend*. The novel's opening sentence is a Conradian aphorism shrouded in Naipaulian bleakness: "The world is what it is; men who are nothing, who allow themselves to become nothing, have no place in it."[12] Ambivalent though it is about whether men "are" or "allow themselves to become" nothing, the statement is unambiguous about the world's inhospitality toward these individuals: they have no place in it. Soon after, we encounter an undeniably Conradian chronotope: "As I got deeper into Africa—the scrub, the desert, the rocky climbs up to the mountains, the lakes, the rain in the afternoons, the mud, and then, on the other, wetter side of the mountains, the fern forests and the gorilla forests—as I got deeper I thought: But this is madness. I am going in the wrong direction. There can't be a new life at the end of this. But I drove on" (4). It is the 1960s and the narrator is Salim, an East Indian refugee fleeing civil war in his home on the eastern coast of Africa where his family have lived as traders for three generations. Being a stateless minority in the midst of a civil war, Salim migrates to another fictional country in central Africa to start his life anew.[13]

But his flight from one troubled country is an arrival into another, for Salim finds that his new home, "like others in Africa, had had its troubles after independence" (3). And such "troubles" persist over the course of the novel. After a few years of relative peace in the town at the bend in the river, a "Second Rebellion" breaks out: "And it was the old war," Salim explains, "the one we were still recovering from, the semi-tribal war that had broken out at independence and shattered and emptied the town. We had thought it over and done with, the passions burnt out. . . . Yet now it was all starting up again" (66–67). Rather than escape this conflict, Salim endures it with a fellow-refugee, Metty, a family servant from his home on the Eastern coast, and Ferdinand, a local friend who, being an ethnic minority, takes refuge with them during the conflict. Though the rebellion is short-lived, so is the peace that replaces it; within a few years civil war returns once more, this time with much more veracity, thereby eliciting Salim to flee again. At the end, Salim escapes just as he did at the beginning, bringing his life in the town at the bend in the river, "demonstrating," as it were, the veracity of his opening aphorism—he has no place in the postcolonial world.

A Bend is often read in relation to Conrad's *Heart of Darkness*. Their formal similarities, such as their chronotopic narrative structures, are striking: Marlow travels down an unnamed West African river into the heart of Africa, while Salim drives to this same location from the Eastern coast. Both narrators meditate (Marlow almost literally, as he sits on the *Nellie* "cross-legged" as a "meditative Bhudda") on the meaning of their journeys retrospectively, the moral of which they know from the start of the narrative.[14] Both narrators detach themselves from the horror that surrounds them: Marlow from the violence of colonial domination, Salim from the violence of postcolonial nationalism. Both narrators conclude their tales in utter despair: Marlow, like Kurtz, begins to comprehend the limits of Europe's civilizing missions, while Salim is disillusioned with the promises of postcolonial modernity. If "darkness" is Conrad's figure for the limits of imperial thinking, then Naipaul's figure for the limits of postcolonial nationalist thinking is the "bend" in the river that obscures that which is to come and is just out of sight—a representational limit announced in the titles of both books.

As illuminating as the intertextuality of these two texts is, the reading that follows reorients *A Bend*'s relationship to Conrad from *Heart of Darkness* to *Nostromo*. My purpose in doing so is not to privilege one text's influence over another's but instead to contrapuntally situate *A Bend* in the long conjoined history of civil war and the civilizing mission—what in *Nostromo* is referred to as "material interests," what Salim calls "business in Africa," and what is today called "development." *Nostromo* and *A Bend in the River* are both preoccupied with historical paralysis at the peripheries, the agent of which is civil war. Like the "blood-thirsty games of murder and rapine" of Conrad's Costaguana, there is nothing "civil" about civil wars in Salim's postcolonial Africa: people are killed, bombs are dropped, cities are destroyed, all to fulfill the desires of power-hungry dictators and rebels. Political tumult stalls the development of the postcolony Salim resides in. All the gains of socioeconomic progress made during times of peace—infrastructure, financial prosperity, cosmopolitanism, intellectual culture—are violently obliterated by civil war, which regresses the country back in developmental time. Civil war, one might recall, was narrated by early Victorians as the motor of history. Disparate figures like Engels, Carlyle, Disraeli, and Gaskell all described a latent civil war to propel England forward in history—be it toward revolution (Engels), annihilation (Carlyle), or resolution (Disraeli and Gaskell). At the end of the nineteenth century, civil war was reinvented as something unique to the imperial peripheries and as a detriment to historical progress. In Conrad's *Nostromo*, civil war's prevalence in the fictional ex-colony of Costaguana is also linked to the forces of history, only now inverted so that it hinders modernization rather than energizes it.

Naipaul revises this schema in the age of decolonization. *A Bend* narrates a series of transitions back and forth from development and its reversal, oscillating between linear progression and regression, the cumulative effect of which is a kind of narrative stasis with no conceivable exit.[15] By emplotting civil war as historical regression and peace as historical progress, *A Bend* formalizes what the World Bank calls "development in reverse" in the shape of a historical novel; it's poetic of national rupture translates the conflict trap into a kind of narrative trap. In doing so, Naipaul's fiction offers an answer to the question of what the historical novel looks like in the age of "development in reverse": rather than constructing a world in which national-historical time moves forward toward an accomplished history, we find the cycles of civil war and international development to stall progress entirely. Narrativizing the conflict trap allows Naipaul to make visible the stakes of postcolonial historicity, which Sanjay Krishnan has helpfully explained is a condition in which "the colonized cannot easily escape the legacy of lies [of colonial modes of reason]; they can only discover more or less effective ways of inhabiting them."[16] Or to put it more specifically for my purposes here, *A Bend*'s poetics of national rupture shows how the burden of postcolonial reason is not to "escape" or break free of the "conflict trap" but to find "more or less effective" ways of inhabiting it. And so it is only within the confines of the "conflict trap," set long ago in the age of empire, that Naipaul narrates the crisis of postcolonial modernity.

For Naipaul, this historical sensibility is less pessimistic than it is tragic. In an extended reading of C. L. R James's *The Black Jacobins*, David Scott argues that in contrast to how anticolonial discourse articulated its politics through a tropics of Romance, "the mode of emplotment of tragedy comports better with a time of postcolonial crisis in which old horizons have collapsed or evaporated and new ones have not yet taken shape."[17] Tragedy, Scott argues, "demands from us more patience for paradox and more openness to chance than the narrative of anticolonial Romanticism does, confident in its striving and satisfied in its own sufficiency. The colonial past may never let go. This is a hard truth."[18] A similar kind of tragic conscription is at the heart of *A Bend*, which is not committed to a politics of escape, transformation, or even slow progress but tragic entrapment in civil war. This is why Naipaul's language is saturated with colonial discourse, why his Africa is nearly indistinguishable from Conrad's, and why his novel refuses to offer an alternative to the interventionist logics of "think tanks."

DEVELOPMENT IN REVERSE

The era Salim enters into in his new home in central Africa is one of peace and economic optimism. "The peace held," he reflects. "People began coming back to the town; and *cité* yards filled up. People began needing the goods which we could supply. And slowly business started up again" (5). The calm allows Salim to establish himself and his business, a small shop. One reason peace "holds" is because of the presence of the army in the town, which Salim explains is as good for business as it is for maintaining political order: "It made for a balance in our town. And a well-paid domesticated army was good for trade. The soldiers spent. They bought furniture, and they loved carpets" (68). Later, in the aftermath of the "Second Rebellion" during a "long peace," the town thrives economically: "Now we were in a period of boom. We felt the new ruling intelligence—and energy—from the capital; there was a lot of copper money around; and these two things—order and money—were enough to give us confidence" (86). *Marchandes* move into the town's *cités*, people from the forest settle in empty lots, and foreign contractors fill up the town's only hotel. Salim's business rises in value tenfold, which he expands from a shop into an import/export trade agency. Even the nature of his business changes. In the beginning he imports material commodities. But during the boom Salim starts trading in abstractions: "I bought and sold quantities long before they arrived; I didn't have to handle them physically or even see them. It was like dealing in words alone, ideas on paper" (88). Salim's friend Mahesh, notorious for failed business endeavors like manufacturing wooden ice cream spoons in a town with no ice cream, finally succeeds in opening a profitable business: a European fast-food franchise called Bigburger. The entire restaurant, Mahesh boasts, is imported: "'They don't just send the sauce, you know, Salim. They send you the whole shop,'" which includes everything from "the milk-shake machines" to the "cups and plates" to the "lovely advertisements: 'Bigburgers—The Big One—The Bigwonderful One,' with pictures of different kinds of Bigburgers" (97). Ildephonse, Mahesh's houseboy who begins working at the restaurant, "loved his Bigburger costume and loved his new job," while the army officials who frequent the eatery "liked the décor and the modernity" (98–99). The economic boom brings a sea change in everyone's lives: "That was what we were like. One day grubbing for food, opening rusty tins, cooking on charcoal braziers and over holes in the ground; and now talking of a million dollars as though we had talked of millions all our lives" (93).

In addition to fulfilling the ambitions of a postcolonial petty bourgeoisie, the economic boom strengthens the state and its institutions. The town is increasingly anchored in the "ruling intelligence of the capital," which rebuilds roads, expands an airfield, and adds a new telephone service (despite it not being needed). Even state institutions begin to exhibit accountability to citizens: "the administration, however hollow, was fuller; there were people you could appeal to. You could get things done, if you knew how to go about it" (87). The most significant federal project is the Domain, a university town built on the wreckage of an old European suburb destroyed in one of the civil wars. Like the economy, the Domain is rebuilt at an even greater scale than the ruin it stands upon: "Among the avenues and new houses, another Africa had been created" (119).[19] Here, "Africans had become modern men who built in concrete and glass and sat in cushioned chairs covered in imitation velvet" (101). And Salim, ever-cautious and endlessly cynical of Third Worldist triumphalism, is himself seduced by the Domain's liberal cosmopolitanism: "I began to get some sense of the social excitements of life on the Domain, of people associating in a new way, being more open, less concerned with enemies and danger, more ready to be interested and entertained, looking for the human worth of the other man" (117–18). Peace might enable infrastructural development and economic prosperity, but it also produces a more democratic society, one in which people look for "the human worth of the other man," not the "dangers" these potential "enemies" pose. One manifestation of this is the sense of belonging people like Salim and Indar (who like Salim is a stateless Indian living in Africa) feel in the Domain: "They [foreigners living on the Domain] looked upon Indar not as a man of our community [the East Indian diaspora] or a refugee from the coast but as one of themselves. It was all a little extraordinary to me" (117). Ever so briefly, Salim begins believing in the promises of Third Worldism: Africa *can* have its own future, and he, a refugee, has a place in this emerging world.

Civic conflict, however, consistently reverses all such gains and optimism. When Salim reflects on the parts of town destroyed by the war that followed independence, he admits that "more unnerving than anything else" was that they used to be "valuable real estate for a while, and now bush again, common ground, according to African practice" (27). The ruins attest to how civic conflict erases economic value. Although the value of the homes was literally "concretized" as property, civil war completely devalues these investments: "The big lawns and gardens had returned to bush; the streets had disappeared; vines and creepers had grown over broken, bleached walls of concrete or hollow clay brick. Here and there in the bush could still be seen the concrete shells of what had been restaurants (Saccone and Speed wines) and nightclubs. One nightclub had been called 'Napoli'; the now meaningless name, printed on the concrete wall, was almost bleached away" (27). An entire society is reduced to ruins by war. And what the rebels leave behind the African bush obliterates. Symbols of European modernization—concrete, suburbs, Saccone, Napoli, wine stores— are overgrown by indigenous flora, their metropolitan names effaced by the sun. The ruins make visible the fragility of economic value in the African forest; no matter how concrete real estate value might be, the landscape resists infrastructural development by devaluing its own commodification.

To Salim, the violence that befalls the town is purposeless, lacks political ambition, and seems solely invested in a politics of erasure. The war that follows independence, he claims, is invested in the "simple rejection" of all institutions:

> At independence the people of our region had gone mad with anger and fear—all the accumulated anger of the colonial period, and every kind of reawakened tribal fear. . . . and at independence they had refused to be ruled by the new government in the capital. It was an instinctive uprising, without leaders or a manifesto. If the movement had been more reasoned, had been less a movement of simple rejection, the people of our region might have seen that the town at the bend in the river was theirs, the capital of any state they might set up. But they had hated the town for the intruders who had ruled in it and from it; and they had preferred to destroy the town rather than take it over. (67)

Independence from colonial rule doesn't trigger a modern postcolonial consciousness but the sum total of accumulated tribal anxieties from the colonial period. This violence is not animated by a particular ideology but is leaderless, devoid of a political program, and instinctually rejects the new postcolonial order of things as though formal independence had never happened. Neither secessionist, nor revolutionary, nor even interested in nationalizing their platform in the capital, the rebellion seeks only to destroy all that which is new. That is to say, its violence is neither law-making nor law-preserving, but law-rejecting.[20] Such nihilism doesn't recode old colonial symbols as much as render them meaningless: "The names of all the main streets had been changed. Rough boards carried the new, roughly lettered names. No one used the new names, because no one particularly cared about them. The wish had only been to get rid of the old, to wipe out the memory of the intruder. It was unnerving, the depth of that African rage, the wish to destroy, regardless of the consequences" (26). Statues, along with their pedestals and railings, are either destroyed or defaced beyond repair. The floodlights used to illuminate monuments to colonial rule are "smashed and left to rust." Such violence, it is important to note, is always tinged with anticolonial motives, for the objects destroyed are the remnants of the old colonial regimes, like statues commemorating the steamer service.

During the Second Rebellion the objects of destruction shift from colonial symbols to development projects undertaken by international organizations like the United Nations. Salim describes how "after the earlier war the United Nations agency had repaired the power station and the causeway at the top of the dam. A metal plaque set on a small stone pyramid, some distance from the dam itself, recorded this fact. That plaque had been defaced, battered with some heavy metal piece, individual letters filed away" (81). Much like how after the first civil war the steamer service is left untouched but the statues commemorating its years of service are defaced, the dam itself is not attacked, only the plaque that named it as a gift from the United Nations. Tellingly, the plaque is not destroyed but its inscription carefully "filed away"—a truly peculiar thing to do in the midst of war (or as an act of war) but which signals the attempt to efface the dam's symbolization as a gift from the developed world. After the rebellion, the dam continues to function as it always did, only in absence of its identity as the product of international development and Western benevolence. And rather than reinscribe the dam's significance, the plaque is left devoid of letters like a void of signification. What unnerves Salim is the "depth" of such erasure and its attention to the sublated aspects of life under colonial rule and the afterlife of such rule in postcolonial times—plaques, street names, and floodlights.

A Bend's rendering of civil unrest differs quite substantially from depictions of armed conflict in the postcolonial war novel, which makes the ideological bases for rebellions, secessions, and revolutions vividly clear. In Weep Not, Child, Ngũgĩ intervenes in how British colonial discourse used civil war as an alibi for deferring Kenyan independence. The Origins and Growth of the Mau Mau (1960), a history of Kenya produced by the British colonial administration commonly known as the "Corfield Report," argues that the Mau Mau gave direction to disenfranchised colonial subjects, offering the "African 'in transition'" a way to return to precolonial traditions in the name of a collective organism—that is to say, national consciousness.[21] The report claims the Mau Mau transformed from an anticolonial movement into one directed at fellow-Kenyans because it "assumed all the known characteristics of an inverted resistance movement, and since it claimed the mantle of a limited national movement directed against the 'invaders,' those who resisted it were the 'quislings' and the traitors. The result was tantamount to a civil war."[22] The report cites the "civil war" as the justification to "maintain law and order" in Kenya, meaning defer Kenyan independence indefinitely.[23] In contrast, Ngũgĩ's *Weep Not, Child* exposes the violence that undergirds the administration's maintenance of "law and order." The main character Njoroge idealizes his school in the midst of the Mau Mau Rebellion because it "was an adobe of peace in a turbulent country. . . . For the first time he felt he would escape the watchful eyes of misery and hardship that had for a long time stared at him in his home. Here he would organize his thoughts and make definite plans for the future."[24] This sanctuary from political and domestic tumult comes undone when the school is complicit in his torture and interrogation concerning his family's connections to the Mau Mau, and whether he too had taken the oath to join the movement. While Ngũgĩ's novel traces the tensions between anticolonial struggles and conflicts within the Gikuyu community, a more recent novel like Adichie's *Half of a Yellow Sun* details the ideological foundations of Igbo nationalism from Odenigbo's declaration that "I was Igbo before the white man came," to its slow institutional escalation to the building of the "Igbo Union Grammar School," and eventually its culmination in the Biafran War.[25] In *Beneath a Lion's Gaze*, Mengiste gives voice to the Ethiopian revolution and counterrevolution through Dawit, a student activist, and his father, Hailu, a prominent doctor. At the cusp of Emperor Haile Selassie's fall, Dawit exclaims, "All along, the emperor has been watching these people die like this. He was there last year, he didn't do anything. This is why we need a change."[26] After Selassie is deposed and the Derg takes power, Hailu reflects on the Ethiopian flag used by the previous regime: "He hooked the flag on the wall furthest from the window where it used to hang before the new regime banned it from public and private display. There was still an outline of its shape on the wall."[27] Knowing the old regime to be dead and its replacement to be equally brutal (which he learns firsthand when taken prisoner and tortured for letting a torture victim die while in his care), the ideological horizon that presents itself to Hailu remains as yet known like the outline of the old flag that remains on the wall. As I argue in the following chapter, while the content of the anti-apartheid revolution is unknown in Gordimer's *July's People*, the existence of a new regime as a historical force is unquestionable. That is to say, while the horizon of South Africa's new regime remains out of view, it is clear to all the characters that it exists somewhere in South Africa, just not within the representative scope of Gordimer's novel. Eleni Coundouriotis has argued that one of the effects of detailing the ideological conditions that create the horrors of war is a separation between the history of the "nation" and the "people": "The focus on human suffering in war often forces us to look up close at the injured body and see from the almost hallucinatory perspective of those with horrific injuries."[28] By dramatizing human suffering at the hands of national ideology in vivid detail, these novels shift "attention to the people as an entity that does not coincide with the novel," and implicitly "points to an outside, or beyond, of war, something beyond the all-determining environment rendered through naturalism."[29]

For all the care and historical fidelity these writers take in their depictions of the ideological bases for political unrest in the postcolony, Naipaul takes equal care to obscure the ideology of sub-Saharan political movements. Salim's inability to see traces of rational politics in the violence that surrounds him has led many to dismiss A Bend for parroting Conrad's Africa, which famously is a place devoid of history and language. Chinua Achebe's is the most well-known of such criticisms, which argues that "Naipaul's method is to ridicule claims to any human achievement in Africa."[30] A Bend in the River, claims Achebe, wholeheartedly endorses Western civilization at the expense of the East: "To ask everybody [not of the West] to shut down their history, pack their bag and buy a one-way ticket to Europe or America is just crazy, to my way of thinking. To suggest that the universal civilization is in place already is to be willfully blind to our present reality and, even worse, to trivialize the goal and hinder the materialization of a genuine universality in the future."[31] Echoing his critique of Heart of Darkness, Achebe finds Naipaul's Africa to be no better than Conrad's, both of which present the continent as incapable of having a history other than the West's.[32]

Said is only slightly more gentle than Achebe. He criticizes Naipaul for becoming "the perfect witness for The New York Review of Books, where he can be counted on to survey the Third World, its follies, its corruption, its hideous problems."[33] What pains Said is that despite his admiration for the Trinidadian writer, Naipaul dismisses postcolonial history along with the promises of "national liberation movements, revolutionary goals, Third worldism."[34] He goes on to contrast Naipaul to writers like Gordimer, whom he finds more generous toward the postcolonial world: "To say that Naipaul resembles a scavenger, then, is to say that he now prefers to render the ruins and derelictions of postcolonial history without tenderness, without any of the sympathetic insight found, say, in Nadine Gordimer's books, rather than to render that history's processes, occasional heroism, intermittent successes; he prefers to indict guerrillas for their pretensions rather than indict the imperialism and social injustice that drove them to insurrection."[35] Said is more sympathetic to *A Bend in the River* in *Culture and Imperialism*, where he acknowledges that Naipaul "successfully dramatizes an ideological position in the West from which it is possible to indict the post-colonial states for having succeeded unconditionally in gaining independence."[36]

MEN WHO ARE NOTHING IN THE WORLD

Achebe and Said overlook Conrad's greatest influence on Naipaul: his main characters are thoroughly limited in their apprehension of the world. Salim is a case in point. As Michael Gorra notes, Naipaul's "argument is the same as Salim's, but his language isn't, and that's precisely why *A Bend in the River* convinces as fiction. When Salim repeats words and phrases, it's not because he has made a conscious choice but because his limited education has given him no others. . . . But he remains something of an ingenue, persistently naive about his own situation."[37] In one of his many Conradian meditations on the meaning—or perhaps more precisely, opacity—of the First and Second Rebellions, Salim reflects: "Such rage! Like a forest fire that goes underground and burns unseen along the roots of trees it had already destroyed and then erupts in scorched land where it has little to feed on, so in the middle of destruction and want the wish to destroy flared up again. And the war, which we had thought dead, was all at once around us" (67).[38] As primitive, instinctual, and non-political as the "rage" might be, Salim's forest-fire metaphor points to a purpose to the violence that exceeds what he—the novel's *narrator*—can fully represent. African rage, like a forest fire, destroys the symbols of colonial modernity that stand in its way (concrete suburbs built for wealthy settlers before independence, nightclubs and Italian restaurants for the town's European residents, monuments to the old empire). But once it has consumed these symbols, it "goes underground" to latently feed off the roots that give life to colonial institutions. This activity, importantly, takes place beneath the surface of society, *out of sight*, and out of the legible domain of politics. In other words, Salim makes it possible to see decolonization as a violent *and* latent affair, both of which are directed toward the old empire's monuments as well as its ideo-logical foundations—the "roots" of the colonial regime that live on after independence. Packaged though it may be in the racist rhetoric of "African rage," "instinctual uprisings," "tribal" motivations, Salim's narration implicitly recognizes that the work of decolonization takes place *beyond his own comprehension.*

Naipaul's tale of the "making and unmaking" of this "half-made society," a narration of the conflict trap, thus achieves what Conrad does with Marlow in *Heart of Darkness*, and the eponymous antihe-roes of *Nostromo* and *Lord Jim*: he formalizes Salim's own constrained place in history and his struggle to comprehend its meaning. As Rob Nixon explains, "By forcing the distinction between the 'primitive' cat-egory of the past and the Western category of history, Naipaul is able to hold Third World societies in one of his classic double-binds: without a sense of history, they can achieve nothing, yet what they tender as their history is something utterly different, amounting to embellishents [*sic*] of the past that either do not evidence achievement or elude descrip-tion in historical terms."[39] Phrases like "African rage" and "instinctual uprisings" may be problematic expressions of barbaric carnality, but they are *Salim's*, and they fill the void of meaning that is otherwise marked by the politics of decolonization—a politics that resists Salim's comprehension.

The reason Salim struggles to comprehend the meaning of the con-flicts that surround him is because he is an outsider to the project of nationalism. His outsiderness is registered in the text by his peculiar historical sensibility. The back-and-forth of development and civil war, building and erasure, postcolonial nationalism and postcolonial civil war, creates an uncanny time-sense for Salim. The suburban ruins (upon which the Domain is later built) just outside of the town are only a few years old, and yet they look to Salim

> like the site of a dead civilization. The ruins, spreading over
> so many acres, seemed to speak of a final catastrophe. But the
> civilization wasn't dead. It was the civilization I existed in and
> in fact was still working towards. And that could make for an
> odd feeling: to be among the ruins was to have your time-sense
> unsettled. You felt like a ghost, not from the past, but from the
> future. You felt that your life and ambition had already been
> lived out for you and you were looking at the relics of that life.
> You were in a place where the future had come and gone. (27)

The ruins are the wreckage of economic development—suburbs, night-clubs, cosmopolitan eateries—a future that had once been. The uprising after independence destroyed this future, returning the landscape to its primordial past. Just as in *Nostromo* where the import of European liberalism and economic development regresses the country back into dictatorships and poverty, no modernizing *telos* exists for Salim, for whom the future can come *and go*. This time-sense worries Salim because it suggests a reversal in the course of history; the forest, briefly brought into the concrete fold of modernity, is returned to what it has always been by civil war. Whatever development takes place during economic booms, whatever progress is achieved, can be entirely reversed by civic conflict: a concrete European suburb is returned to the African forest. The effect of this reversal is a troubling sense of anachronism: objects promising a future and yet which manifest as relics of a bygone era. On the one hand, the concrete shells attest to an era of prosperity where the forces of modernization appeared to be taking hold. Suburban debris marks the horizon of European modernity, one that Salim aspires to. On the other hand, their status as shells of their former structures attests to the fragility and reversibility of this notion of modernity—they appear as though from the past. Civil war negates the triumph of European civilization; it is the *uncivil* event that swallows the gifts of European civility back into the heart of darkness.

David Lloyd has argued that the figure of the ruin in contemporary Ireland represents "the image of a continuing violence or ruination that afflicts at once the present and the unsubsumed remnants of the past. . . . The ruins stand as a kind of uneroded sill that both recalls destruction and comes into conjunction with the obstinate refusal in the present to accept that there are no alternatives."[40] "Out of such images," Lloyd continues, "there emerges an alternative conception of history, not rendered as the record of a gradually imposed civility but as transforming the melancholy of loss into a refusal to let go of the possibilities of the past."[41] The ruins created in the conflict trap speak of a different relationship to the past. For in *A Bend*, it is the future that is in ruins. The ruins that pepper the landscape are not relics of the past but of a future that had once been. Indeed, the time-sense Salim describes is closer to the contradictions Achille Mbembe sees at the heart of the African experience of modernity:

> African social formations are not necessarily converging toward a single point, trend or cycle. They harbor the possibility of a

variety of trajectories neither convergent or divergent but inter-
locked, paradoxical. More philosophically, it may be supposed
that the present *as experience of time* is precisely that moment
when different forms of absence become mixed together:
absence of those presences that are no longer so and that one
remembers (the past), and absence of those others that are yet
to come and are anticipated (the future). . . . The contemporary
African experience is that this emerging time is appearing in
context today—in which the future horizon is apparently closed,
while the horizon of the past has apparently receded.[42]

In *A Bend*, the "future horizon" promised by international development and commerce in the postcolony is "closed" to the degree that it
has become the past. That is to say, the future has become anachronistic and obsolete. However, this future is the only horizon Salim knows
to move toward. And so rather than narrating a transition *out* of the
conflict trap, Salim's narrative is entrapped within its own coordinates,
embracing impasse as its condition rather than its point of departure.
Or to put it in Naipaul's own terms, impasse is the starting point, and
the rest its demonstration.

And herein lies Naipaul's most prescient observation in *A Bend*:
the figure of the refugee is inextricably linked to development and its
reversal in civil war. The ghostly time-sense Salim describes is a product of the cycles of development and regression that befall the developing world, the conflict trap. Recognizing he is a stateless minority
at the cusp of more civil unrest, Salim buys the last available ticket
out of town on the river steamboat. Attached to the steamer is a passenger barge packed with local townspeople who are also presumably
fleeing—refugees in the making. Their collective escape is jeopardized
when the boat is attacked at night: "At the time what we saw was
the steamer searchlight, playing on the riverbank, playing on the passenger barge, which had snapped loose and was drifting at an angle
through the water hyacinths at the edge of the river. The searchlight
lit up the barge passengers, who, behind bars and wire guards, as yet
scarcely seemed to understand that they were adrift. Then there were
gunshots" (278).[43] The searchlight is turned off and Salim contemplates, "The air would have been full of moths and flying insects. The
searchlight, while it was on, had shown thousands, white in the white
light" (ibid.). Salim's departure is shrouded in uncertainty. Though we
know he makes it out alive because the story is told retrospectively, his

escape is far from a clean break. His departure comes at the cost of leaving behind Metty, a family servant/friend who lived with him in the town and whose statelessness means he is almost certainly going to be killed in the oncoming violence. More immediately, the reason his steamboat pulls away from the attackers is because the link between it and the passenger/refugee barge is severed—leaving the reader with the image of its inhabitants trapped behind "behind bars and wire guards" in darkness amid gunfire, as precarious as the thousands of moths whose visibility is contingent on the searchlight shining upon them. Salim's escape completes Naipaul's demonstration of the novel's opening "truth": unable to make himself into anything, allowing himself to be reduced once more to a refugee, Salim has no place in this world. *A Bend in the River* ends where it began, at the bend in the river.

Such pessimism is precisely why Naipaul can seem completely complicit with the World Bank's ideology: Salim has no faith in Africa's future; the future properly belongs to Europe. But it is crucial to remember that *A Bend* is equally pessimistic about the effectiveness of international intervention, which it shows to be completely useless in "solving" civic unrest through development. The World Bank's paradigm of civil war and development suggests that if things had turned out differently for the developing world, the latter could have avoided being ensnared within the conflict trap. In contrast, Salim's narration in *A Bend* suggests that this choice was never there. The product is a historical novel that doesn't move toward an accomplished history because that moment of arrival has already passed. Naipaul's novel thus completes the inversion of Victorian narratives of civil war, which saw it to be a progressive force in history. Civil war in *A Bend* instead takes the postcolony nowhere. *But neither does economic development or international intervention.* The nation Salim describes is not, as Balibar puts it, "the culmination of a long historical project," nor does it move forward toward a progressivist future. Instead, the first, second, and third rebellions are simply repetitions of an old pattern of economic booms and wartime busts, development and its reversal. The promise of historical transitions in *A Bend* points to a future that can, *and has*, come and gone.

CHAPTER 7

Postcolonial Interregnum

Anticipating the end of the apartheid regime in the early 1980s, Nadine Gordimer declared that "the sun that never set over one or other of the nineteenth-century colonial empires of the world is going down finally in South Africa."[1] Gordimer famously characterized this imperial dusk, the "final" end of colonialism, as an "interregnum." South Africa, she explains, is at the cusp of postcoloniality and therefore caught between "two social orders but also between two identities, one known and discarded, the other unknown and undetermined."[2] Gordimer inherits her idea of the interregnum from Antonio Gramsci, whose brief and enigmatic statement on the topic serves as the epigraph to her 1981 novel, *July's People*: "The old is dying and the new cannot be born; in this interregnum there arises a great diversity of morbid symptoms."[3] More than an epigraph, Gramsci's statement structures the plot of Gordimer's novel, which is set in the midst of a fictional civil war between the apartheid government and black revolutionaries. The civil war Gordimer depicts pushes South Africa to the thresholds of postcoloniality: the end of apartheid rule and the seizure of state power by the country's non-white majority. In other words, the figure of national rupture for Gordimer concerns civic conflict between whites and blacks as well as the transition between two regimes, the apartheid past and a postcolonial future.

At the foreground of Gordimer's novelization of the interregnum is a white middle-class South African family, the Smaleses, who seek refuge in a rural village, the home of their black servant July (Mwawate). For a novel set amid a civil war, it is surprising just how little of the war is in fact represented in *July's People*. All the reader and the main characters are privy to are military planes flying almost inaudibly high and occasional radio reports of the violence far away in the cities. We instead see what Susan Pearsall has described as a transformation of "a state of civil war into the boredom of the barely literate, the grunginess of the unwashed body, the vapid communications of the long married."[4] Quotidian though it may be, the interregnum becomes the occasion for an intensification of relations of labor, throwing what Abdul JanMohamed calls the "sublated aspects of the master-slave relationship" into sharp relief.[5] Throughout the novel, the Smaleses and July struggle to recalibrate their relationship to better fit the historical interstice they find themselves in, where servants have become hosts to their desperate masters. This struggle is especially apparent between July and Maureen, the Smaleses' matriarch. Both recognize the changed circumstances of their relationship, yet fall back on old habits of master and servant—habits that in their new uncertain context appear unsettlingly anachronistic. At the end of the novel, an unmarked helicopter arrives in the village carrying July and his people's "saviours or murderers."[6] These concluding passages are the novel's most mysterious: Maureen runs toward the helicopter despite not knowing who sits inside it. The reader is left in suspense, not knowing how things end (or begin anew), whether the Smaleses will be restored to their status as the benefactors of apartheid or if a new regime will transform their relationship to July and South Africa more generally. The uncertainty of Maureen's fate is dramatized for readers, who like her must suspend the desire for resolution and endure what J. Hillis Miller has described as the "disquieting power" of "unreadability."[7] By rendering the interregnum both content and form of the novel, South Africa's historical uncertainty is mirrored in the ambiguity of the story's conclusion.

The interregnum was a leitmotif in much of Gordimer's writings in the late apartheid years and featured prominently in her discussions of the place of the white writer in the anti-apartheid movement. Gordimer describes her role as one of "inescapable responsibility," where "the white, as writer and South African, does not know his place 'in history' at this stage, in this time."[8] The white South African, claims Gordimer, has no way of knowing whether he/she has a place in South Africa's post-apartheid future and yet must work toward this destination.[9] Her arrival at the impasse of the interregnum is the product of an arc in her fiction from themes of departure to those of arrival.[10] *The Conservationist* (1974) interrogates the self-preservative impulses of Mehring, a wealthy Afrikaner who slowly loses his property and power in a time of democratization. Her following novel, *Burger's Daughter* (1979), is set in the midst of the anti-apartheid movement of the 1970s and concludes with the protagonist Rosa Burger, daughter of an influential activist, finding her place and role in the political movement at the thresholds of revolution. Though this revolution finally arrives in *July's People*, whether it succeeds or not remains unclear. The thematic arc from collapse to action to transition is unmistakable in Gordimer's writing, yet none of these novels touches upon "the future" in the sense of prescription or prediction.[11]

Gordimer was not alone in her characterization of this period and the ambivalent place of white South Africans within it. In his 1985 study, anthropologist Vincent Crapanzano characterized the 1980s as a condition of "waiting" for white South Africans, where "waiting means to be oriented in time in a special way. It is directed towards the future . . . in waiting, the present is always secondary to the future. It is held in expectation. It is filled with suspense. It is a sort of holding action—a lingering."[12] As in the interregnum, the future remains unattainable, with the present paralyzed in a "holding action." Neil Lazarus similarly describes the fiction of late apartheid white writers, stating: "In contrast with the revolutionary idealism of much contemporary black South African theorizing, the openness to the future of white intellectuals begins to seem less like an openness than an ambivalence."[13] Ambivalence is how the death of the old and birth of the new comes to be written by white South African intellectuals who must negotiate the conundrum of being, as Gordimer put it, "a minority within a minority" by belonging to (and therefore being complicit with) the regime while opposing it.[14] It is important to note, however, that black South African fiction was far from homogeneous. As Martin Trump notes, "There is no complacent vision of a unitary black society" in black fiction during the 1970s and 1980s, the themes of which ranged from depictions of everyday life for those living under apartheid, as, for example, in Miriam Tlali's *Muriel at Metropolitan* (1975) and Zoë Wicomb's *You Can't Get Lost in Cape Town* (1988), to narrations of explicitly political themes as, for example, in Mongane Serote's *To Every Birth Its Blood* (1981).[15] Hence Njabulo Ndebele claimed in 1990 that South African politics and literary culture was like a play with multiple scripts: "The problem is that the South

African stage, at this moment, is full of actors with many competing scripts. Hitherto there had been, as it were, only one legitimate actor with his one legitimate script. . . . But after years of persistent pressure, the dominant actor has finally yielded some space on the stage, and we are witnessing a frantic entrance of new actors, all carrying their own scripts. . . . What is in the scripts now? This is the foremost question of our times."[16]

Writing at the cusp of the post-apartheid era in 1994, Ndebele remains pessimistic about how to "script" the country's future because "at this time when the spirit of reconciliation is supposed to bring South Africans together, South Africans don't know one another as a people. Can we as a nation write the novel of the future under these conditions? If so, what are the preconditions for such novels to be written? What does it take for us to know one another? What *will* it take?"[17] Uncertain about what the nation and its literature will look like after apartheid, Ndebele describes a temporality almost identical to Gordimer's notion of regnal impasse: "The past is knocking constantly on the doors of our perceptions, refusing to be forgotten, because it is deeply embedded in the present. To neglect it at this most crucial of moments in our history is to postpone the future."[18] Even with a clear view of the post-apartheid future, Ndebele too turns to an interregnal time-sense to make legible a regime that still cannot be born.

In contrast, white South African fiction during the 1980s thematized and formalized the problem of historical complicity with the apartheid regime and storytelling.[19] Coetzee's *Waiting for the Barbarians* (1980) is perhaps the most obvious text within this constellation. The novel's narrator, a magistrate working at the frontier of a fictitious empire, observes that "Empire dooms itself to live in history and plot against history. One thought alone preoccupies the submerged mind of Empire: how not to end, how not to die, how to prolong its era."[20] The magistrate instead wishes "to live outside the history that Empire imposes on its subjects, even its lost subjects. I never wished it for the barbarians that they should have the history of Empire laid upon them."[21] Coetzee returns to these themes in *The Life and Times of Michael K* (1983), which like *July's People* is set during a fictional civil war in South Africa. The main character, Michael K, flees the war and travels from Cape Town into the *veldt* to live "in a pocket outside time."[22] But once there, he finds that the search for such pockets reproduces the desires of white settlers: "He could understand that people should have retreated here and fenced themselves in with miles and miles of silence; he could understand that they should have wanted to bequeath that privilege of so much silence to their children and grandchildren in perpetuity (though by what right he was not sure); he wondered whether there were not forgotten corners and angles and corridors between fences, land that belonged to no one yet. Perhaps if one flew high enough, he thought, one would be able to see."[23] To locate such a place untouched by the history of colonialism, K must inhabit a perspective from above. But this perspective recalls the optics of colonial authority (a god's point of view), for the very next sentence is shown to be of the very theater of war K is escaping from: "Two aircraft streaked across the sky from south to north leaving vapour trails that slowly faded, and a noise like waves."[24] Caught between a legacy of settler colonialism and the political turmoil saturating the country in the present, K undertakes a life that strives to be forgotten by history, seeking to leave no trace of himself behind.

André Brink folds this problem of historical situatedness into a question of writing and storytelling in *States of Emergency* (1988). The premise of the novel is the narrator's desire to write "a love story untarnished by politics," specifically in the midst of the political turmoil that saturated South Africa in the 1980s.[25] Framed as a story within a story, the narrator undertakes numerous false starts, middles, and endings in his own writing, dramatizing his inability to narrate a story isolated from the political milieu. When he eventually commits to a beginning to a love story, it concerns an affair between a writer and his student who are brought together by the declaration of a state of emergency by the apartheid government. In other words, their story's entire condition of possibility is the state of emergency that enables the beginning to their tale rather than a suspension of it—as it certainly is at juridical and national-temporal registers.[26] But at the end of Brink's novel, the narrator admits to giving up on writing the love story he initially set out to, concluding, "I find myself back where I started."[27] The end returns the writer to the beginning, when the narrative that is yet to be written is still yet to come. Far from a failure, this return to the beginning inscribes a future still open to possibilities. Thus the concluding sentence of Brink's novel (a sentence fragment no less) reads: "Perhaps only the freedom, the openness, the open-endedness, the endlessness . . . of a country for which the future is still possible, a love not yet circumscribed, a story not yet written."[28]

For Gordimer, Coetzee, and Brink alike, narratives of national rupture take on a variety of forms. In *Michael K*, the civil war is the horizon of history and politics that K runs away from. In *States of Emergency*, South Africa's political turmoil forecloses the possibility of a life outside of politics and history. *July's People* narrates the interregnum as the occasion for the demystification of class and race relations under apartheid. But in all these cases, narratives of national rupture allowed white writers to make visible a crisis of historical transition during an especially uncertain epoch of South African history. All their novels sense an ending to the apartheid regime but also defer what exactly this ending will look like. In the process, they, as Elleke Boehmer explains, "give us deaths or near deaths . . . and escapes, but without clear destinations, departures which are headed for culs-de-sac, caught in a void."[29] In what follows, I focus on *July's People* to see how Gordimer's poetics of national rupture narrates the interregnum and in the process asks how can one understand the plot of a historical transition when it has an unreadable destination? What does a historical novel look like when the historical period depicted is one in which no particular regime is dominant? As discussed earlier, Lukács's historical novel narrativizes an accomplished history. But if this is the case, then what does a historical novel look like when this history hasn't been accomplished yet, as is certainly the case in South Africa in the 1980s?

INTERREGNUM: A FIELD OF INTELLIGIBILITY

Before considering these questions further, it is helpful to elaborate on Gramsci's idea of the interregnum in some detail, for whom it is first and foremost a field of intelligibility. Like his Marxist (and even non-Marxist) predecessors, war is less of an event for Gramsci and more of a lens with which to make class antagonisms visible beneath states of assumed peace. In his brief entry on the interregnum in his prison writings, Gramsci reflects on the ideological void that followed Italy's post–World War I political climate, when it became apparent that existing ideological structures were no longer valid yet no clear alternative presented itself to the masses. What is most characteristic of such a period is the recognition that the frameworks of society are politically unviable. During this period, ruling parties "dominate" through force rather than lead ideologically, a tendency that only further alienates the masses from the ideologies they are already skeptical of: "physical depression will lead in the long run to a widespread scepticism, and a new 'arrangement' will be found." Later, "The death of old ideologies takes the form of scepticism with regard to all theories and general formulae; of application to the pure economic fact (earnings, etc.), and to a form of politics which is not simply realistic in fact (this is always the case) but which is cynical in its immediate manifestation."[30] Gramsci describes a state of skeptical inaction rather than revolutionary discord. The interregnum doesn't usher in a new regime, only widespread "cynicism" of existing ideologies and institutions.

Gramsci's notion of the interregnum departs from earlier Marxist figurations of war in that it is less about a tropics of race war—the Manichean conflict between two historically conjoined groups—as about a tension between past and an as-yet-illegible future. While race wars thrust history forward, the interregnum stalls all progress. This impasse is created because of the detachment of history and (predominant) ideologies. Consequently, the interregnum describes a period of clarity more than anything else, only a kind of clarity in which there are no solutions to social woe. That is to say, the clarity afforded by the interregnum operates retrospectively toward older regimes but not necessarily toward the formation of new alternatives; its field of intelligibility concerns a knowledge about the limits and outdatedness of dominant (as opposed to "leading") ideologies. If the old party's ideologies were hegemonic, in the interregnum it is the "cynicism" and "skepticism" toward these old ideologies that become hegemonic. Only when such disillusionment "leads" (as opposed to the older regime's ideologies that have had to resort to forms of domination) is there "the possibility and necessity of creating a new culture." Gramsci is far from triumphalist, for the "new culture" he speaks of is only ever a *possibility*, not a reality. And this possibility is legible only to the degree that the dominant regimes of the present have, as Gramsci states elsewhere, "become mummified and anachronistic."[31] Gramsci does not have in mind confident revolutionary statements or predictions but a space of critical "cynicism" and "skepticism"—a space and time of repudiation and rejection.

Gramsci's account of the interregnum differs quite substantially from statist versions. For example, Giorgio Agamben's notion of the *iustituim* is "not defined as a fullness of powers, a pleromatic state of law, as in the dictatorial model, but as a kenomatic state, an emptiness and standstill of the law."[32] In Gramsci's interregnum, law is not at a "standstill" but proliferates in what Walter Benjamin might call a "rotten" form because it fails to mask the violent underbelly of law.[33] Similarly, one can distinguish Gramsci's idea of the interregnum from the openness that Slavoj Žižek sees in periods of regime change, such as the overthrow of Ceausescu in Romania. Žižek describes "rebels waving the national flag with the red star, the Communist symbol, cut out, so that instead of the symbol standing for the organizing principle of the national life, there was nothing but a hole in its center."[34] This moment is open to possibilities for Žižek because it is *without* ideology, hegemony, and sovereignty. Although Gramsci's interregnum is open to possibilities, this openness looks back at the uselessness of existing regimes, not forward to potential histories. In other words, what the interregnum makes visible are the limits of historical comprehension, describing more of an impasse than a transition between regimes—much like what Benjamin meant by a "present which is not a transition."[35]

Gordimer understood the interregnum at a sociopolitical register.[36] In "Living in the Interregnum," she insists that those working against apartheid must do more than merely overthrow the apartheid government as an entire way of life has to be rethought: "from the all-white Parliament to the all-white country club and the separate 'white' television channels, it is not a matter of blacks taking over white institutions, it is one of conceiving institutions . . . that reflect a societal structure vastly different from that built to the specifications of white power and privilege."[37] The obvious barrier for Gordimer was finding a way to take part in such a movement without reinscribing the privilege that apartheid had historically afforded her and the "segment of white South African society" to which she belonged.[38] And more than an institutional problem, Gordimer saw apartheid to be "above all a habit."[39] By "habit," she means the permeation of apartheid ideology into the everyday unconscious of white South Africa.[40] To think beyond habits is to transform their unconscious repetitions into conscious ones, that is to say, to be aware of one's habits. Lazarus finds this to be characteristic of late apartheid literature, which doesn't undertake "writing *for* revolution" as much as "writing *against* apartheid."[41] For Gordimer, this meant dramatizing the habits of apartheid: "If we live out our situation consciously, proceeding from the Pascalian wager that the home of the white African exists, know that this depends also on our finding our way there out of the perceptual clutter of curled photographs of master and servant relationships, the 78 *rpms* of history repeating the conditioning of the past."[42] The post-apartheid future for white South Africans must come "out of the 78 *rpms* of history" that reinscribe the system of apartheid. A departure from apartheid's cyclical repetitions cannot come through a straightforward exit or stoppage of its rotary replication but from within the limits of the spinning record's axis. R. Radhakrishnan has helpfully described this problem as: "How to narrativize 'coevalness' while inhabiting a single chronotope."[43]

In *July's People*, the reader is alerted to the historical impasse of the interregnum in a brief reference to Alessandro Manzoni's *The Betrothed* (1827), which not coincidentally features prominently in Lukács's own study of the historical novel. In an early chapter, Maureen cannot finish reading Manzoni's novel because "the transport of the novel, a false awareness of being within another time, place and life that was the pleasure of reading, for her, was not possible. She *was* in another time, place, consciousness" (29). Michael Neill has helpfully called this the Smaleses' "temporal dislocation," which refers to the disjuncture between epistemological and the interpretive registers, where, for example, Maureen's capacities for reading fall short because she is "in another time, place, consciousness."[44] This is why when Maureen finally finishes *The Betrothed* in a later chapter, the narrator comments that Manzoni's novel holds no meaning for her because "she had regained no established point of a continuing present from which to recognize her own sequence" (139). Not having the coordinates to determine when exactly the "continuing present" exists (the old or the new), Maureen's anxiety lies in her points of reference (or lack thereof) rather than the actual sequence of historical events. That is to say, the problem is neither hers nor Manzoni's novel but the interregnal time *July's People* and its characters inhabit. In context of the historical novel, such a genre can only makes sense when the reader reads from the standpoint of an accomplished history, which is precisely what Gordimer argued South Africans lacked during the 1980s.

The beginning of *July's People*, in fact, establishes the historico-temporal dislocation of the interregnum. The first lines of the novel take the form of a question spoken in broken English—thereby racially marking its speaker—who is immediately after identified as July: "You like to have some cup of tea?" (1). The quotidian nature of such a question is then made explicit: "July bent at the doorway and began that day for them as his kind has always done for their kind" (1). July's "bend," a gesture of subservience, is routine in his relationship to his white employers. Immediately after, the narrator transports the reader to similar settings: "the knock on the door. Seven o'clock. In governor's residences, commercial hotel rooms, shift bosses' company bungalows, master bedrooms *en suite*—the tea-tray in black hands smelling of

Lifebuoy soap" (1). This scene is of middle-class banality where July's labor is his condition on account of his black hands. The knock on the door is the comforting signal that no matter what the context— hotel rooms or bedrooms—July will bring his employers their tea in the morning.

Such scenes of bygone bourgeois domesticity are interrupted with an incomplete sentence, "the knock on the door," and beginning on the following line the narrator states "no door, an aperture in thick mud walls, and the sack that hung over it looped back for air, sometime during the short night. *Bam, I'm stifling; her voice raising him from the dead, he staggering up from his exhausted sleep*" (1). The narrative disrupts the routine of morning tea by repeating the same encounter in an entirely different context. In what is a clear reference to the novel's epigraph, Bam and Maureen are somewhere between life and death, one rising from it, the other suffocating. The motive behind July's bend is also questioned, as he may very well do so because he is entering through an "aperture." This opening is equally a reference to the dying regime as it is to the unknown future to come, for as Brian Macaskill has pointed out, the "knock on the door" performs "a setting apart" of the past and present.[45] The sentence "the knock on the door" is left incomplete as it lacks a full stop, and a new sentence begins on a new line, "no door." This second line begins uncapitalized, implying that it is a continuation of another sentence, yet the reader does not know what the sentence is. "no door," in other words, does not have an origin, it is displaced and begins anew. Much like the Smaleses who awaken disoriented among "a bald fowl with chicks cheeping," this sentence too is "jolted out of chronology," left incomplete and detached from its origins (4). Phrases that seemed routine now connote something very different to the reader: "the knock on the door," instead of signifying the comforting repetition of morning tea, now carries with it the anxiety that "knocks on the door" bring when one is hiding—which of course the Smaleses are as they live in constant fear that they will be found by black revolutionaries. The absent knock on the door splits the text by "jolting" the past out of chronology into the present, thereby putting the Smaleses in a place and time where the language they know from "back there" seems to have far less valence and effectiveness than it used to. The knowledge that these words are anachronistic makes sense to the reader only because of their existence in the interregnum. The contradiction here is that to understand something as anachronistic—as originating in a period not belonging to the present—presupposes a more contemporary epistemology, a present that is distinct from the past. Yet this knowledge cannot in fact be translated into the novel's lexicon. The Smaleses' rule that July must always knock transforms from servitude into the servant's hospitality; the protocols of master-servant relations morph into those of host-guest. The field of intelligibility afforded by Gordimer's narration of the interregnum, as in Gramsci, is premised on making visible the limits of what one knows. That is to say, it is a field of intelligibility into limits rather than new horizons.

THINKING IN ANACHRONISMS

Knowing limits, however, is a way of knowing what lies beyond. For unlike in Gramsci where the new "cannot" be born, the new regime has indeed arrived in *July's People*, only it remains just beyond the novel's field of vision. Instead, the novel defines the negative space for this future by repeating the anachronisms that permeate the novel and hence produces an unutterable awareness of the new regime. Gordimer's text indicates that the "new" has arrived in history, only its characters' historicity means they cannot fully comprehend what this "new culture" could be. The narrator of *July's People*, for example, assumes a new politics to have already been born out of the interregnum when discussing the difficulties Bam—Maureen's husband—has adapting to his new historical location, for he "struggled hopelessly for words that were not phrases from back there, words that would make the truth that must be forming here, out of the blacks, out of themselves. He sensed for a moment the great drama hidden in the monotonous days, as she was aware, always, of the yellow bakkie hidden in the sameness of the bush. But the words would not come. They were blocked by an old vocabulary" (127). The key word is "blocked" as it implies that the old vocabulary that Maureen and Bam rely upon is in fact the very obstacle between them and the legibility of the present.[46] They try over and over again to catch a radio signal in English that puts the civil war around them in the familiar terms of the old regime: "'rural backwardness', 'counter-revolutionary pockets', 'failure to bring about peaceful change inevitably leading to civil war'—she knew all that, she had heard all that before it happened. And now it had happened, it was an experience that couldn't be forethought" (127). The civil war exceeds the language they know, and this crisis takes place not because these words can't capture the "reality" of the Smaleses' experience but because these mummified words from "back there" block words that properly belong to the present. The novel posits the existence and contemporaneity of a new language, but resists representing it because of the continued "domination" (as opposed to "leading") of the dated language of apartheid. Older forms of colonial reason obstruct representations of the new regime.[47]

By allowing its characters to be conscious of these shifts—albeit fleetingly—the novel identifies a type of knowing that is elusive to its own lexicon, as it cannot put the "sense" of the future into any words. By narrating the interregnum in the manner that it does, *July's People* formalizes a limit of intelligibility—a literary epistemology of not-knowing. The text, like Bam, must instead turn to a past vocabulary—the "78 rpms of history"—in order to articulate an "awareness" of the future. The deployment of an anachronistic language echoes Marx's opening to the *Eighteenth Brumaire* (which could itself be said to be about an interregnum) where he makes the analogy between the historical arrival of a new regime and the difficulties of learning a new language as one's own: "a beginner who has learnt a new language always translates it back into his mother tongue, but he has assimilated the spirit of the new language and can freely express himself in it only when he finds his way in it without recalling the old and forgets his native tongue in the use of the new."[48] "Conjured spirits," "borrowed names, battle cries, costumes," and "mother tongues" all serve to palliate and regulate the possibilities that political upheaval brings. Words from "back there," "names, battle cries," block and obscure a new lexicon. Although "the content [of the interregnum] goes beyond the phrase," its language can nevertheless obscure the meaning of its content.

The Smaleses' difficulty in "adapting" to the new regime's lexicon characterizes much of their frustrations with being in July's village. The children crave commodities like Coca-Cola and fight over the toys they brought from "back there," Maureen wishes she had disposable sanitary napkins and asks July to get medicine from the town nearby. However, as has been discussed in much of the criticism on the novel, despite these initial difficulties the children are soon able to "pick up the habits" of the village children, such as a cough they all share, wiping themselves with stones, and even speaking some phrases of "their language." Their prized toy cars are later exchanged for homemade wire carts with the other boys of the village.[49] Bam and Maureen, tellingly, have a much harder time letting go of the past. Over the course of the novel their bakkie—a recreational vehicle from their previous life—becomes a no-man's-land between the old and new regimes of power, for while it represents the Smaleses' idyllic past it also represents a newer, more independent future for July, who in addition to learning to drive also plans to use it in the future to open a grocery store. During their arguments with July about the bakkie, July refers to himself as Maureen's "boy," a "weapon" she had openly expressed hostility toward "back there" (70). "Boy" upsets Maureen's liberal sensibilities because it throws her relationship with July in the sharp relief of master-servant. July's insistence on using "boy" forces her to come up with a better term to capture their current relationship: "If I ask you for the keys now it's not the key of the kitchen door! It's not as a servant you've got them. Is it? But a friend" (72). She hopes July will see that she recognized his dignity: "If she had never before used the word 'dignity' to him it was not because she didn't think he understood the concept, didn't have any—it was only the term itself that might be beyond his grasp of the language" (72). However, what follows is *precisely* a scene of humiliation: "He produced the keys in his palm. 'Fifteen years I'm work for your kitchen, your house, because my wife, my children, I must work for them. Take it'" (72). July submits. As with the tea tray, he offers her the keys. But the act is also a retort, for he summarizes their history together: he works because he has to; he produces the keys because he has to.

Maureen's inability to reorient herself to the time of the interregnum manifests at the level of language. When waking up in July's village for the first time, Maureen remains disoriented from the journey, for she "closed her eyes again and the lurching motion of the vehicle swung in her head as the swell of the sea makes the land heave underfoot when the passenger steps ashore after a voyage" (2–3). The vehicle in question is the yellow bakkie the Smaleses escaped in with July. The narrator explains the vehicle's significance in apartheid South Africa: "It makes a cheap car-cum-caravan for white families, general Afrikaners, and their half-brother coloureds who can't afford both. For more affluent white South Africans, it is a second, sporting vehicle for purposes to which a town car is not suited" (5). When Bam brought the bakkie home as a gift for himself for his fortieth birthday, "they stood around it indulgently, wife and family, the children excited, as it seemed nothing else could excite them, by a new possession. Nothing made them so happy as buying things" (6).

This stable memory of the bakkie contrasts with the hallucinatory, ever-changing perception of the present by Maureen. The disorientation that she feels upon waking up in July's home is caused primarily by the bakkie, which "contains her" even after their journey is over. Despite having disembarked the night before, Maureen continues to inhabit the bakkie for she feels seasick. Moreover, this seasickness is characterized as "delirium," which causes her to "rise and sink, in and out of lucidity" (3). In other words, the seasickness she feels is in the realm of expression, for it is on the axis of *lucidity* that Maureen experiences this disorientation, implying that it is her ability to speak that the bakkie alters.

Having obstructed her ability to speak, the seasickness also alters her perception of the world around her. Instead of hearing the "faintest sound in the world" produced by a "bald fowl with chicks cheeping," Maureen can only hear the incessant rattling of the bakkie: "The swaying shuddering, thudding, flinging stops, and the furniture of life falls into place. The vehicle was the fever. Chattering metal and raving dance of loose bolts in the smell of the children's car-sick. She rose from it for gradually longer and longer intervals. At first what fell into place was what vanished, the past" (3). The bakkie, here the *fever* that alters perception, *blocks* the legibility of the "room" she is currently in—a hallucinatory symptom produced in the form of a reliance on words from the past. The only furniture in the room is a car seat extracted from the bakkie itself, implying that it is a piece of "furniture of life" from "back there" that "falls into place" first. The bakkie is immediately after blamed for this hallucination: "as if the vehicle had made a journey so far beyond the norm of a present it divided its passengers from that the master bedroom *en suite* had been lost, jolted out of chronology as the room where her returning consciousness properly belonged: the room that she had left four days ago" (3–4). This "temporal dislocation" illustrates how Maureen "properly belongs" to the past, yet finds herself in the present and as with the lost knock on the door of the opening scene, she is "jolted out of chronology."[50] But what is crucial to remember is that it is the bakkie that creates aphasia. Maureen's perception is out of joint not because she *resists* adapting to a new order but because she is *contained* within the bakkie, or more accurately, her words are contained by it. Her detachment from the world around her is caused by the weight of this vocabulary from "back there" that carries with it a force that splits the past and present of the novel.

Maureen struggles with language throughout the novel. When she insists to July that she can take care of herself in her new surroundings, the narrator observes: "The guest protesting at giving trouble; he and she caught the echo of those visitors who came to stay in her house and tipped him when they left" (10). Similarly, after July returns from a local store with new batteries, Maureen says, "Oh how marvelous. How clever to remember," a phrase they both recognize from "back there" when the Smaleses' friends brought over flowers or chocolates (55). The significance of these batteries lies in the fact that they power the radio Bam and Maureen use to search for stations in "their language." But as Maureen reflects, the irony is that "not even a new battery would bring the voices from back there if the radio station should be hit" (55). The historico-political reality forming in the interregnum—the birth of the new regime—is a constant reminder to Maureen that the old regime continues to die, and yet it is upon this anachronistic landscape that Bam and Maureen exclusively reside.[51]

The novel's manner of working through this impasse is to turn and return to anachronistic habits, specifically, the trope of the "knock on the door." One particular "knock" occurs when a vehicle arrives in the village late one night (we find out later that this is July and Daniel in the bakkie). Maureen steps out into the rain to shower after Bam's "deathly tiredness drained him of all apprehension" (48). In complete darkness,

> She turned as if she were under a shower faucet. Soon her body was the same temperature as the water. She became aware of being able to see; and what she saw was like the reflection of a candle-flame behind a window-pane flowing with rain, far off. The reflection moved or the glassy ripples moved over it. But it existed—the proof was that there was a dimension between her and some element in the rain-hung darkness. Where it was, the rain must have thinned: and now she saw a twin faint, needled beams, traveling. They progressed slowly, and because there was no other feature to be made out between her and them, seemed half-way up the sky. The sense of direction came to her, from the luminous trace: she stuck a pin where there was no map. (48–49)

Maureen's gesture is out of place and time, for there are no windows or faucets in July's village, and her "turn" might be seen as toward the past. Within her habitual perception of the present-as-past, Maureen becomes aware of "something" but is not able to describe what this "something" is. Noticing a light in the distance, she sees it as a *reflection* of a candle flame "behind a window-pane," implying that the candle is not outside of this fictional room she inhabits but is right next to her. As it turns out, the light source in question is the bakkie being driven by July and Daniel, which appears adjacent to her despite its distance "far off." The vehicle's movement produces the effect of "glassy ripples" that Maureen sees rather than the actual rain that streams down her fictional window. The bakkie, in other words, *refracts* the *reflection* Maureen sees because what she perceives as a representation of objective reality is in fact one that is mediated and modified by *something*—namely the movement of the bakkie. Despite being unable to define or name what this something is, she remains aware of its existence and it remains unutterable, muted, elusive yet present.

The bakkie too performs a contradictory movement in the scene, for although it is returning to the village from afar it is also going to an unknown location by appearing adjacent to Maureen. July and Daniel took the bakkie without the Smaleses' permission, and their return signals the handing-back of the vehicle to its old proprietors. But it also marks the altered circumstances in which it returns—the keys are in July's hands. Identical to "the knock on the door," July's arrival is both a return to old conditions as well as the possibility of a transformation in his relationship to the Smaleses. However, rather than deferring the creation of the new regime exclusively to July, the scene insists upon Maureen's conscription to this new regime. As the bakkie's return is indirectly described from her point of view, it is possible to read the "window-pane flowing with rain" as also framing her perspective from *within* the bakkie driving in the rain. July's defiant return to the village—an act that signals the arrival of a radical shift in the master-servant dialectic—is a future Maureen is inescapably implicated in. If Gramsci claims that the interregnum signifies "a possibility *and necessity* of creating a new culture," then it is the "necessity" of such a project that the scene alerts us to.[52] The new regime is adorned in old "costumes" (the bakkie in which the servant dutifully returns to his masters with much-needed supplies from the shops in town), yet in a manner where a new regime is simultaneously driven toward.

Gordimer's narrative of the interregnum thus makes it possible to sense how the "awareness" of a new regime, indeed of the future that is "as yet not presentable," is one whose location remains illegible in the text. As the bakkie comes closer its headlamps illuminate Maureen so that her world is perceivable again. The description of this light is equally telling because its beams morph into needles—indeed, the "pin" that she subsequently uses to find her way back to the hut. But there is no map to stick a pin into. The bakkie gives Maureen the ability to navigate her way back to the hut, but does so without actually allowing for a cartographic representation of where she is going: "there was no map." Her destination and route have no discernible or intelligible sequence. Consistent with the maritime metaphors that have been encountered before, the vessel that left her seasick returns with her "lifebuoy," after which Maureen "slept, like a drowning case in the coarse warmth of the rescuers' blanket wrapped around her, on her car seat" (49). Having dramatized the paralyzed transit of the interregnum, the scene reveals what JanMohamed calls "the parasitic nature of the master," for having "sensed" the birth of the new, Maureen, who until a few moments ago was as cold as the landscape around her, is warmed by the "rescuer's blanket" (140).

The coordinates between old to the new—indeed the "readability" or "sequence" of the interregnum—remains elusive to the very end of the novel, where yet another "knock on the door" takes place when Maureen is said to "*feel* some change in the fabric of subconsciously identified sounds and movements that make the silence" (157; emphasis added). Soon after, a helicopter arrives in the village: "A high ringing is produced in her ears, her body in its rib-cage is thudded with deafening vibration, invaded by a force pumping, jigging in its monstrous orgasm—the helicopter has sprung through the hot brilliant cloud just above them all, its landing gear like spread legs, battling the air with whirling scythes" (158). Maureen feels the presence of the helicopter first, and once in sight, it is through the senses that the helicopter finds its way on the page. What follows has been the subject of an exhaustive debate regarding the conclusion of the novel: Maureen runs toward the helicopter while leaving her family behind. As tempting as it is to set aside the ending in favor of focusing on lesser-discussed parts of the novel, the subject of this chapter requires some attention to the scene.

Nicholas Visser has argued that the arrival of the helicopter is an intertext with W. B. Yeats's "Leda and the Swan." Similarities in the expressions as well as the style of the two texts lead Visser to conclude that Maureen's flight is above all an "annunciation."[53] He elaborates: "the imminent convergence of Maureen and the helicopter, like the convergence of Leda and the god-swan, heralds a new civilization, a new epoch for South Africa that cannot, particularly from within a moment of interregnum, be described but only be symbolically prefigured in a

prophetic gesture of revolutionary optimism."[54] Visser's characterization of Maureen's flight as a "symbolic prefiguration" is a key point
because it is to say that the text encrypts the future to come. As he goes
on to say, "Maureen has been overtaken by something far larger than
herself, than her self."[55] For Visser, Maureen is drawn to the helicopter
for reasons that neither she nor the reader understands.

In contrast to Visser, I would stress that the arrival of the helicopter
is a repetition of prior "knocks on the door" and not the signaling
of the arrival of a new regime. In much the same way as Maureen
was "stifling" in the "knock on the door" of the opening scene, "fear
climbs her hand-over-hand to throttle, hold her" in this final scene
(159). Similarly, Maureen's inability to identify the returning bakkie is
echoed in the ending when "she could not have said what colour [the
helicopter] was, what markings it had, whether it holds saviours or
murderers; and—even if she were to have identified the markings—for
whom" (158).[56] Finally, just as Maureen "was aware, always, of the yellow bakkie hidden in the sameness of the bush," she senses the helicopter's presence despite its camouflage in the bush: "she can still hear the
beat, beyond those trees and those, and she runs towards it. She runs"
(160). All is foreshadowed *and* foreclosed by the "knock" that began
as an instruction to July, and eventually became a habit that lived on
in the time of the interregnum. The ending, like the beginning, is yet
another knock on the door—an arrival whose content remains beyond
the thresholds of legibility.

Far from the historical "dead end" that the novel has been criticized
for, or even the "revolutionary standpoint" from where this ending
is supposedly narrated, *July's People* first and foremost seems to be
about *when* it is read. Just as Maureen struggles to read Manzoni's
novel because she lives in the interregnum, the interregnal poetics of
July's People must also find a way to read without the coordinates
and sequence with which to make sense of the narrative. Interpreting
the interregnum, indeed, requires the reader to defer the temptation
to transcend the text's limitations, the desire for narrative closure. In
Conrad's "tale of civil war," this desire was for the triumph of economic development and the completion of Costaguana's arrival into
capitalist modernity. In Gordimer, this desire is to arrive at the postcolonial, which, of course, is kept out of reach. At work in the text is
a politics of transition that repudiates the comfort zone of tidy transitions from the old to the new, for it deliberately obscures the temporal
registers and axes upon which to make sense of the interregnum as a

linear transition. Entrapped within its own narrative coordinates, the novel turns and returns to colonial anachronisms to find a way to its postcolonial destination, one that is everywhere and nowhere.

The ending of *July's People* echoes the ending of *A Bend in the River*. Maureen leaves her *family and servant* behind, running toward an unmarked helicopter; Salim leaves his *family servant* Metty behind, traveling to an unknown destination. Maureen runs toward her "saviors or murderers"; Salim knows it is better to risk his life in escape than stay in town. But the crucial difference between these two conclusions rests on the distinction David Scott identifies between anticolonial romance and postcolonial tragedy. Although Gordimer doesn't allow the reader to know whether a new regime is born at the end of the novel, its existence in history is unquestioned. Bam and Maureen are aware of the "new words forming" in the interregnum, only they cannot translate this awareness into cognizable signs. Although the new regime has been born, what is at stake in the novel is whether it can stay alive and be made legible to those who properly belong to the old regime, namely, the Smaleses. And Gordimer's ending, vague though it is, nevertheless frames Maureen's flight as a triumphant embrace of historical transformation. Maureen no longer waits for the future to become legible to her but instead boldly runs toward it—not knowing what it has in store for her. In contrast, Salim's departure is shrouded in tragedy. Metty, like the barge passengers, is doomed. Ferdinand, who helped Salim escape, has an uncertain fate. And Salim's escape is not a valiant embrace of an uncertain future but a suspenseful journey on a steamboat in complete darkness, enveloped instead in the sound of gunshots and the knowledge that the lives of the barge passengers are as good as the moths that fill the air. Gordimer's interregnum, despite being an impasse, ends in a romantic flourish—certain that the new is at the very least a viable option for the future of South Africa, there *is* a knock on the door. The ending of *A Bend* has no such romance, for as the novel makes clear, such futures have already "come and gone" for those who have no place in the world.

Global Civil War

In recent years, the idea of an international civil war has gained some traction within political philosophy and yielded a very different understanding of political rupture. Agamben, for example, begins *State of Exception* by declaring: "Faced with the unstoppable progression of what has been called a 'global civil war,' the state of exception tends increasingly to appear as the dominant paradigm of government in contemporary politics."[1] Schmitt is in many ways the originator of this formulation, arguing in his lectures on guerrilla warfare that the proliferation of the "irregular enemy" and "irregular warfare" in the twentieth century deterritorialized classical warfare into a global problem. V. I. Lenin and Mao Tse-Tung, according to Schmitt, were the first to render civil war an international possibility.[2] In a different philosophical tradition but to a similar end, Michael Hardt and Antonio Negri claim that war "is becoming the primary organizing principle of society, and politics merely one of its means or guises. What appears as civil peace, then, really only puts an end to one form of war and opens the way for another."[3] Citing the proliferation of war in late twentieth-century rhetoric like "war on poverty" and "war on drugs" (and we may now add phrases like "war on Christmas" and "war on terror"), Hardt and Negri argue that "the enemies are posed not as specific nation-states or political communities or even individuals but rather as abstract concepts or perhaps as sets of practices."[4] Carlo Galli similarly notes that the globalization of war by the war on terror has created a "global civil war."[5] Instead of a war between or within states, this new kind of conflict is between "two global functions, two networks that overlap with one another more than they oppose each other," which are "both deterritorialized and in search of a politically legitimated identity."[6]

Such conceptions of civil war, while helpful in thinking about the state and sovereignty in the age of hyper-globalization, too easily gloss over the unevenness with which narratives of civil war are deployed—an unevenness the chapters of this book have attempted to highlight and track. I have argued throughout this book that civil war has for some time been global in that it is implicated in the politics of empire. But to assume that civil war is globally diffuse, homogeneously distributed, or even molecular omits how narratives of civil wars often function in the service of nationalist politics. Because narratives of national rupture have historically offered a counterintuitive way to make the nation legible, they have also always been involved in the delineation and sometimes contestation of national boundaries. Making the nation legible goes hand in hand with making the asymmetries of power within and between nations legible. For the early Victorians, England's latent civil war between the classes offered a way to define a civilized national identity against the "savage" Irish. Similarly for jingoists like Kipling and Doyle, the "civility" of the Boer War, a war between "fellow-citizens" of the British empire, stemmed from the fact that the conflict was reserved for "sahibs," thereby excluding colonized subjects from participation and membership in Greater Britain. More recently, the World Bank, along with academic disciplines like the political sciences, define the Global South through its proclivity towards civil war. But each of these instances also demonstrates how the territorial boundaries drawn by narratives of national rupture are always unstable. When Carlyle distinguishes the condition of England question from the Irish question by narrating England's latent fratricide, he also undermines this distinction by showing the fratricidal "cash-nexus" to disregard national difference. When Kipling writes a tale about the "white man's war," he describes the savagery of the British war effort. When Conrad reinvents civil war as symptomatic of a lack of development in his fictional country of Costaguana, he also shows this incivility to be unthinkable in isolation from the failures of New Imperialism and the civilizing mission more generally. And as Naipaul's own "tale of civil war" demonstrates, the figure of the refugee is as much a product of the failures of postcolonial nationalism as he is of international interventionism.

To conclude this study, I want to consider the final scene of *A Bend in the River* in light of the most recent conjuncture of civil war and nationalism. If we recall, Naipaul's novel ends with Salim leaving a central African state at the dawn of yet another civil war. It is the mid-1970s, and an uprising has polarized the country Salim lives in. His property is seized, his wealth turned over to the authorities (by a family servant, no less), and his friend Ferdinand warns him that he is likely to be killed if taken prisoner. Lacking a place in the town at the bend in the river, lacking a place in Africa, Salim flees once more. Stateless and "flagless," Salim is no longer able to sustain a life in the war-torn periphery. He must yield to the "waves of history" that initially brought his Indian Muslim family to the shores of East Africa in the previous century, which later pushed him into the center of Africa, and which are now forcing him to the shores of Europe, far away from civil war in the heart of darkness.

This is arguably *the* story of the twentieth century: the story of the refugee.

Today, however, civil war appears to have followed the refugee back to his birthplace in Europe. Nearly forty years after Salim's journey, we might conjecture that we know where Salim and millions others like him escaping civil war end up: Istanbul. Lesbos. Mioni. Tabanove. Röszke. Vienna. Munich. Calais. London. Houston. Refugees are said to have brought an international civil war to the doorsteps of the West. The late twentieth-century notion that civil war is unique to the developing world has buckled under the pressure of human migration from the formerly colonized world to the metropole. Accompanying these human movements has been the efflorescence of far-right political movements across Europe and the United States whose platforms are explicitly anti-immigrant and almost always anti-Muslim. Muslim immigrants (or those who resemble them in the eyes of the Right)— Naipaul's Salim, for all we know!—are said to have brought an uncivil civil war to the West's secular society.

Ironically, Salim's creator is at the vanguard of Europe and the United States' recent xenophobia. In an article about the civil wars in the Middle East, Naipaul argues that ISIS is the Fourth Reich. His essay begins by listing horrific acts of violence perpetrated by ISIS, including murder, torture, crucifixions, the demolition of historic sites, young girls being forced into sexual slavery, and men being thrown off cliffs for suspected homosexuality. "Yes," Naipaul explains, "all these scenes could have taken place in several continents in the medieval world, but they were captured on camera and broadcast to anyone with access to the internet. These are scenes, of yesterday, today and tomorrow in our own world."[7] Far from "development in reverse," as the World Bank would have it, Naipaul understands ISIS as violently returning the world to the Middle Ages. Citing Islam's supposedly innate opposition to European culture, he pits prophets of the Enlightenment like "Descartes, Leibniz and Newton" against the Bangladeshi immigrant, claiming the latter is drawn to Islam over secular values because of the "simplicity that a simple and singular upbringing craves. That is why they go. And volunteer for death, and die."[8] And then he advocates for the bombing of Syria and Iraq: "With air support from the West, they [the Iraqi and Irani governments] may manage to push Isis back. Such an offensive . . . has to be urgently expanded. Isis has to be seen as the most potent threat to the world since the Third Reich. Its military annihilation as an anti-civilisational force has to now be the objective of a world that wants its ideological and material freedoms."[9] Indeed, the survival of western civilization (here assumed to be seamlessly universal) rests on the defeat of ISIS's "anti-civilizational" existence. Doing so, the logic goes, will eradicate the Muslim immigrant's object of desire—"simplicity"—and force him to endure the hardships of cultural assimilation into Britain's secular, "by-and-large egalitarian system."[10] In stark contrast to how Naipaul-the-novelist meditates on the contradictions and limits of development, Naipaul-the-essayist is the civilizing mission's biggest proponent.

And Naipaul is far from alone. Greece's Golden Dawn, which has gained significant popularity in recent years, claims Greece is in a "new type of civil war" between refugees and anarchists on the one hand, and Greek nationalists like themselves on the other.[11] Patriotic Europeans Against the Islamization of the West (PEGIDA) has enjoyed significant popularity in Germany since its formation in 2014. PEGIDA is unambiguous about the danger immigrants, especially Muslim minorities, pose to Europe: the "religious wars" in the Middle East have created a "global civil war" of which Europe is the most recent victim.[12] Following the terrorist attacks in Nice in 2016, the head of France's DGSI (Direction Générale de la Sécurité Intérieure) declared that French citizens were "on the verge of civil war" with far-right extremist (Muslim) immigrants.[13] Having been expunged by the advent of capitalist modernity in the West, uncivil war is said to be knocking on the door of the birthplace of modern civilization, of the citizen, of civil war.

For the left, civil war continues to function as a field of intelligibility into the politics of nationalism and empire. Étienne Balibar, for example, has recently turned to the category of civil war to think about the conjuncture of the refugee crisis and terrorist attacks in Europe. In his response to the Paris attacks in November 2015, Balibar calls the closure of Europe's borders to those seeking refuge an act of civil war: "Above all, 'westerners' and 'easterners' *together* must *construct* the language of a new universalism by taking the risk of speaking on behalf of one another. The closure of borders, their imposition, being to the detriment of the multiculturalism of our societies across the region, already constitutes a civil war."[14] Balibar draws upon, indeed reinvents, a long tradition of Marxist thought (one that arguably dates to its formative moment in Engels's first study of the "social war" in industrial society) that has turned to civil war to understand the relations of force that organize society. Balibar's invocation of civil war blurs the boundary between the domestic and the foreign, Europe and its former colonies. But more importantly, his language suggests a different axis upon which to consider political affiliation. His use of "civil war" differs from that of Agamben, Galli, Hardt, Negri, and others, in that Europe's "civil wars" are premised on creating asymmetries between West and East, developed and undeveloped nations, citizens and refugees. Far from molecular and diffuse, "civil war," for Balibar, is *the closure of borders*. Paradoxically, his use of the term extends civic protection to those who are stateless. For by claiming the *closure* of borders to be an act of civil war, he envisions a fictive *civis*, one in which "westerners" and "easterners" (terms that are already in question given the quotation marks Balibar uses) are fellow-citizens. For how else could the closure of borders be an act of "civil war" if those standing on either side of these boundaries were not already fellow-citizens, or at the very least members of the same polity? The "war" that Balibar refers to is simply the refusal of rights to fellow-citizens of this fictive polity. His turn to the language of national rupture therefore serves to expand the idea of Europe because it presupposes a political community across national borders. Only this expansion is not territorial in the imperial sense but what Balibar has elsewhere called a "demographic enlargement"—European citizens and refugees are "fellow-citizens."[15] The "civil war" Balibar speaks of then refers to a fictive polity that both exceeds the borders of the nation-state and links oppositional categories, citizen and refugee, in a different, if impossible, political relationship.[16]

However, recent criticisms of the actual closure of borders to refugees and Muslim immigrants refract Balibar's call for "demographic enlargement" into a justification for the international division of labor. Following the U.S. government's "Muslim ban" of January 2017 (Executive Order 13769), nearly a hundred technology corporations filed an amicus brief opposing the ban on the basis that it impedes business. "People who choose to leave everything that is familiar," the brief declares, "and journey to an unknown land to make a new life necessarily are endowed with drive, creativity, determination—and just plain guts."[17] The "energy" these intrepid migrants bring to the United States "is a key reason why the American economy has been the greatest engine of prosperity and innovation in history."[18] In other words, the suit argues for the reopening of borders while retaining geopolitical difference between an innovative West and tumultuous East. So vast is this difference that it takes heroic efforts—"just plain guts"—to embrace the American dream, a way of life supposedly alien to these "driven," "creative," and "determined" workers. The naiveté of the suit rests on the notion that such vast migrations are merely difficult decisions—"people who choose to leave"—and not forced expulsions or escapes undertaken in duress. To the titans of Silicon Valley, Salim's escape at the end of *A Bend in the River* would read triumphantly "gutsy" (how exactly they might read Metty's lack of choice in leaving civil war–torn Africa, one can only imagine).

The lawsuit crystalizes its vision for the world in the phrase "immigrant-entrepreneurs."[19] One cannot help but read this phrase alongside another, the "citizen-subject," especially given that the occasion for the lawsuit is the most recent crisis of statelessness. The brief supplants the unalienable rights of the citizen-subject and the principle of equality with entrepreneurial prowess. No longer a juridical subject, the immigrant/refugee is reduced to a work ethic. Most perniciously, the suit implies a correspondence between the experience of statelessness and professional expertise. For these aliens to American culture and democracy are defined by the horrors they have witnessed and escaped—horrors that engine the immigrant-entrepreneur's "drive," "creativity," and "determination" to succeed in a foreign land. By this logic, civil wars in the Orient fuel capitalism. The East is still a career.

Notes

INTRODUCTION

1. Chimamanda Ngozi Adichie, *Half of a Yellow Sun* (New York: Anchor Books, 2006), 228.

2. See Émile Benveniste, "Deux Modèles Linguistiques de la Cité," in *Problèmes de Linguistique Générale*, vol. 2 (Paris: Gallimard, 1974), 272–80.

3. World Bank, *Breaking the Conflict Trap: Civil War and Development Policy* (Washington, DC: World Bank, 2003), ix.

4. Ibid.

5. Ibid., 53–54.

6. Ibid., ix.

7. A "new wave" of scholarship on civil war emerged in the 1990s within the field of conflict resolution. See Stathis Kalyvas, "'New' and 'Old' Civil Wars: A Valid Distinction?" *World Politics* 54, no. 1 (October 2001): 99–118; Paul Collier and Nicholas Sambanis, "Understanding Civil War: A New Agenda," *Journal of Conflict Resolution* 46, no. 1 (2002): 3–12; James D. Fearon and David D. Laitin, "Ethnicity, Insurgency, and Civil War," *American Political Science Review* 97, no. 1 (February 2003): 75–90.

8. See Nicholas Sambanis, "What Is Civil War? Conceptual and Empirical Complexities of an Operational Definition," *Journal of Conflict Resolution* 48, no. 6 (December 2004): 814–58; Patrick Regan, *Civil Wars and Foreign Powers: Outside Intervention in Intrastate Conflict* (Ann Arbor: University of Michigan Press, 2002); Melvin Small and J. David Singer, *Resort to Arms: International and Civil Wars, 1816–1980* (Beverly Hills, CA: Sage, 1982).

9. Jacob Mundy's scholarship is exceptional in this regard. His interventions represent the only voice from within the political sciences that offers a critique of recent social scientific approaches to the study of civil war. As

he notes, "Given the incoherence in these various conceptualizations of civil war, it is not surprising that an insurgent discourse has emerged. Growing out of the same international political milieu that witnessed a spike in armed conflicts in the 1990s, a group of scholars began to lay claim on a new ontology of war. . . . The irony of most critiques of the new wars thesis is that they rest upon the assumption that categories such as civil war are conceptually coherent across the literature, which . . . is clearly not the case." "Deconstructing Civil Wars: Beyond the New Wars Debate," *Security Dialogue* 42, no. 3 (2011): 282–83. See also Jacob Mundy, *Imaginative Geographies of Algerian Violence: Conflict Science, Conflict Management, Antipolitics* (Stanford: Stanford University Press, 2015), 31–45.

10. Donald M. Snow argues in his revealingly titled book, *UnCivil Wars* (1996), that contemporary civil wars in the peripheries are "less principled in political terms, less focused on the attainment of some political ideal. They seem more vicious and uncontrolled in their conduct. . . . Rampages by groups within states against one another with little or no apparent ennobling purpose or outcome; they are, indeed, uncivil wars." *UnCivil Wars: International Security and the New Internal Conflicts* (Boulder, CO: Lynne Rienner, 1996), 1–2.

11. For the World Bank's position on intervention, see especially chapter 5 of *Breaking the Conflict Trap*, 121–72. For a critique of similar policies from almost two decades before the Bank's report, see Mahmood Mamdani, "How Not to Intervene in Internal Conflicts," *Security Dialogue* 20, no. 4 (1989): 437–40.

12. Edward Said, *Orientalism* (New York: Vintage, 1979), 3.

13. *The Letters of Charles Dickens*, ed. Graham Storey and Kathleen Tillotson, vol. 8, *1856–1858* (Oxford: Clarendon Press, 1995), 459–60. See also Grace Moore, *Dickens and Empire: Discourses of Class, Race, and Colonialism in the Works of Charles Dickens* (Aldershot: Ashgate, 2004); Christopher Herbert, *The War of No Pity: The Indian Mutiny and Victorian Trauma* (Princeton: Princeton University Press, 2009); Gautam Chakravarty, *The Indian Mutiny and the British Imagination* (Cambridge: Cambridge University Press, 2004). Tellingly, when the term "civil war" was used by Victorians in the context of the Mutiny, it described instances of Britons massacring allies of the British army. See General Hope Grant's reflections on the Mutiny in *Incidents in the Sepoy War: 1857-8* (Edinburgh: William Blackwood and Sons, 1873), 234–35.

14. Karl Marx, *The Civil War in the United States* (New York: International Press, 1971), 81; John Stuart Mill, *The Contest in America* (Boston: Little, Brown, 1862), 30–31.

15. For an account of Victorian understandings of civility as sociability, see Christopher Lane, *Hatred and Civility: The Antisocial Life in Victorian England* (New York: Columbia University Press, 2004); Kent Puckett, *Bad Form: Social Mistakes and the Nineteenth-Century Novel* (Oxford: Oxford University Press, 2008). For a discussion of civility as a Foucauldian disciplinary technique in the British empire, see Anindyo Roy, *Civility and Empire: Literature and Culture in British India, 1822–1922* (London: Routledge, 2005).

16. For an etymological study of the term "civilization," see Émile Benveniste, "Civilization: A Contribution to the History of the World," in *Problems in General Linguistics* (Miami: Miami University Press, 1973), 289–96.

17. Norbert Elias, *The Civilizing Process: Sociogenetic and Psychogenetic Investigations*, trans. Edmund Jephcott (Malden, MA: Blackwell, 1982), 5.

18. Étienne Balibar, *Politics and the Other Scene*, trans. Christine Jones, James Swenson, and Chris Turner (London: Verso, 2002), 30n36. Roy argues that nineteenth-century British discourses of civility created a "differential dynamic" with the colonies, edifying metropolitan ideas of civility against the presumed incivility of the colonial subject. *Civility and Empire*, 8.

19. The messiness of terms like "Orient," "periphery," "Third World," "developing nations," and "Global South" is inherent to the archive I am examining. When I use these terms in this book, I refer less to geographical coordinates (which are static) than geopolitical demarcations (which are dynamic and elastic) between the West and the non-West. While the Orient is typically applicable to places like the Middle East, Asia, and North Africa (and to a lesser degree sub-Saharan Africa), I use it to describe Latin American settings like the Banda Orientál in William Henry Hudson's *The Purple Land* (1885) and Joseph Conrad's Costaguana in *Nostromo* (1904) because I see the same dynamic between Occident and Orient operative there.

20. See David Armitage's overview of the concept of civil war in political thought from ancient Rome to the present in *Civil War: A History in Ideas* (New York: Alfred A. Knopf, 2017).

21. For a study of how literature functions as a counterdiscourse to the social sciences and think-tank discourse, see John Marx, *Geopolitics and the Anglophone Novel, 1890–2011* (Cambridge: Cambridge University Press, 2012). I discuss Marx's intervention at greater length in Chapters 6 and 7.

22. Michel Foucault, *The Punitive Society*, trans. Graham Burchell, ed. Bernard Harcourt (New York: Palgrave Macmillan, 2015), 29.

23. Ibid., 31.

24. Étienne Balibar and Immanuel Wallerstein, *Race, Nation, Class: Ambiguous Identities*, trans. Chris Turner (London: Verso, 1991), 86. Balibar's notion is not unlike Cornelius Castoriadis's understanding of the "social imaginary" in *The Imaginary Institution of Society*, trans. Kathleen Blamey (Cambridge, MA: MIT Press, 1987). Stathis Gourgouris adapts Castoriadis's thought for the study of nationalism, noting that "a society's imaginary is the 'ground' of that society's institution. . . . Moreover, while providing the 'ground' for society's coherence, this social imaginary cannot ever exist outside the bounds of that society; it is, in other words, also instituted by that society." *Dream Nation: Enlightenment, Colonization, and the Institution of Modern Greece* (Stanford: Stanford University Press, 1996), 14.

25. Benedict Anderson, *Imagined Communities: Reflections on the Origins and Spread of Nationalism*, rev. ed. (London: Verso, 2006), 7. For critiques of Anderson's thesis, see Partha Chatterjee, "Whose Imagined Community?" in *The Nation and Its Fragments* (Princeton: Princeton University Press, 1993), 3–13; Gayatri Chakravorty Spivak, *Nationalism and the Imagination* (Kolkata: Seagull Books, 2010), 83–84.

26. Achille Mbembe argues that "contemporary forms of subjugation of life to the power of death (necropolitics) profoundly reconfigure the relations among resistance, sacrifice, and terror. . . . The notion of biopower is insufficient to account for contemporary forms of subjugation of life to the power of death." "Necropolitics," trans. Libby Meintjes, *Public Culture* 15, no. 1 (2003): 39–40.

27. For a discussion of civil war's conceptual proximity to revolution, see Hannah Arendt, *On Revolution* (London: Penguin, 1963); David Armitage, "Every Great Revolution Is a Civil War," in *Scripting Revolution: A Historical Approach to the Comparative Study of Revolutions*, ed. Keith Michael Baker and Dan Edelstein (Stanford: Stanford University Press, 2015), 57–68.

28. Mahmood Mamdani, "The Politics of Naming," *London Review of Books* 29, no. 5 (2007): 5–8. For Mamdani's analysis of the Sudanese civil war in the context of international interventionism, see *Saviours and Survivors: Darfur, Politics, and the War on Terror* (Cape Town: HSRC Press, 2009).

29. Ernst Renan, "What Is a Nation?" in *Nation and Narration*, ed. Homi Bhabha (London: Routledge, 1990), 11.

30. Homi Bhabha makes a similar point in his reading of Renan but criticizes Anderson for assuming the homogeneity of the nation's historiographic imagination. *The Location of Culture* (London: Routledge, 1994), 159–60. For a similar account of forgetting civil war in the context of ancient Greece, see Nicole Loraux's study of *stasis* in *The Divided City: On Memory and Forgetting in Ancient Athens*, trans. Corinne Pache and Jeff Fort (New York: Zone Books, 2001). While Loraux speaks of a very different kind of political assemblage from the nation, the *polis* of classical Greece, her description of the need to forget *stasis* is markedly like Anderson's analysis of the reassurance of fratricide.

31. Anderson, *Imagined Communities*, 26.

32. Paul Ricoeur sees this as operating in a polarity between two kinds of memory: "It is in relation to this exclusion—to this primordial not-now—of the past nevertheless retained that a new kind of polarity is suggested within the not-now of memory itself. This is the polarity of primary and secondary memory of retention and reproduction." *History, Memory, Forgetting*, trans. Kathleen Blamey and David Pellauer (Chicago: University of Chicago Press, 2004), 35. By "reproduction," Ricoeur means those memories that have faded away but can still come back. In contrast, "Retention still hangs onto the perception of the moment. . . . It is re-presentation. It is the same melody but heard 'as it were'" (ibid.). For an account of the tension between history and memory, see Pierre Nora, "Between History and Memory: *Les Lieux de Mémoire*," trans. Marc Roudebush, *Representations* 26 (1989): 7–24; Eelco Runia, *Moved by the Past: Discontinuity and Historical Mutation* (New York: Columbia University Press, 2014), 17–48.

33. A recent special issue of *American Historical Review* titled "Ending Civil Wars" points to the problem of closure in the historicization of civil wars. See Alex Lichtenstein, ed., *American Historical Review* 120, no. 5 (December 2015): 1682–1837.

34. Michel Foucault, *"Society Must Be Defended,"* trans. David Macey, ed. Mauro Bertani and Alessandro Fontana (New York: Picador, 2003), 15. It

should be noted that Foucault simply uses Clausewitz's formulation as a counterpoint to help illustrate the innovation of race war discourse, which in fact preceded the publication of Clausewitz's *On War* (1832).

35. Hannah Arendt, *The Origins of Totalitarianism* (New York: Harvest Books, 1976), 159.

36. Arthur Conan Doyle, *The Great Boer War* (London: Smith, Elder, & Co., 1901), 527.

37. Timothy Brennan puts it succinctly: "It was the *novel* that historically accompanied the rise of nations by objectifying the 'one, yet many' of national life, and by mimicking the structure of the nation, a clearly bordered jumble of languages and styles." "The Nation Longing for Form," in *Nation and Narration*, ed. Homi K. Bhabha (London: Routledge, 1990), 49.

38. Jonathan Culler, "Anderson and the Novel," in *Grounds of Comparison: Around the Work of Benedict Anderson*, ed. Jonathan Culler and Pheng Cheah (New York: Routledge, 2003), 48.

39. Such possibilities, David Lloyd notes, often have a "regulative function." *Anomalous States: Irish Writing and the Post-Colonial Moment* (Durham: Duke University Press, 1993), 154. In a rebuttal of Anderson's privileging of the novel as the vessel of the nationalist ideal, Lloyd states that in the case of Ireland, "the dialogism of the novel is not confined to its production of an anti-*imperial* national culture but also involves . . . the subordination of alternative narratives within a multiply voiced national culture. For the novel not only gives voice to formally voiceless national elites, but also disenfranchises other possible voices" (ibid.).

40. György Lukács, *The Historical Novel*, trans. Hannah Mitchell and Stanley Mitchell (London: Merlin Press, 1962), 23, 24.

41. Ibid., 24.

42. Balibar and Wallerstein, *Race, Nation, Class*, 100.

43. Jed Esty, *Unseasonable Youth: Modernism, Colonialism and the Fiction of Development* (Oxford: Oxford University Press, 2011).

44. Anderson, *Imagined Communities*, 86.

45. Giorgio Agamben, *State of Exception*, trans. Keven Attell (Chicago: University of Chicago Press, 2005), 2.

46. Thomas Hobbes, *Leviathan* (London: Penguin, 1985), 233. See also Foucault's reading of *Leviathan* in *"Society Must Be Defended,"* 87–114. The English Civil War is also the focus of Hobbes's lesser-known work *Behemoth, or, The Long Parliament*, ed. Ferdinand Tönnies (Chicago: University of Chicago Press, 1990).

47. Carl Schmitt, *The Concept of the Political*, trans. George Schwab (Chicago: University of Chicago Press, 1996), 32, 47.

48. Giorgio Agamben, *Homo Sacer: Sovereign Power and Bare Life*, trans. Daniel Heller-Roazen (Stanford: Stanford University Press, 1998), 178.

49. Ibid., 177.

50. Giorgio Agamben, *Stasis: Civil War as a Political Paradigm*, trans. Nicholas Heron (Stanford: Stanford University Press, 2015), 16. For a very different but highly illuminating study on the Greek idea of civil war, or *stasis*, see Loraux, *The Divided City*.

51. Michel Foucault, *The History of Sexuality, Volume 1: An Introduction*, trans. Robert Hurley (New York: Pantheon Books, 1978), 89.

52. Mary Poovey, *Making a Social Body* (Chicago: University of Chicago Press, 1995), 4; Linda Colley, *Britons: Forging the Nation: 1707–1837*, rev. ed. (New Haven: Yale University Press, 2012).

PART I

1. With the exception, perhaps, of Edward Said, for whom earlier texts like *The Order of Things* and *Archeology of Knowledge* were more influential. See, for example, Said, *Beginnings: Intention and Method* (New York: Columbia University Press, 1975), 277–343.

2. Nathan K. Hensley's *Forms of Empire: The Poetics of Victorian Sovereignty* (Oxford: Oxford University Press, 2016) is unique in this regard. Other works that make use of Foucault's lectures include Nancy Armstrong, "Gender Must Be Defended," *South Atlantic Quarterly* 111, no. 3 (2012): 529–47; and Zarena Aslami, *The Dream Life of Citizens: Late Victorian Novels and the Fantasy of the State* (New York: Fordham University Press, 2012).

3. Foucault, *"Society Must Be Defended,"* 58.

4. Ibid., 237.

5. Ibid., 58.

6. Ibid., 51.

7. Ibid., 69.

8. Ibid., 65–66. Such "race thinking," as Hannah Arendt calls it, connotes one half of a dialectic in which two races cohabit the same polity and national institutions. *Origins of Totalitarianism*, 158–75.

9. Foucault, *"Society Must Be Defended,"* 77.

10. For one of the most substantial studies of biopolitics and nineteenth-century British studies, see Emily Steinlight, "Dickens's 'Supernumeraries' and the Biopolitical Imagination of Victorian Fiction," *NOVEL: A Forum on Fiction* 43, no. 2 (2010): 227–50. For a discussion of governmentality in Victorian literature and culture, see Lauren Goodlad, *Victorian Literature and the Victorian State: Character and Governance in a Liberal Society* (Baltimore: Johns Hopkins University Press, 2003).

11. Foucault defines biopolitics as the power to "make live and let die," a departure from forms of sovereignty that derived their power for the right to "take life or let live." The inversion marks a turning point at which sovereignty became a mode of governance of entire human populations. Foucault only offers a sketch of biopolitics in *"Society"* but elaborates and develops the concept at much greater length in *The History of Sexuality: Volume 1*, as well as in his subsequent courses (albeit in revised form), now published as *Security, Territory, Population* (1977–78) and *The Birth of Bio-Politics* (1978–79).

12. Ann Laura Stoler has argued that the lectures differ from *The History of Sexuality* because they are focused not on the productive elements of biopower but on a built-in self-defensiveness of bourgeois society: "One of the more riveting themes of the lectures, on the production of 'internal enemies' within the body politic, alters our reading of *The History of Sexuality* in yet

another way. Foucault's finer tracing in the lectures of a 'racism that a society will practice against itself' provides a strong rationale for two of his claims: that the biopolitical management of life was a critical bourgeois project and that the management of sexuality was crucial to it. His contention in *The History of Sexuality* that the affirmation of the bourgeois self was secured through specific technologies centered on sexuality emerges in the lectures as part of a specific set of strategies not only of self affirmation . . . but self-defense of a bourgeois society against the internal dangers it has produced." *Race and the Education of Desire: Foucault's "History of Sexuality" and the Colonial Order of Things* (Durham: Duke University Press, 1995), 92.

13. W. L. Burn coined the phrase in *The Age of Equipoise: A Study of the Mid-Victorian Generation* (London: Allen and Unwin, 1964). For a more recent revisitation of Burns's thesis, see Martin Hewitt, ed., *An Age of Equipoise? Reassessing Mid-Victorian Britain* (Burlington, VT: Ashgate, 2001); Francesco Marroni, *Victorian Disharmonies: A Reconsideration of Nineteenth-Century English Fiction* (Rome: John Cabot University Press, 2010).

14. For a study of the Victorian discourse of "two nations" and the crisis of national unity, see Shiela M. Smith, *The Other Nation: Poor in English Novels of the 1840s and 1850s* (Oxford: Clarendon Press, 1980).

15. Anonymous, "Review of *London Labour and the London Poor*," *Christian Observer* 52 (1852): 236.

16. Charles Dickens, *Sketches by Boz* (London: Penguin, 1995), 96.

17. Friedrich Engels, *The Conditions of the Working-Class in England* (Oxford: Oxford University Press, 2009), 135.

18. Similarly, when Jane Eyre contemplates her plight in Gateshead, she echoes the tumult that saturated Europe in the 1840s: "Unjust!—unjust! . . . What a consternation of soul was mine that dreary afternoon! How all my brain was in tumult, and all my heart in insurrection! Yet in what darkness, what dense ignorance, was the mental battle fought!" Charlotte Brontë, *Jane Eyre* (London: Penguin Classics, 2006), 19.

19. Elizabeth Gaskell, *North and South* (London: Penguin Classics, 1996), 84.

20. Franco Moretti, *Atlas of the European Novel: 1800–1900* (London: Verso, 1998), 17–18.

21. Poovey, *Making a Social Body*, 4.

22. Colley, *Britons*, 373–84. See also Linda Colley, "Britishness and Otherness: An Argument," *Journal of British Studies* 31, no. 4 (1992): 309–29.

CHAPTER 1

1. Walter Benjamin, *The Writer of Modern Life: Essays on Charles Baudelaire*, ed. Michael W. Jennings (Cambridge, MA: Harvard University Press, 2006), 40.

2. Ira Katznelson, *Marxism and the City* (Oxford: Clarendon Press, 1992), 153–54.

3. Henri Lefebvre, *The Production of Space*, trans. Donald Nicholson-Smith (Oxford: Blackwell, 1991), 84.

4. Ibid., 85.

5. Engels, *The Conditions of the Working-Class in England*, 36. Subsequent citations appear parenthetically in the text.

6. Alexis de Tocqueville, *Journeys to England and Ireland*, trans. George Lawrence and K. P. Mayer (New Haven: Yale University Press, 1958), 108.

7. Henry Mayhew, *London Labour and the London Poor* (London: Griffin, Bohn, and Company, 1861), 2.

8. Engels remained interested in war throughout his career. For more on the role of war in his later works, see *The Role of Force in History: A Study of Bismarck's Policy of Blood and Iron*, ed. Ernst Wangermann (New York: International Publishers, 1968). See also Azar Gat, "Clausewitz and the Marxists: Yet Another Look," *Journal of Contemporary History* 27, no. 2 (1992): 363–82.

9. Benjamin Disraeli will pick up on the trope of conquest in *Sybil, or, The Two Nations*, which I discuss at length in Chapter 3.

10. This is not to say that Marx never talks about civil wars as historical events. In his writings on 1848 in France and the American Civil War, he consistently describes revolution and counterrevolution as a historical episode rather than an ongoing latent war. See *The Civil War in France: The Paris Commune* (New York: International Publishers, 1988); and *The Civil War in the United States*.

11. Étienne Balibar, "Marxism and War," *Radical Philosophy* 160 (2010): 9.

12. Lukács, *The Historical Novel*, 173, 175–76.

13. Karl Marx and Friedrich Engels, *Collected Works*, vol. 39, *1852–1855* (New York: International Publishers, 1983), 473.

14. Foucault, *"Society Must Be Defended,"* 48.

15. Foucault notes that Clausewitz was in fact responding to the discourse of race war, which significantly preceded him. For a fuller sense of Clausewitz's intervention, see Étienne Balibar, "Reflections on *Gewalt*," *Historical Materialism* 17 (2009): 99–125.

16. See Pasquale Pasquiano, "Political Theory of War and Peace: Foucault and the History of Modern Political Theory," *Economy and Society* 22, no. 1 (1993): 77–88.

17. Foucault, *"Society Must Be Defended,"* 50–51.

18. For a reading of Engels's understanding of visibility and structural violence, see Yves Winter, "Violence and Visibility," *New Political Science* 34, no. 2 (2012): 195–202.

19. Balibar, "Marxism and War," 10–11.

20. Karl Marx and Friedrich Engels, *The Marx-Engels Reader*, 2nd ed., ed. Robert Tucker (New York: W. W. Norton, 1978), 474.

21. Balibar, "Marxism and War," 11.

22. Marx, *The Civil War in the United States*, 81.

23. Karl Marx, *Capital: A Critique of Political Economy*, vol. 1, trans. Ben Fowkes (New York: Vintage, 1977), 412–13.

24. Eduard Bernstein, *The Preconditions for Socialism*, trans. and ed. Henry Tudor (Cambridge: Cambridge University Press, 1993), 1–8.

25. Georges Sorel, *Reflections on Violence*, ed. Jeremy Jennings (Cambridge: Cambridge University Press, 1999), 47–48. Joshua Clover has recently

argued that since the global financial crisis of 1973, the strike is vanishing as the horizon of class war, giving way instead to a return of the riot. See *Riot. Strike. Riot: The New Era of Uprisings* (New York: Verso, 2016).

26. Rosa Luxemburg, *The Essential Rosa Luxemburg: "Reform or Revolution" and "The Mass Strike,"* ed. Helen Scott (Chicago: Haymarket Books, 2008), 111–81.

27. V. I. Lenin, "The Russian Revolution and Civil War," in *Collected Works*, vol. 26 (Moscow: Progress Publishers, 1972), 28–42.

28. The exception for Benjamin is what he calls "sovereign violence," which breaks the cycle of violence and law of "mythical violence," and founds a new historical epoch. "Critique of Violence," in *Reflections*, trans. Edmund Jephcott (New York: Schocken Books, 1986), 287. See also Jacques Derrida, "Force of Law," in *Deconstruction and the Possibility of Justice*, ed. Drucilla Cornell, Michael Rosenfield, and David G. Carlson (London: Routledge, 1992), 3–67.

29. Antonio Gramsci, *Selections from the Prison Notebooks*, trans. and ed. Quintin Hoare and Geoffrey Nowell Smith (New York: International Publishers, 1971), 175–85. The importance of these categories is evident in Partha Chatterjee's history of Indian anticolonial nationalism in *Nationalist Thought and the Colonial World* (Minneapolis: University of Minnesota Press, 1986), 43–49.

30. Mao Tse-Tung, *On Protracted War*, 3rd ed. (Peking: Foreign Languages Press, 1967); Carl Schmitt, *Theory of the Partisan: Intermediary Commentary on the Concept of the Political*, trans. G. L. Ulmen (New York: Telos Publishing, 2007), 39.

31. Étienne Balibar, "In War," *openDemocracy*, November 16, 2015, https://www.opendemocracy.net/can-europe-make-it/etienne-balibar/in-war. I will return to Balibar's formulation of an "international civil war" in the coda of this book.

32. Balibar, "Marxism and War," 9.

33. Ibid.

34. Alan Robinson, *Imagining London, 1770–1900* (New York: Palgrave Macmillan, 2004), 80.

35. For a study of realist narration's origins in the journalistic sketch, see J. Hillis Miller, "The Fiction of Realism: *Sketches by Boz, Oliver Twist*, and Cruikshank's Illustrations," in *Victorian Subjects* (Durham: Duke University Press, 1991), 119–77; see also Amanpal Garcha, *From Sketch to Novel: The Development of Victorian Fiction* (Oxford: Oxford University Press, 2008).

36. Louis Althusser and Étienne Balibar, *Reading Capital*, trans. Ben Brewster (New York: Verso, 2009), 21.

37. James Buzard, *Disorienting Fiction: The Autoethnographic Work of Nineteenth-Century British Novels* (Princeton: Princeton University Press, 2005), 12.

38. Dickens, *Sketches by Boz*, 71.

39. Steven Marcus, *Engels, Manchester and the Working Class* (New York: Vintage, 1975), 98.

40. Aruna Krishnamurthy, "'More than Abstract Knowledge': Friedrich Engels in Industrial Manchester," *Victorian Literature and Culture* 48, no. 2 (2000): 428.

41. Ibid., 444.

42. Engels's seemingly "native knowledge" of Manchester was also made possible by a fellow-foreigner, Mary Burns, an Irish factory worker. For a discussion of Burns's influence on Engels, see Marcus, *Engels, Manchester, and the Working Class*, 98–100.

43. Michel de Certeau, *The Practice of Everyday Life*, trans. Steven Randall (Berkeley: University of California Press, 1984), 116.

44. Much has been written about whether Engels's descriptions accurately represent Manchester in the 1840s. Richard Dennis, for example, goes so far as to call Engels's descriptions of the modern city "propagandist" because "it was important to Engels that all towns should be alike, since to convince his readers of the universality of the class struggle and the need for revolution he needed to demonstrate the universality of unscrupulous landlords, exploitation in the market place and exploitation at work." *English Industrial Cities of the Nineteenth Century: A Social Geography* (Cambridge: Cambridge University Press, 1984), 24. Even official reports of the 1840s sought to "demonstrate that problems (sanitary reform, cheap housing, model bye-laws) everywhere were the same" because they "were prepared in the expectation of national legislation or central government intervention" (ibid.). See also David Ward, "Victorian Cities: How Modern?" *Journal of Historical Geography* 2, no. 1 (1975): 135–51.

45. de Certeau, *The Practice of Everyday Life*, 120.

46. Ibid.

47. Ibid., 119.

48. Moretti, *Atlas of the European Novel*, 84.

49. Ibid., 84–86.

50. Charles Dickens, *Oliver Twist* (London: Penguin, 2003), 283.

51. Dickens, *Sketches by Boz*, 92.

52. Ibid., 94.

53. Ibid.

54. Jonathan Grossman, *Charles Dickens's Networks: Public Transport and the Novel* (Oxford: Oxford University Press, 2013), 64–69. Grossman argues that essential to Boz's depiction of a singular society are public forms of connectivity, such as public transport, to which Dickens devotes several sketches.

55. Charles Dickens, *Bleak House* (London: Penguin, 1996), 903.

56. D. A. Miller, *The Novel and the Police* (Berkeley: University of California Press, 1988).

57. Frank Kermode, *The Sense of an Ending: Studies in the Theory of Fiction* (New York: Oxford University Press, 1967).

CHAPTER 2

1. "The Manifesto of the Communist Party" declares: "The bourgeoisie, wherever it has got the upper hand, has put an end to all feudal, patriarchal, idyllic relations. It has pitilessly torn asunder the motley feudal ties that bound man to his 'natural superiors', and has left remaining no other nexus between

man and man than naked self-interest, than callous 'cash payment'" (*The Marx and Engels Reader*, 475). Marx and Engels revised their praise for Carlyle in a review of the *Latter-Day Pamphlets*, where they proclaim that while his earlier writings were "revolutionary," his later work was theological. See Karl Marx and Frederick Engels, *Collected Works*, vol. 10, *1849–51* (New York: International Publishers, 1978), 301–10. See also Lukács's account of the rise of reactionary rhetoric in the post-1848 period in *The Historical Novel*, 177–78.

2. Thomas Carlyle, *"Chartism" and "Past and Present"* (London: Chapman and Hall, 1843), 36. Subsequent citations appear parenthetically in the text.

3. Ferdinand Tönnies, *Community and Civil Society*, trans. Jose Harris and Margaret Hollis (Cambridge: Cambridge University Press, 2001), 17.

4. Jean-Joseph Goux explains that the universal equivalent has a centralizing function in society: "The general equivalent functions as head and capital of a divided territory from which it is barred as empty, omnipotent center. Supplanting the diversity of relationships among elements in this univocal, exclusive relationship to the general equivalent which *magnetizes* or *funnels* toward its ideal center all value relationships, making them its tributary rays." Jean-Joseph Goux, *Symbolic Economies: After Marx and Freud*, trans. Jennifer Curtiss Gage (Ithaca: Cornell University Press, 1990), 45. For a discussion of Carlyle, Goux, and secularism, see John M. Ulrich, *Signs of Their Times: History, Labor, and the Body in Cobbett, Carlyle, and Disraeli* (Athens: Ohio University Press, 2002), 88–95.

5. This is one of Engels's major criticisms of Carlyle in his review of *Past and Present*: "What Carlyle says about Democracy, incidentally, leaves little to be desired. . . . Democracy, true enough, is only a transitional stage, though not towards a new, improved aristocracy [as Carlyle suggests], but towards real human freedom." Marx and Engels, *Collected Works*, vol. 39, *March 1843–August 1844* (London: Lawrence and Wishart, 1975), 466. For an account of Carlyle's move toward conservatism over his career, see Chris R. Vanden Bossche, *Carlyle and the Search for Authority* (Columbus: Ohio University Press, 1991).

6. Although Carlyle's depiction of the capitalist might seem extreme, it should be remembered that his biblical metaphor renders the worker into a mere victim who doesn't resist the Millowner; he is as innocent and passive as the unknowing Abel. I will return to the ideological effects of such a characterization later.

7. Hobbes, *Leviathan*, 223.

8. See also Jan Mieszkowski, "How to Do Things with Clausewitz," *Global South* 3, no. 1 (2009): 18–29.

9. In classical Greek thought, civil war hinges on the word *stasis*, which, unlike its English homonym, describes a precarious state of rest that is the product not of immobility but a tumultuous balance between competing and antagonistic forces. Loraux, *The Divided City*, 93–122. See also Nicole Loraux, "Reflections of the Greek City on Unity and Division," in *City-States in Classical Antiquity and Medieval Italy: Athens and Rome, Florence and*

Venice, ed. Anthony Molho, Kurt Raaflaub, and Julia Emlen (Stuttgart: Franz Steiner, 1991), 33–52; Dimitris Vardoulakis, "The Ends of Stasis: Spinoza as a Reader of Agamben," *Culture, Theory and Critique* 51, no. 2 (2010): 145–56.

10. Franco Moretti, *Signs Taken for Wonders: Essays in the Sociology of Literary Forms* (London: Verso, 1983), 84.

11. Catherine Gallagher calls this "bioeconomics," in which "'Life' is both the ultimate desideratum and the energy or force that circulates through organic and inorganic nature." *The Body Economic: Life, Death, and Sensation in Political Economy and the Victorian Novel* (Princeton: Princeton University Press, 2006), 3. As I argue later, Carlyle's treatment of financial metaphors in *Past and Present* creates what Gallagher calls "somaeconomics," which is deeply rooted in British empiricism as a theory of action complementing Lockean epistemology: "just as we know only what comes through the senses, we are motivated primarily through the sensations (bodily and mental) of pleasure and pain" (ibid., 4).

12. See Mary Poovey's *Making a Social Body* and Pamela Gilbert, *Mapping the Victorian Social Body* (Albany: State University of New York Press, 2004).

13. John Plotz, *The Crowd: British Literature and Public Politics* (Berkeley: University of California Press, 2000), 137.

14. Ibid., 144.

15. Dickens, *Bleak House,* 107.

16. See also Joseph Childers, "Carlyle's *Past and Present,* History, and a Question of Hermeneutics," *Clio* 13, no. 3 (1984): 247–58; Erin M. Gross, "Reading Cant, Transforming the Nation: Carlyle's *Past and Present,*" in *Victorian Transformations: Genre, Nationalism and Desire in Nineteenth-Century Literature,* ed. Bianca Tredennick (Farnham: Ashgate, 2011), 95–114.

17. For a fuller account of the debates regarding the politics surrounding Peterloo and specifically its historiography, see Robert Poole, "'By the Law of the Sword': Peterloo Revisited," *History* 91, no. 302 (2006): 254–76.

18. E. P. Thompson, *The Making of the English Working Class* (New York: Vintage, 1966), 687; see also Thompson, *Making History: Writings on History and Culture* (New York: New Press, 1994), 185.

19. James Chandler, *England in 1819: The Politics of Literature Culture and the Case of Romantic Historicism* (Chicago: University of Chicago Press, 1998), 84. See also Dror Wahrman, *Imagining the Middle Class: The Political Representation of Class in Britain, c. 1780–1840* (Cambridge: Cambridge University Press, 1995), 200–214.

20. Nancy Armstrong, *Desire and Domestic Fiction: A Political History of the Novel* (Oxford: Oxford University Press, 1990), 169.

21. Thompson, *Making History,* 687, 689.

22. Peter Linebaugh and Marcus Rediker argue that the image of the hydra has a long relationship to class struggles, particularly in the context of British imperialism: "From the beginning of English colonial expansion in the early seventeenth century through the metropolitan industrialization of the early nineteenth, rulers referred to the Hercules-hydra myth to describe the difficulty of imposing order on increasingly global systems of labor." Peter Linebaugh and Marcus Rediker, *The Many-Headed Hydra: Sailors, Slaves,*

Commoners and the Hidden History of the Revolutionary Atlantic (Boston: Beacon Press, 2000), 3.

23. This is not to suggest that statistical abstractions are not the only means by which Carlyle represents the Insurrection. As Plotz notes, "We are not, in Carlyle's account, witnessing labor organized behind a rational collection of grievances. Action is taken away from men here, and vested in time . . . , taken away from time and vested in machines . . . , taken away from machines and vested in Parliament . . . , taken away from Parliament and vested in ambiguous statistical abstractions . . . , taken away from abstractions and vested in weapons . . . , taken away from weapons and vested in natural phenomena." Plotz, *The Crowd*, 139–40.

24. György Lukács, *History and Class Consciousness: Studies in Marxist Dialectics*, trans. Rodney Livingstone (Cambridge, MA: MIT Press, 1971), 91.

25. Michael Klotz likens statistical representation to novelistic realism, for both provide "a means of representing those individuals who do not possess any extraordinary or radically atypical features." "Manufacturing Fictional Individuals: Victorian Social Statistics, the Novel, and *Great Expectations*," *NOVEL: A Forum on Fiction* 46, no. 2 (2013): 215. But where the forms of representation differ is the novel's valorization of the individual as a character: "Like novelistic writing, statistical description sets out to produce a capacious and inclusive view of humanity, though at a comparatively diminished level of individual description" (ibid.). Hence Carlyle is unconcerned about the individuals who were a part of Peterloo—they are abstracted into quantifiable units of "calculation."

26. Alain Desrosières, *The Politics of Large Numbers: A History of Statistical Reasoning*, trans. Camille Naish (Cambridge, MA: Harvard University Press, 2002), 61.

27. Audrey Jaffe, *The Affective Life of the Average Man: The Victorian Novel and the Stock Market Graph* (Columbus: Ohio State University Press, 2010), 2. For recent work on the role of statistics in literary representation, specifically as they relate to Realism, see Jesse Rosenthal, "The Large Novel and the Law of Large Numbers, or, Why George Eliot Hates Gambling," *ELH* 77, no. 3 (Fall 2010): 777–811; Catherine Gallagher, "George Eliot: Immanent Victorian," *Representations* 90, no. 1 (2005): 61–74.

28. Jaffe, *The Affective Life of the Average Man*, 12.

29. E. P. Thompson, "Time, Work-Discipline, and Industrial Capitalism," *Past and Present* 38 (1967): 56–97; Paul Glennie and Nigel Thrift, "Reworking E. P. Thompson's 'Time, Work-Discipline and Industrial Capitalism,'" *Time Society* 5 (1996): 275–99.

30. Peter Brooks, *Reading for the Plot: Design and Intention in Narrative* (Cambridge, MA: Harvard University Press, 1992), 12.

31. Paul Ricoeur, "Narrative Time," *Critical Inquiry* 7, no. 1 (1980): 178–79. Brooks succinctly paraphrases Ricoeur's notion of plot as a "shaping function." *Reading for the Plot*, 14.

32. Paul Ricoeur, *Time and Narrative*, vol. 1 (Chicago: University of Chicago Press, 1990), 67.

33. Ibid.

34. Ibid.

35. Brooks, *Reading for the Plot*, 26.

36. Thomas Carlyle, *Historical Essays*, ed. Chris R. Vanden Bossche, Joel J. Brattin, and D. J. Trela (Berkeley: University of California Press, 2005), 7.

37. Ibid., 8.

38. Paul E. Kerry and Marylu Hill argue that for Carlyle "narrative is an unavoidable yet inadequate medium that filters our understanding. This tension between its necessity and its inadequacy highlights the importance of constant mediation." Paul E. Kerry and Marylu Hill, *Thomas Carlyle Resartus* (Teaneck, NJ: Fairleigh Dickinson University Press, 2010), 149.

39. John D. Rosenberg, *Carlyle and the Burden of History* (Cambridge, MA: Harvard University Press, 1986), 29–30.

40. Carlyle, *Historical Essays*, 19.

41. Hayden White notes that for Carlyle, representation requires "a twofold movement of thought and imagination . . . by which things are first apprehended in their *similarity* to other things *and then* grasped in their uniqueness, or *difference*, from everything else." *Metahistory: The Historical Imagination in Nineteenth-Century Europe* (Baltimore: Johns Hopkins University Press, 1973), 148.

42. See Ann Rigney, *Imperfect Histories: The Elusive Past and the Legacy of Romantic Historicism* (Ithaca: Cornell University Press, 2001), 99–120.

43. J. Hillis Miller, *Victorian Subjects* (Durham: Duke University Press, 1991), 304.

44. Brooks, *Reading for the Plot*, 38.

45. Matthew Arnold, *Culture and Anarchy* (Oxford: Oxford University Press, 2006).

46. Edward Said importantly notes that Arnold's idea of culture is better understood as *national* culture. "Secular Criticism," in *The World, the Text, and the Critic* (Cambridge, MA: Harvard University Press, 1983), 1–30.

47. Poovey, *Making a Social Body*, 65–66.

48. See Roger Swift, "Thomas Carlyle, *Chartism*, and the Irish in Early Victorian England," *Victorian Literature and Culture* 29, no. 1 (2001): 67–83.

49. Engels, *The Conditions of the Working-Class in England*, 102.

50. Mary Jean Corbett, *Allegories of Union in Irish and English Writing, 1790–1870: Politics, History, and the Family from Edgeworth to Arnold* (Cambridge: Cambridge University Press, 2000), 87.

51. Ibid. See also Luke Gibbons, *Transformations in Irish Culture* (Notre Dame: University of Notre Dame Press, 1996), 150–53.

52. Simon Gikandi, *Maps of Englishness: Writing Identity in the Culture of Colonialism* (New York: Columbia University Press, 1996), 60.

53. Thomas Carlyle and John Stuart Mill, *The Nigger Question and the Negro Question*, ed. Eugene R. August (New York: Appleton Century-Crofts, 1971), 8.

54. Engels, *The Conditions of the Working-Class in England*, 103.

55. Ibid., 104–5.

56. Gaskell, *North and South*, 176.

57. Ibid., 409.

58. David Lloyd, *Nationalism and Minor Literature: James Clarence Mangan and the Emergence of Irish Cultural Nationalism* (Berkeley: University of California Press, 1987), 12–13.

CHAPTER 3

1. Balibar and Wallerstein, *Race, Nation, Class*, 86.

2. Ibid.

3. Shahid Amin understands this distinction as between "event" and "metaphor." The former is the episode that remains "fixed in time," while the latter is what untethers the episode from chronology, making it resonate with subsequent events. Mediating the relationship between these two is the nationalist master narrative, which constructs a "selective national amnesia in relation to specified events which would fit awkwardly, even seriously inconvenience, the nearly woven pattern." *Event, Metaphor, Memory: Chauri Chaura, 1922–1992* (Berkeley: University of California Press, 1995), 19–20.

4. Balibar and Wallerstein, *Race, Nation, Class*, 86.

5. James Anthony Froude, who wrote biographies of both Disraeli and Carlyle, went so far as to say that "the opinions of Benjamin Disraeli, if we take 'Sybil' to be their exponent, were the opinions of the author of 'Past and Present.'" *Lord Beaconsfield* (London: Sampson Low, Marston, Searle and Rivington, 1891), 92. Disraeli's respect for Carlyle was unrequited. Froude writes that Carlyle thought of Disraeli "as a fantastic ape," for he "detested Jews, and looked on Disraeli as an adventurer fishing for fortune in Parliamentary waters. His novels he despised. His chains and velvets and affected airs he looked on as the tawdry love of vulgar ornament characteristic of Houndsditch" (ibid., 84).

6. Benjamin Disraeli, *Sybil, or, The Two Nations* (Oxford: Oxford University Press, 1981), 171. Subsequent citations appear parenthetically in the text.

7. This is in contrast to the more prevalent narrative in the early nineteenth century that saw the Norman Conquest as having beneficial long-term effects. See Karine Bigand, "French Historiography of the English Revolution Under the Restoration: A National or Cross-Channel Dialogue?" *European Journal of English Studies* 14, no. 3 (2010): 249–61.

8. For an overview of early nineteenth-century histories of the rise of the middle class quite different from that of race war discourse, see Wahrman, *Imagining the Middle Class*, 333–52.

9. See Étienne Balibar, "The Genealogical Scheme: Race or Culture?" *Trans-Scripts* 1 (2011): 1–9.

10. For a discussion of Disraeli's historical imagination, see Peter Jupp, "Disraeli's Interpretation of History," in *The Self-Fashioning Disraeli, 1818–1851*, ed. Charles Richmond and Paul Smith (New York: Cambridge University Press, 1999), 131–51.

11. The narrator identifies himself as Disraeli by way of a reference to *Vindication of the English Constitution* (London: Saunders and Otley, 1835), which Disraeli published ten years prior to *Sybil*.

12. Ulrich, *Signs of Their Times*, 109.

13. White, *Metahistory*, 146. Rosemary Bodenheimer has similarly suggested that the novel's narrative energy is fundamentally historical. She explains that "the narrative motion is a theory of history in action. . . . Thus the narrative of *Sybil* works in a number of interlocking ways to excise the present while asserting that it has been here all along. Disraeli's expansions of historical time are meant to suggest a seamless line running back through English history to Jehovah, while his double readings of contemporary events contrive to read those continuities as muffled within politics." Bodenheimer, *The Politics of Story*, 187.

14. Daniel Bivona, *Desire and Contradiction: Imperial Visions and Domestic Debates in Victorian Literature* (Manchester: Manchester University Press, 1990), 13.

15. Peter Brooks's study of melodrama argues that such narratives begin in a "space of innocence" that is subsequently invaded by a villain, "the troubler of innocence." *The Melodramatic Imagination: Balzac, Henry James, Melodrama, and the Mode of Excess* (New Haven: Yale University Press, 1975), 29. The intrusion bifurcates the world of the novel into two moralities—virtue and villainy, a "Manichean structure" that finds its resolution in the defeat of evil and restoration of virtue. Disraeli's historical account has a similar structure, for the medieval past acts as a "space of innocence" when English community thrived. Fratricide corrupts this space, and its agent is Henry VIII.

16. For Disraeli's views on the New Poor Law, see Martin Fido, "The Treatment of Rural Distress in *Sybil*," *Yearbook of English Studies* 5 (1975): 153–63.

17. For more on the Victorian fascination with England's medieval past, see Alice Chandler, *A Dream of Order: The Medieval Ideal in Nineteenth Century English Literature* (London: Routledge, 1971), 152–83.

18. Disraeli, *Vindication of the English Constitution*, 93.

19. For a discussion of the "natural aristocracy" in *Sybil*, see Albert Tucker, "Disraeli and the Natural Aristocracy," *Canadian Journal of Economics and Political Science* 28, no. 1 (1962): 1–15.

20. For a discussion of *Sybil*'s turn to India as a counterpoint to the condition of England question, see Suzanne Daly, *The Empire Inside: Indian Commodities in Victorian Domestic Novels* (Ann Arbor: University of Michigan Press, 2014), 54–56.

21. Carolyn Betensky describes the symmetry as one where the two nations "in their isolation and difference . . . *mirror* each other in their knowledge of and animus toward the other." *Feeling for the Poor: Bourgeois Compassion, Social Action, and the Victorian Novel* (Charlottesville: University of Virginia Press, 2010), 68.

22. Robert O'Kell goes so far as to say that dispossession is "the structural framework of the novel." "Two Nations or One?: Disraeli's Allegorical Romance," *Victorian Studies* 30, no. 2 (1987): 219.

23. For a fuller account of the influences on Disraeli's work, see Shiela M. Smith, "Willenhall and Wodgate: Disraeli's Use of Blue Book Evidence," *Review of English Studies* 13, no. 52 (1962): 368–84; and Martin Fido, "'From His Own Observation': Sources of Working Class Passages in Disraeli's *Sybil*," *Modern Language Review* 72, no. 2 (1977): 268–84.

24. Arendt, *The Origins of Totalitarianism*, 161, 163.

25. Ibid., 162.

26. For a thorough account of the Norman Conquest in the Victorian imagination, see Asa Briggs, "Saxons, Normans and Victorians," in *The Collected Essays of Asa Briggs* (Brighton: University of Sussex Press, 1985), 2:215–35.

27. For a discussion of Foucault, race war, and *Ivanhoe*, see Stoler, *Race and the Education of Desire*, 74–75.

28. Walter Scott, *Ivanhoe* (Oxford: Oxford World's Classics, 2010), 7.

29. Lukács's summation of Scott's fiction contends that his historical novels charted the entirety of English history: "out of the struggle of the Saxons and Normans there arose the English nation, neither Saxon nor Norman; in the same way the bloody Wars of the Roses gave rise to the illustrious reign of the House of Tudor, especially that of Queen Elizabeth; and those class struggles which manifested themselves in the Cromwellian Revolution were finally evened out in the England of today, after a long period of uncertainty and civil war, by the 'Glorious Revolution' and its aftermath." *The Historical Novel*, 32.

30. Scott, *Ivanhoe*, 9.

31. Ibid., 9–10.

32. Ibid., 9.

33. For a study Scott's influence on Disraeli, Thierry, Carlyle, and Macaulay, especially in their understandings of the idea of conquest, see Claire A. Simmons, *Reversing Conquest: History and Myth in Nineteenth-Century British Literature* (New Brunswick, NJ: Rutgers University Press, 1990).

34. Thomas Macaulay, *The History of England from the Ascension of James II* (London: J. M. Dent & Sons Ltd., 1906), 2:10.

35. Augustin Thierry, *The History of the Conquest of England by the Normans*, trans. William Hazlitt (London: David Bogue, 1847), 1:xxviii.

36. Ibid., 309.

37. Foucault, *"Society Must Be Defended,"* 50.

38. Lukács, *The Historical Novel*, 177.

39. Ibid., 176.

40. Thierry, *The Conquest of England*, xix.

41. Ibid., xix–xx.

42. Scott, *Ivanhoe*, 9. Balibar notes that the "linguistic community" that the nation institutes is fully concrete because it "connects individuals with an origin which may at any moment be actualized and which has as its content the *common act* of their own exchanges, of their discursive communication, using the instruments of spoken language and the whole, constantly self-renewing mass of written and recorded texts." *Race, Nation, Class*, 97. See also Balibar's discussion of Fichte's idea of the "internal border" in *Masses, Classes, Ideas: Studies on Politics and Philosophy Before and After Marx*, trans. James Swenson (London: Routledge, 1994), 61–84.

43. Macaulay, *History of England*, 12.

44. Ibid.

45. Thierry, *The History of the Conquest of England by the Normans: Its Causes and Consequences, in England, Scotland, Ireland, and on the Continent*, trans. William Hazlitt (London: David Bogue, 1847), 2:391–92.

46. Jennifer Sampson makes the compelling claim that Disraeli "seeks to affect the future by replaying past events with a difference, but his battleground is 'English minds' rather than English soil." "*Sybil*, or the Two Monarchs," *Studies in Philology* 95, no. 1 (1998): 98.

47. Catherine Gallagher, *The Industrial Reformation of English Fiction* (Chicago: University of Chicago Press, 1985), 215–16.

48. Chris R. Vanden Bossche, *Reform Acts: Chartism, Social Agency and the Victorian Novel, 1832–1867* (Baltimore: Johns Hopkins University Press, 2014), 90.

49. In *Sybil*'s conclusion, the narrator describes the riot as entering a nostalgic place in the national-historical imagination of England, for the townspeople of Marney subsequently "tell wonderful stories of the "great stick-out and the riots of '42" (420).

50. See Betensky, *Feeling for the Poor*; Vanden Bossche, *Reform Acts*, 98; Patrick Parrinder, *Nation and Novel: The English Novel from Its Origins to the Present Day* (Oxford: Oxford University Press, 2006), 170; Bodenheimer, *The Politics of Story*, 168–88; and O'Kell, "Two Nations or One?" 214. Others have maintained that the novel doesn't resolve but in fact reproduces England's internal divisions. See Daniel R. Schwarz, *Disraeli's Fiction* (New York: Palgrave Macmillan, 1979), 124; Gallagher, *The Industrial Reformation of English Fiction*, 216; Patrick Brantlinger, *The Spirit of Reform* (Cambridge, MA: Harvard University Press, 1977), 104; Corbett, *Allegories of Union in Irish and English Writing*, 86–87.

51. Bivona, *Desire and Contradiction*, 13.

52. Balibar and Wallerstein, *Race, Nation, Class*, 100.

53. Raymond Williams, *Culture and Society: 1780–1950* (New York: Columbia University Press, 1983), 109. For a recent rereading of Williams's claim, see Carolyn Lesjak, *Working Fictions: A Genealogy of the Victorian Novel* (Durham: Duke University Press, 2006).

PART II

1. John Acton, *The History of Freedom and Other Essays* (London: Macmillan, 1907), 290.

2. Ibid.

3. Charles Wentworth Dilke, *Greater Britain: A Record of Travel in English-Speaking Countries* (New York: Harper and Brothers, 1869), vii.

4. J. R. Seeley, *The Expansion of England: Two Courses of Lectures* (London: Macmillan, 1914).

5. While these three writers share this assumption, I will delineate their differences in the following chapter.

6. Thomas Macaulay, *Speeches by Lord Macaulay* (London: Oxford University Press, 2008), 359.

7. Dilke, *Greater Britain*, 528.

8. It is important to remember that as inclusive as such a project seems, it was also invested in deferring the colony's arrival into modernity. When Dilke describes an Indian rendition of "Romeo and Juliet, in the Maratta tongue,"

he is as horrified as he is comforted by its failure to stay true to Shakespeare's original. Shakespeare might allow Britons to retain their cultural identity overseas, but he is opaque enough to remain inaccessible to the colonized. John Plotz illuminatingly paraphrases Dilke's response: "Shakespeare travels well *with* us, but let us not be too quick to wish him well among the natives." *Portable Property: Victorian Literature on the Move* (Princeton: Princeton University Press, 2008), 22.

9. Dipesh Chakrabarty, *Provincializing Europe: Postcolonial Thought and Historical Difference* (Princeton: Princeton University Press, 2000), 6.

10. For a discussion of vitalism in nationalist thought, see Pheng Cheah, *Spectral Nationality: Passages of Freedom from Kant to Postcolonial Literatures of Liberation* (New York: Columbia University Press, 2003).

11. For a discussion of "invasion literature," see Moretti, *Atlas of the European Novel*, 130–40.

12. See James Bryce, *Studies in History and Jurisprudence* (New York: Oxford University Press, 1901), 1–123; and James Bryce, *The Holy Roman Empire* (London: Macmillan, 1905).

13. For a comparative reading of the relationship between realism and historicity in the metropole and colony, see Ranajit Guha, "The Colonial City and Its Time(s)," *Indian Economic and Social History Review* 45, no. 3 (2008): 329–51.

14. Charles Dickens, "The Niger Expedition," *Miscellaneous Papers* (Cambridge: Cambridge University Press, 2009), 62.

15. Joseph Conrad, *Heart of Darkness* (London: Penguin, 2012), 14.

16. Ibid., 15.

17. See, for example, Gikandi, *Maps of Englishness*, 157–89; Esty, *Unseasonable Youth*; David Trotter, "Modernism and Empire: Reading *The Waste Land*," *Critical Quarterly* 28, no. 1–2 (1986): 143–53.

18. Quoted in V. I. Lenin, *The Essential Works of Lenin*, ed. Henry Christman (New York: Dover, 1987), 229.

19. Ibid., 268–69.

CHAPTER 4

1. J. A. Hobson, *The War in South Africa: Its Causes and Effects* (New York: Macmillan, 1900), 48.

2. For a discussion of this crisis of loyalty, see Melissa Free, "Fault Lines of Loyalty: Kipling's Boer War Conflict," *Victorian Studies* 58, no. 2 (2016): 314–23.

3. For a discussion of imperial citizenship within Greater Britain and its contestation by non-white British subjects, see Sukanya Banerjee, *Becoming Imperial Citizens: Indians in the Late-Victorian Empire* (Durham: Duke University Press, 2010); and Daniel Gorman, *Imperial Citizenship: Empire and the Question of Belonging* (Manchester: Manchester University Press, 2006).

4. Martin Booth, *The Doctor and the Detective: A Biography of Arthur Conan Doyle* (New York: Minataur Books, 1997), 227.

5. Doyle, *The Great Boer War*, 72–73.

6. Ibid., 527.

7. Britain was not the only European power that undertook such a project. Gary Wilder offers a similar account of Greater France in *The French Imperial Nation-State: Negritude and Colonial Humanism Between the Two World Wars* (Chicago: University of Chicago Press, 2005).

8. Doyle, *The Great Boer War*, 72.

9. Ibid., 79.

10. Patrick Brantlinger, *Victorian Literature and Postcolonial Studies* (Edinburgh: Edinburgh University Press, 2009), 38.

11. It is historically significant that the First Anglo-Boer War raised none of these concerns for Britons. The reason is undoubtedly because in 1870 the idea of a "Greater Britain" was far less of a reality than by the end of the century. Carl Schmitt locates the conflation of metropolitan and colonial territory in the juridical discourse of western Europe as an effect of the Congo Conference of 1885. He explains that because "the status of state territory in the sense of European international law—European soil—no longer was distinguishable from overseas, colonial—non-European—soil, then the whole spatial structure of European international law had to be abandoned, because the bracketing of internal, interstate European wars had an essentially different content than did the pursuit of colonial wars outside Europe." *The Nomos of the Earth: In the International Law of the Jus Publicum Europeanum*, trans. G. L. Ulmen (New York: Telos Publishing, 2003), 220.

12. See Paula M. Krebs, *Gender, Race and the Writing of Empire: Public Discourse and the Boer War* (Cambridge: Cambridge University Press, 2003).

13. Anthony Stokes, *A View of the Constitution of the British Colonies in North America and the West Indies at the time the Civil War Broke Out on the Continent of America* (London: B. White, 1783) makes this explicit in its very title. See also J. G. A. Pocock, *Virtue, Commerce, and History* (Cambridge: Cambridge University Press, 1985) and *Barbarism and Religion*, vol. 4 (Cambridge: Cambridge University Press, 2005); Andrew Jackson O'Shaughnessy, *An Empire Divided: The American Revolution and the British Caribbean* (Philadelphia: University of Pennsylvania Press, 2000). I am grateful to Chris Taylor for pointing me to these texts.

14. Dilke, *Greater Britain*, vii. See also J. A. Froude, *Oceana: England and her Colonies* (London: Longmans, Green and Co., 1886).

15. See Duncan Bell, *The Idea of Greater Britain* (Princeton: Princeton University Press, 2007).

16. Plotz, *Portable Property*, 3. Plotz emphasizes the centrality of cultural objects such as the Bible or strawberries in England's portability. For the purposes of my argument, I focus less on the export of such commodities and more on the export of national culture and institutions.

17. Dilke, *Greater Britain*, vii.

18. Ibid., 227.

19. Dilke implicitly suggests that British nationhood was a unified whole, lacking diversity and divisions within. For more on the demographics of nineteenth-century Britain, see Laura Tabli, "A Homogeneous Society? Britain's Internal 'Others' 1800–Present," in *At Home with the Empire*, ed.

Catherine Hall and Sonya O. Rose (Cambridge: Cambridge University Press, 2007), 53–76.

20. Dilke, *Greater Britain*, 385.

21. Ibid.

22. Ibid., 227.

23. Anderson, *Imagined Communities*, 21.

24. Dilke, *Greater Britain*, 390. It is important to note that Dilke's emphasis on citizenship and civic education is indicative of a broader late Victorian shift toward a language of citizenship that increasingly referred to the duties individuals owed to their national community and its empire. This manifested not only in public discourse but also in schools, which underscored the importance of voting in the domestic arena, as well as the responsibility of maintaining the British empire. But while the figure of the citizen was mobilized for nationalist ends in the metropole, at stake was who counted as citizens. Sukanya Banerjee has illuminatingly shown how at the moment the notion of an "imperial citizenship" gained currency, so did claims to British citizenship by Indians. Banerjee argues that "it was the *potential* of their [British Indians'] position as subjects that was at stake, and it was a testing of the strength of this potential that yielded articulations and understandings of what it is to be a citizen in ways that animated the discourse of citizenship not only for Indians, but for Britons as well" (*Becoming Imperial Citizens*, 5). Debates around the citizenship of British Indians—which were sometimes successful as in the case of Dadabhai Naroji—not only called into question what citizenship meant for non-British subjects in the colonies but recast how metropolitans understood their own national and civic identity.

25. The supplement, Derrida maintains, is always an "*exterior* addition," and can both complete and substitute the whole. Jacques Derrida, *Of Grammatology*, trans. Gayatri Chakravorty Spivak (Baltimore: Johns Hopkins University Press, 1998), 145. In the case of Greater Britain, while America is exterior to Britain, it completes Britain's natural project of imperial expansion.

26. See David Armitage and Peter Burroughs, "John Robert Seeley and British Imperial History," *Journal of Imperial and Commonwealth History* 1 (1972): 191–211.

27. David Armitage, "Greater Britain: A Useful Category of Historical Analysis?" *American Historical Review* 104, no. 2 (1999): 430.

28. Seeley, *The Expansion of England*, 51.

29. Ibid., 16.

30. Seeley recognizes the fictiveness and ideological character of racial unity when he clarifies that a "community of race" is in fact "the *belief in* a community of race." *The Expansion of England*, 220; emphasis added.

31. Ibid., 8, 43.

32. Ibid., 40–41.

33. This is precisely why America is absent from Seeley's Greater Britain (and in fact is seen to be, alongside the Russian empire, a rival to the British empire).

34. Henry John Temple Palmerston, "On the Affairs in Greece," in *The Life and Correspondence of Henry John Temple Viscount Palmerston*, ed. Evelyn Ashley (London: Richard Bentley and Son, 1879), 2:160.

35. Note the slippage in Palmerston's language from *civis*, meaning fellow-citizen, to imperial subjecthood. The former describes a horizontal affiliation, while the latter a vertical relationship to a sovereign. For a discussion of the conjuncture of these two categories, see Étienne Balibar, "Citizen Subject," in *Who Comes After the Subject?* ed. Eduardo Cadava, Peter Connor, and Jean-Luc Nancy (New York: Routledge, 1991), 33–57.

36. Seeley, *The Expansion of England*, 87.

37. Ibid., 288.

38. Ibid., 73–74. Technological limitations, Seeley argues, are why America was lost to Greater Britain, which in the eighteenth century could not sustain cultural and political continuity over transatlantic distances.

39. Seeley's faith in the telegraph was doubtless a sign of the times. Between the publishing of *Greater Britain* and *The Expansion of England*, the total length of telegraph wires in the world had increased almost twelvefold, with the vast majority belonging to Britain. For an extended discussion of the geopolitical implications of the transatlantic telegraph, see Daniel R. Headrick, *The Invisible Weapon: Telecommunications and International Politics, 1851–1945* (New York: Oxford University Press, 1991). For a discussion of the telegraph in relation to the idea of Greater Britain, see Duncan Bell, "Dissolving Distance: Technology, Space, and Empire in British Political Thought, 1770–1900," *Journal of Modern History* 77, no. 3 (September 2005): 523–62; Aaron Worth, "Imperial Transmissions: H. G. Wells, 1897–1901," *Victorian Studies* 53, no. 1 (2010): 65–89. For a study of how such information impacted literary form, see Richard Menke, *Telegraphic Realism: Victorian Fiction and Other Information Systems* (Stanford: Stanford University Press, 2008).

40. Seeley, *The Expansion of England*, 63.

41. Ibid., 255–56.

42. See C. A. Bayly, *The Birth of the Modern World: 1780–1914* (Malden, MA: Blackwell, 2004); Gary B. Magee and Andrew S. Thompson, *Empire and Globalisation: Networks of People, Goods and Capital in the British World, 1850–1914* (Cambridge: Cambridge University Press, 2010); Alan Lester, *Imperial Networks: Creating Identities in Nineteenth-Century South Africa and Britain* (London: Routledge, 2001); and Simon J. Potter, "Webs, Networks, and Systems: Globalization and the Mass Media in the Nineteenth and Twentieth Century British Empire," *Journal of British Studies* 46, no. 3 (July 2007): 621–46.

43. Aaron Worth makes the important point that the study of imperial networks has illuminated much about the empire's reach and hegemony but also "kept the colonial world at the margins." "Imperial Transmissions," 68.

44. Charles Wentworth Dilke, *The Problems of Greater Britain* (London: Macmillan, 1890), 289.

45. It is notable that South Africa is conspicuously absent from Dilke's *Greater Britain*, being mentioned only twice—once in relation to slavery, the other to emphasize the teachability of English to native populations. Ibid., 338, 539.

46. Seeley, *The Expansion of England*, 49.

47. Ibid.

48. Rudyard Kipling, *The Letters of Rudyard Kipling*, vol. 3, *1900–1910*, ed. Thomas Pinney (Iowa City: University of Iowa Press, 1990), 15.

49. Garett Stewart, *Reading Voices: Literature and the Phonotext* (Berkeley: University of California Press, 1990), 5.

50. Jacques Derrida, *Margins of Philosophy*, trans. Alan Bass (Chicago: University of Chicago Press, 1982), 5.

51. Theodor Adorno, *Notes to Literature*, vol. 1, trans. Shierry Weber Nicholsen (New York: Columbia University Press, 1991), 198.

52. Kipling's homophonic play is therefore quite different from the way in which Marjorie Perloff understands Eugene Jola's multilingual poetics, which introjects foreign words as a means to reinvent "English as a magnet language, pulling in those particles . . . so as to produce a dense mosaic of intertextual references," the politics of which were directed at an increasingly fascistic monolingual horizon of Nazism. *Differentials: Poetry, Poetics, Pedagogy* (Tuscaloosa: University of Alabama Press, 2004), 88.

53. I borrow the term "semantic proximity" from Paul Ricoeur, "The Metaphoric Process," *Critical Inquiry* 5, no. 1 (1978): 143–59.

54. Perhaps not coincidentally, the term "friction" has been used by critics to describe both homophonic play between text and sound and the effect of contact zones in the context of globalization. For the former, see Stewart, *Reading Voices*, 5; for the latter, see Anna Lowenhaupt Tsing, *Friction: An Ethnography of Global Connection* (Princeton: Princeton University Press, 2005).

55. Said adapts his idea of the "contrapuntal" from Western classical music, in which "various themes play off one another, with only a provisional privilege being given to any particular one; yet in the resulting polyphony there is concert and order, an organized interplay that derives from the themes, not from a rigorous melodic or formal principle outside the work." *Culture and Imperialism* (New York: Vintage, 1994), 32, 51.

56. See Cicely Palser Havely, "A Sahibs' War," *Kipling Journal* 68, no. 272 (December 1994): 12–22; Philip Holden, "Halls of Mirrors: Mimicry and Ambivalence in Kipling's Boer War Short Stories," *Ariel* 28, no. 4 (1997): 91–110; St. John Damstra, "Attacking the Boers in the Style of Kipling Sahib," *Kipling Journal* 82, no. 329 (2008): 10–25; Malvern van Wyk Smith, "Telling the Boer War: Narrative Indeterminacy in Kipling's Stories," *South African Historical Journal* 41 (1999): 349–69; and *Drummer Hodge: The Poetry of the Anglo-Boer War, 1899–1902* (Oxford: Oxford University Press, 1978). For a thorough account of Kipling's revisions to *Kim* during the writing of his Boer War tales, see Margaret Peller Feeley, "The *Kim* That Nobody Reads," *Studies in the Novel* 13, no. 3 (Fall 1981): 266–81.

57. Rudyard Kipling, *The Collected Works of Rudyard Kipling*, vol. 7, *Traffics and Discoveries* (New York: Doubleday, Doran and Company, 1941), 71. Subsequent citations of this text appear parenthetically.

58. Ivan Kreilkamp, *Voice and the Victorian Storyteller* (Cambridge: Cambridge University Press, 2005), 4.

59. Gayatri Chakravorty Spivak, *A Critique of Postcolonial Reason: Toward a History of the Vanishing Present* (Cambridge, MA: Harvard University Press, 1999), 162.

60. David Stewart, "Orality in Kipling's *Kim*," *JNT: Journal of Narrative Technique* 13, no. 1 (Winter 1983): 54.

61. John Marx, *The Modernist Novel and the Decline of Empire* (Cambridge: Cambridge University Press, 2005), 2.

62. Elleke Boehmer, *Empire, the National, and the Postcolonial: Resistance in Interaction* (Oxford: Oxford University Press, 2002), 2.

63. Ibid., 12.

64. Pradip Kumar Datta, "Interlocking Worlds of the Anglo-Boer War in South Africa/India," *South African Historical Journal* 57 (2007): 37.

65. Recent work on the connections between India and South Africa during the Boer War include Thomas R. Metcalf, *Imperial Connections: India and the Indian Ocean Arena, 1860–1920* (Berkeley: University of California Press, 2007); Isabel Hofmeyr and Michelle Williams, eds., "South Africa–India: Connections and Comparisons," special issue, *Journal of Asian and African Studies* 44, no. 1–2 (2009): 1–165; Isabel Hofmeyr, "Universalizing the Indian Ocean," *PMLA* 125, no. 3 (2010): 721–29; Hester Blum, "The Prospect of Oceanic Studies," *PMLA* 125, no. 3 (2010): 670–77.

66. For more on the materiality of Kipling's publications and the commodification of jingo poems like "The Absent Beggar" and "Tommy song" into handkerchiefs, mugs, and tea towels, see Elleke Boehmer, "The Worlding of the Jingo Poem," *Yearbook of English Studies* 41, no. 2 (2011): 41–57.

67. Bhabha, *The Location of Culture*, 87–88.

68. Ibid.

69. Kaori Nagai, *Empire of Analogies: Kipling, India and Ireland* (Cork: Cork University Press, 2006).

70. Rudyard Kipling, *The Collected Works of Rudyard Kipling*, vol. 26, *The Five Nations* (New York: Doubleday, Doran and Company, 1941), 294.

71. Ibid., 293.

72. Ibid.

73. Smith, "Telling the Boer War," 356.

74. Rudyard Kipling, *Kim* (New York: Penguin Classics, 2011), 40, 25, 171.

75. Ian Baucom writes that in *Kim*, Kipling "acknowledges that the empire has founded itself on a bordered epistemology and confronts the limit of colonial knowledge. In doing so, the novel, along with the reader, becomes aware of the existence of the unmapped and the unmappable within the cartography of imperialism." *Out of Place: Englishness, Empire, and the Locations of Identity* (Princeton: Princeton University Press, 1999), 97.

CHAPTER 5

1. Joseph Conrad, *Nostromo: A Tale of the Seaboard* (Oxford: Oxford University Press, 2007), 292. Subsequent citations appear parenthetically in the text.

2. One could understand Gould's concern in terms of the slippage between mimicry and mockery that Homi Bhabha argues is at the heart of the civilizing mission. In Bhabha's account, the colonial other is produced by the West as a mimic of the West so that it is "almost the same, *but not quite*" (*The Location*

of Culture, 88–89). In the process, the colonized's mimicry of the colonizer's norms slips into a mockery of them; resemblance becomes menace. Gould's impression of Costaguana is not dissimilar. Costaguana makes a mockery of Enlightenment ideals, the solution to which for Gould is more imperialism—a project Conrad's novel reveals to be flawed.

3. For an account of finance capital in *Nostromo*, see Cannon Schmitt, "Rumor, Shares, Novelistic Form: Joseph Conrad's *Nostromo*," in *Victorian Investments: New Perspectives on Finance and Culture*, ed. Nancy Henry and Cannon Schmitt (Bloomington: University of Indiana Press, 2008).

4. See Benita Parry, *Conrad and Imperialism: Ideological Boundaries and Visionary Frontiers* (London: Macmillan, 1983); Christopher GoGwilt, *The Invention of the West: Joseph Conrad and the Double-Mapping of Europe and Empire* (Stanford: Stanford University Press, 1995), 190–218; Stephen Ross, *Conrad and Empire* (Columbia: University of Missouri Press, 2004); Luz Elena Ramirez, *British Representations of Latin America* (Gainesville: University Press of Florida, 2007).

5. I am, of course, referring to Peter Brooks's account of narrative desire in *Reading for the Plot*, and Frank Kermode's study of narrative closure in *Sense of an Ending*.

6. Naipaul helpfully points out that Conrad's fiction has explicit theses and arguments. These arguments are invariably evident early in the plot, which allows Conrad to meditate on their meaning in the narrative itself. See V. S. Naipaul, "Conrad's Darkness and Mine," in *Literary Occasions: Essays* (New York: Vintage, 2003), 162–80. I will discuss this essay at greater length in the following chapter.

7. William Henry Hudson, *The Purple Land* (New York: Grosset and Dunlap, 1904), 8.

8. Ibid., 6

9. Ibid., 9.

10. Ibid., 243–44.

11. To be clear, I am not suggesting, as Michael Hardt and Antonio Negri do, that the twentieth century sees a shift from "imperialism" to "Empire," a shift that accompanies the decline of the nation-state. Michael Hardt and Antonio Negri, *Empire* (Cambridge, MA: Harvard University Press, 2001), xii. Rather, my point is that while the centers of imperial rule are deterritorialized—no longer London or Britain but also the United States—the places to rule—like Costaguana—remain clearly defined as peripheral nation-states. Today, these countries include the long list of developing nations that the World Bank deems to be caught in a "conflict trap."

12. Evelyn Barring Cromer, "The Government of Subject Races," in *Political and Literary Essays: 1908–1913* (London: Macmillan, 1913), 29–30.

13. Ibid., 30.

14. Arendt, *The Origins of Totalitarianism*, 213. For an account of the role of the bureaucrat in late Victorian imperial thought, see Daniel Bivona, *British Imperial Literature, 1870–1940: Writing and the Administration of Empire* (Cambridge: Cambridge University Press, 1998), 99–130.

15. Arendt, *The Origins of Totalitarianism*, 216–17.

16. J. A. Hobson, *Imperialism: A Study* (Ann Arbor: University of Michigan Press, 1965), 127.

17. Cromer, "The Government of Subject Races," 4.

18. *The Communist Manifesto* in fact, uses the very term "epoch" to characterize historical periods: "Our epoch, the epoch of the bourgeoisie . . . has simplified the class antagonism . . . , into two great classes directly facing each other: Bourgeoisie and Proletariat." Marx and Engels, *The Marx and Engels Reader*, 474.

19. Claire Rosenfield, *Paradise of Snakes: An Archetypical Analysis of Conrad's Political Novels* (Chicago: University of Chicago Press, 1967), 48.

20. Avrom Fleishman, *Conrad's Politics: Community and Anarchy in the Fiction of Joseph Conrad* (Baltimore: Johns Hopkins University Press, 1967), 162.

21. Leslie Bethell explains that "by the 1870s, major portions of Latin America came to offer a much more hospitable—which is to say reliable—investment climate for foreign capital than they had hitherto, reinforcing the basic cultural affinity that gave Latin America closer and broader links with the capital-exporting countries than were enjoyed by Asia, Africa or the Middle East." *The Cambridge History of Latin America*, vol. 4, *c. 1870–1930* (Cambridge: Cambridge University Press, 2008), 5.

22. Hobson, *Imperialism*, 49.

23. Focusing more on the relationship between the economy and *Nostromo*'s narrative structure, Joshua Gooch argues that "the narrative economy and political economy form a unique dynamic of repetition as material interests subsume Sulaco's economy into a credit-based economy of the world market. This intersection of political and narrative economies inflects the novel's rhetorical texture and drives its plotting and characterization." "'The Shape of Credit': Imagination, Speculation, and Language in *Nostromo*," *Texas Studies in Literature and Language* 52, no. 3 (Fall 2010): 269.

24. Said, *Beginnings*, 117.

25. Aaron Fogel, *Coercion to Speak: Conrad's Poetics of Dialogue* (Cambridge, MA: Harvard University Press, 1985), 94.

26. Critics and popular editions of *Nostromo* take pains to either retell the history of Costaguana or append chronologies of the salient historical events that take place in the novel. For an excellent reassembly of Costaguana's history, see Irving Howe, *Politics and the Novel* (New York: Horizon Press, 1957), 102–7. For the most detailed chronology of the country's history as well as a map of Sulaco, see Ian Watt, *Joseph Conrad: Nostromo* (Cambridge: Cambridge University Press, 1988).

27. Pamela H. Demory, "*Nostromo*: Making History," *Texas Studies in Literature and Language* 35, no. 3 (Fall 1993): 321.

28. Said, *Beginnings*, 114.

29. John Marx suggests that when such histories are inserted into literary texts, they register how literature itself offers a counterdiscourse by populating stories with experts distinct from those in think tanks. He writes, "Fiction strives to make their expertise intelligible as specialized knowledge every bit as consequential as that of development economists and political theorists. In

doing so, failed-state fiction may be said to promote a dramatic revision of the division of labor that abides in policy circles. . . . But when fiction broaches the question of who qualifies as an expert in the first place, it identifies a problem political science has yet to fully think through. Fiction claims a special understanding of state politics by demonstrating an ability to rethink the hierarchical arrangements of meritocratic rule" (*Geopolitics and the Anglophone Novel*, 87–88). While I agree with Marx's argument, my point here is to show how the expertise Conrad features in *Nostromo* is about the limits of solving politico-economic problems in the East—a theme I continue to develop in the following two chapters.

30. A notable exception is Charles Gould, who Pamela Demory argues, is unconcerned with history: "The only history he is interested in are the facts of the San Tomé mine's recent past" ("*Nostromo*: Making History," 326). But this is to assume that developmental historicism (which Gould is entirely subsumed by) is *not* a historical consciousness. As I argue throughout this chapter, Gould's mission is to eradicate the uneven development of the colonial periphery—a task thoroughly committed to the historicism that the civilizing mission is premised on.

31. Seamus O'Malley, *Making History New: Modernism and Historical Narrative* (London: Oxford University Press, 2015), 4.

32. Ibid., 19.

33. Perry Anderson, "From Progress to Catastrophe: The Historical Novel," *London Review of Books* 33, no. 15 (July 2011), 24.

34. Hayden White, *Figural Realism: Studies in the Mimesis Effect* (Baltimore: Johns Hopkins University Press, 1999), 74.

35. Ibid., 81–82.

36. Howe, *Politics and the Novel*, 103–4.

37. Nicholas Visser, "Crowds and Politics in *Nostromo*," *Mosaic* 23, no. 2 (1990): 3.

38. Christopher GoGwilt makes a comparison between the *Eighteenth Brumaire* and *Nostromo* but also states, by way of Fanon, where Conrad departs from Marx: "*Nostromo*'s extraordinary meditation on revolution may in part stem from a reaction against the spirit of Marx . . . the very nature of Conrad's reaction points also to the imaginative power of his engagement with revolutionary discourses, anticipating the way Frantz Fanon will stretch Marxist analysis to address the colonial problem" in which the *lumpenproletariat* loom especially large. *The Invention of the West*, 192.

39. Parry, *Conrad and Imperialism*, 112.

40. Visser, "Crowds and Politics in *Nostromo*," 5–6.

41. The term "singular modernity," of course, is Fredric Jameson's, who poses the thesis that "Modernity is not a concept, philosophical or otherwise, but a narrative category." *A Singular Modernity: Essay on the Ontology of the Present* (London: Verso, 2002), 40. I evoke Jameson's thesis to call attention to the metaphor of railway-tracks-as-historical progress that Conrad deploys—a metaphor that brings together a classical symbol of industrial modernity (the train) and modernity's singular trajectory (the train track). The metaphor reveals how Costaguana's "own" modernity is not suppressed by Europe's

civilizing mission but invented as such by capital. As Dipesh Chakrabarty puts it, "We do not have a choice in the matter [of being a part of Europe's universalist modernity], even when the problem does not admit of any permanent resolutions" (*Provincializing Europe*, 180). Chakrabarty's point is that while "the rule of capital" is everywhere in the world, this is not to say that everyone is at home in capital equally. It is the attempt to make an ex-colony at home in capital—a process otherwise known as the civilizing mission—that is the burden of Conrad's text. For a different reading of Jameson and Chakrabarty, see Esty, *Unseasonable Youth*, 199–201; see also Sanjay Krishnan, "V. S. Naipaul and Historical Derangement," *Modern Language Quarterly* 73, no. 3 (September 2012): 448–49.

42. Referred to as the "Ingléz of Sulaco," Gould is identifiably English because of his clothes, which look "as though he had come this moment to Costaguana at his easy swift *pasitrote*, straight out of some green meadow at the other side of the world" (38). It is precisely this retention of English culture overseas that John Plotz calls this the "portability" of late Victorian English national identity.

43. Peter Smith notes that Gould "represents the dominant political theory of Anglo-Saxon tradition. Accordingly, he comes not with the weapons of the conqueror, but armed only with a contract." *Public and Private Value: Studies in the Nineteenth Century Novel* (Cambridge: Cambridge University Press, 1984), 190.

44. All that remains of the waterfall is a watercolor sketch by Emilia Gould composed during the mine's construction, thereby preserving Sulaco's primordial existence within the representational matrix of the Goulds' civilizing mission.

45. And even when war eventually breaks out in the rest of the country, business continues as usual in Sulaco: "every three months the silver escort had gone down to the sea as if neither the war nor its consequences could ever affect the ancient Occidental state secluded beyond its high barrier of the Cordillera. All the fighting took place on the other side of that mighty wall of serrated peaks lorded over by the white dome of Higuerota" (99).

46. Fredric Jameson, *The Political Unconscious: Narrative as a Socially Symbolic Act* (Ithaca: Cornell University Press, 1981), 278.

47. Said, *Beginnings*, 135.

48. Conrad, *Heart of Darkness*, 80.

49. Said, *Culture and Imperialism*, 30.

50. Luz Elena Ramirez argues that *Nostromo*'s conclusion shows Costaguana revolting against European interests, and suggests a new trajectory to its history (*British Representations of Latin America*, 98–99). I find instead that the narrative's enclosure within stillness forecloses the possibility of such a departure.

51. Albert J. Guerard, *Conrad the Novelist* (Cambridge, MA: Harvard University Press, 1958), 178.

52. Ibid., 198.

53. Paul B. Armstrong similarly notes that "Nostromo is not so much a realistic representation of a given historical situation as a paradigm of political

processes—a model through which Conrad explores the ontology of the social world." *The Challenge of Bewilderment: Understanding and Representation in James, Conrad, and Ford* (Ithaca: Cornell University Press, 1987), 155.

54. As the previous chapter argues, this lesson was something Kipling—the poet of empire—began to recognize at the turn of the century.

55. Aijaz Ahmed, *In Theory: Nations, Classes, Literatures* (London: Verso, 2008), 103.

PART III

1. *Anil's Ghost* has, in fact, been criticized for its lack of detail about the Sri Lankan Civil War. See Qadri Ismail, "A Flippant Gesture Towards Sri Lanka: A Review of Michael Ondaatje's *Anil's Ghost*," *Pravada* 6, no. 9 (2000): 24–29.

2. Michael Ondaatje, *Anil's Ghost* (New York: Vintage International, 2000), 17.

3. Ibid., 55.

4. For a discussion of the novel's relationship to history and the archive, see Antoinette Burton, "Archive of Bones: *Anil's Ghost* and the Ends of History," *Journal of Commonwealth Literature* 38, no. 1 (2003): 39–56.

5. Ondaatje, *Anil's Ghost*, 151.

6. Lukács, *The Historical Novel*, 53.

7. Ondaatje, *Anil's Ghost*, 274–75.

8. Ibid., 285–86.

9. For an overview of the postcolonial historical novel, see Hamish Dalley, *The Postcolonial Historical Novel: Realism, Allegory, and the Representation of Contested Pasts* (London: Palgrave Macmillan, 2014).

10. This is by no means an exhaustive list within Anglophone literature, let alone literary traditions in languages other than English.

11. Lukács, *The Historical Novel*, 53.

12. See also Jed Esty, "Global Lukács," *NOVEL: A Forum on Fiction* 42, no. 3 (2009): 366–72.

13. By "historicism," I am referring to Dipesh Chakrabarty's use of the term in *Provincializing Europe*, which he defines as "what made modernity or capitalism look not simply global but rather as something that became global *over time*, by originating in one place (Europe) and then spreading outside it. This 'first in Europe, then elsewhere' structure of global historical time was historicist" (7).

14. Marx, *Geopolitics and the Anglophone Novel*, 65.

15. Ibid., 48.

16. Adichie, *Half of a Yellow Sun*, 541.

17. Marx, *Geopolitics and the Anglophone Novel*, 87–88.

CHAPTER 6

1. I borrow this phrase from R. Radhakrishnan's essay, "Derivative Discourse and the Problem of Signification," *European Legacy* 7, no. 6 (2002): 790.

2. Naipaul, "Conrad's Darkness and Mine," 168.

3. Ibid., 173.

4. Ibid., 170–71. For a discussion of the derivation and deviation of anti-colonial nationalism from European nationalism, see Chatterjee, *Nationalist Thought and the Colonial World*.

5. Said, *Orientalism*, 40.

6. Naipaul's recognition of his own implication in Conrad's darkness is evident in the shift in title for his essay. When first published in *The Return of Eva Peron*, the essay's title was initially "Conrad's Darkness" and only later revised as "Conrad's Darkness and Mine."

7. Conrad, *Nostromo*, 373.

8. Ibid., 374.

9. Naipaul, "Conrad's Darkness and Mine," 177.

10. The problem of historicizing "secondhand" societies is in many ways the premise of *The Loss of Eldorado*, Naipaul's two-part history about the making of his home island, Trinidad. Naipaul writes that for a place like Port of Spain, "History was the Trinidad five-cent stamp: Ralegh discovering the Pitch Lake. History was also a fairytale not so much about slavery as about its abolition, the good defeating the bad. . . . In the records the slave is faceless, silent, with an identification rather than a name. He has no story." *The Loss of Eldorado: A Colonial History* (New York: Vintage, 1997), 354.

11. See Peggy Nightingale's discussion of despair in Naipaul's fiction in *Journey Through Darkness: The Writing of V. S. Naipaul* (St. Lucia: University of Queensland Press, 1987), 201–20.

12. V. S. Naipaul, *A Bend in the River* (New York: Vintage, 1989), 3. Subsequent citations appear parenthetically in the text.

13. Just as Conrad's choice of the fictional country of Costaguana as the setting for *Nostromo* has led a number of scholars to conjecture which South American country it was "really" about, so has Naipaul's decision to set *A Bend in the River* in a seemingly nameless town in a fictional central African country. See Linda Prescott, "Past and Present Darkness: Sources for V. S. Naipaul's *A Bend in the River*," *Modern Fiction Studies* 30, no. 3 (Autumn 1984): 547–59; Bruce King, *V. S. Naipaul*, 2nd ed. (New York: Palgrave Macmillan, 2003), 118–35. Most agree that Naipaul's inspiration for *A Free State* as well as *A Bend in the River* was Mobutu's Zaire. For Naipaul's reflections on Mobutu, see "A New King for the Congo," *New York Review of Books*, June 26, 1975.

14. Conrad, *Heart of Darkness*, 3, 89.

15. For more on the plotlessness of *A Bend in the River*, see Imran Coovadia, *Authority and Authorship in V. S. Naipaul* (New York: Palgrave Macmillan, 2009), 30–35; Ronald Blaber, "'This Piece of Earth': V. S. Naipaul's *A Bend in the River*," in *A Sense of Place in the New Literatures in English*, ed. Peggy Nightingale (St. Lucia: University of Queensland Press, 1986), 61–67.

16. Sanjay Krishnan, "Edward Said, Mahmood Mamdani, V. S. Naipaul: Rethinking Postcolonial Studies," *Modern Fiction Studies* 58, no. 4 (Winter 2012): 820. See also Krishnan, "V. S. Naipaul and Historical Derangement."

17. David Scott, *Conscripts of Modernity: The Tragedy of Colonial Enlightenment* (Durham: Duke University Press, 2004), 168.

18. Ibid., 220.

19. While Naipaul suggests that the development projects undertaken are by and large capitalist, Maaza Mengiste's *Beneath a Lion's Gaze* points out how such projects were equally driven by the Soviet Union. Ethiopia, we are told, has "fallen victim to the Cold War scramble for the Horn of Africa," and so the novel depicts the USSR's role in arming the Derg, as well as building prisons, all "necessary step[s] in our progress." *Beneath a Lion's Gaze* (New York: W. W. Norton, 2010), 117, 133, 125.

20. Walter Benjamin argues that all human violence seeks to either create law or protect it ("Critique of Violence," 287). But Salim questions the very premise of the law in the town at the bend in the river, "To talk of trouble was to pretend there were laws and regulations that everyone could acknowledge. Here there was nothing" (58).

21. F. D. Corfield, *The Origins and Growth of the Mau Mau* (Nairobi, 1960), 284.

22. Ibid.

23. Ibid.

24. Ngũgĩ wa Thiong'o, *Weep Not, Child* (Johannesburg: Heinemann Publishers, 1987), 108.

25. Adichie, *Half of a Yellow Sun*, 25, 47.

26. Mengiste, *Beneath a Lion's Gaze*, 50.

27. Ibid., 145.

28. Eleni Coundouriotis, *The People's Right to the Novel: War Fiction in the Postcolony* (New York: Fordham University Press, 2014), 10.

29. Ibid., 20, 23.

30. Chinua Achebe, *Home and Exile* (New York: Anchor Books, 2000), 88.

31. Ibid., 91. Selwyn R. Cudjoe argues that while Naipaul's earlier writing is indeed committed to thinking the potentiality of the postcolonial world, by *A Bend*, his perspective has regressed into a spokesperson for the West: "The blame of colonialism and imperialism is removed from its external, exploitative source and made into an internal flaw of the colonized. This is the central position that *A Bend in the River* seeks to demonstrate. Because such a position is more concerned with ideas and opinions than with sensibility and experience, the novel emerges as a political document rather than a fictional text, and this is its major difficulty." *V. S. Naipaul: A Materialist Reading* (Amherst: University of Massachusetts Press, 1988), 191–92. While I agree with Cudjoe's analysis, I am less convinced by the claim that *A Bend* is "a political document," only because Naipaul's nonfiction has a very different politics than his fiction. A more nuanced relationship between these two categories must be considered in Naipaul's fiction.

32. Chinua Achebe, "An Image of Africa: Racism in Conrad's *Heart of Darkness*," in *Hopes and Impediments: Selected Essays* (New York: Anchor Books, 1990), 1–20. Rob Nixon touches on Achebe's concern with Naipaul, and clarifies that the latter "distinguishes between the past and history." Naipaul associates the former, which is unique to "half-made societies" in the colonial peripheries, "with the regressive myths and fantasies that 'tribal'

societies fabricate about themselves," while history is "a precondition for and product of human achievement" that originates in and belongs to the West. *London Calling: Postcolonial Mandarin* (Oxford: Oxford University Press, 1992), 119.

33. Edward Said, *Reflections on Exile, & Other Literary and Cultural Essays* (Cambridge, MA: Harvard University Press, 2002), 100.

34. Ibid.

35. Ibid.

36. Said, *Culture and Imperialism*, 265. Sanjay Subrahmanyam diverges from Said slightly when he presents Naipaul as fundamentally naive, a virtue he finds essential to Naipaul's value as an author: "With his clarity of expression and utter lack of self-awareness, he [Naipaul] provides a window into a world and its prejudices: he is thus larger than himself." "Where Does He Come From?" *London Review of Books* 29, no. 21 (November 2007): 9.

37. Michael Gorra, *After Empire: Scott, Naipaul, Rushdie* (Chicago: University of Chicago Press, 1997), 107.

38. Homi Bhabha offers a productive account of the idea of "civilization" in the writings of Naipaul in "Naipaul's Vernacular Cosmopolitanism," *Chronicle of Higher Education* (October 26, 2001), B13.

39. Nixon, *London Calling*, 120.

40. David Lloyd, *Irish Times: Temporalities of Modernity* (Dublin: Field Day Files, 2008), 4.

41. Ibid., 5.

42. Achille Mbembe, *On the Postcolony* (Berkeley: University of California Press, 2001), 16.

43. Naipaul has, of course, written such a scene before in *In a Free State* (1971), whose opening also describes an overcrowded steamboat that was "like a refugee ship. . . . They were Egyptian Greeks. They were traveling to Egypt, but Egypt was no longer their home. They had been expelled; they were refugees." V. S. Naipaul, *In a Free State* (New York: Vintage, 2002), 1.

CHAPTER 7

1. Nadine Gordimer, *The Essential Gesture*, ed. Stephen Clingman (London: Penguin, 1988), 262.

2. Ibid., 269–70.

3. Gramsci, *Selections from the Prison Notebooks*, 276. In Joseph A. Buttigieg's translation, these lines read: "If the ruling class has lost consensus, that is, if it no longer 'leads' but only 'rules'—it possesses sheer coercive power—this actually means that the great masses have become detached from traditional ideologies, they no longer believe what they previously used to believe." Antonio Gramsci, *Prison Notebooks*, trans. Joseph A. Buttigieg (New York: Columbia University Press, 1991), 2:32. It is important to contextualize Gramsci's prison writings as well as situate them within Anglophone academic discourse. Written under extreme conditions, Gramsci's prison writings are fragmentary, disorganized, and coded so as to avoid his censors, and moreover never intended for publication. It is with this in mind that his concept of the

interregnum, like any portion of these writings, must be read. But much of what is typically thought to be Gramsci's engagement with the idea of "interregnum" is located in what Quentin Hoare and Geoffrey Nowell Smith compiled as the final section of Gramsci's "chapter" on the State and Civil Society titled "'Wave of Materialism' and 'Crisis of Authority.'" Although the Hoare and Smith selections have been organized into what Gramsci scholars agree are the salient features of his work ("subaltern classes," "intellectuals," etc.), as Buttigieg has pointed out, "the more accurately an editor's choices and textual arrangements reflect the broad consensus of the scholarly community, the greater the likelihood that the ensuing anthology will further propagate, or at the very least confirm and reinforce, already established opinions and entrenched interpretations." Joseph Buttigieg, "Philology and Politics: Returning to the Text of Antonio Gramsci's *Prison Notebooks*," *Boundary2* 21, no. 2 (1994): 114. There is thus a tendency to reproduce traditional readings of Gramsci by relying exclusively on the (heavily) edited selections of the *Selected Writings of the Prison Notebooks*. I will therefore do my best to shuttle between the selected works that have gained significant currency in the Anglophone academy and Buttigieg's own ongoing translation of the *Quaderni del Carcere* in hopes to more completely, but also more critically, read Gramsci's idea of interregnum.

4. Susan Pearsall, "'Where the Banalities Are Enacted': The Everyday in Gordimer's Novels," *Research in African Literatures* 31, no. 1 (Spring 2000): 95.

5. Abdul R. JanMohamed, *Manichean Aesthetics: The Politics of Literature in Colonial Africa* (Amherst: University of Massachusetts Press, 1983), 140.

6. Nadine Gordimer, *July's People* (New York: Penguin, 1981), 158. Subsequent citations appear parenthetically in the text.

7. J. Hillis Miller, *Reading Narrative* (Norman: University of Oklahoma Press, 1998), 98.

8. Gordimer, *The Essential Gesture*, 278–76.

9. For J. M. Coetzee's discussion of the white writer in South Africa, especially before the 1960s, see *White Writing: On the Culture of Letters in South Africa* (New Haven: Yale University Press, 1988).

10. See also Nadine Gordimer, *Conversations with Nadine Gordimer*, ed. Nancy Topping Bazin and Marilyn Dallman Seymour (Jackson: University Press of Mississippi, 1990).

11. See also Gordimer's short story "Loot" in *Loot and Other Stories* (London: Penguin, 2004), which thematizes and formalizes a brief period of lawlessness in the midst of civilizational calamity.

12. Vincent Crapanzano, *Waiting: The Whites of South Africa* (New York: Random House, 1985), 43.

13. Neil Lazarus, "Modernism and Modernity: T. W. Adorno and Contemporary White South African Literature," *Cultural Critique* 5 (1986–87): 146.

14. Gordimer, *The Essential Gesture*, 272.

15. Martin Trump, "Part of the Struggle: Black Writing and the South African Liberation Movement," in *Rendering Things Visible: Essays on South*

African Literary Culture, ed. Martin Trump (Athens: Ohio University Press, 1990), 180. For a discussion of these two poles in black South African fiction, see Njabulo S. Ndebele, "Turkish Tales and Some Thoughts on South African Fiction," in *South African Literature and Culture: Rediscovery of the Ordinary* (Manchester: Manchester University Press, 1994).

16. Njabulo S. Ndebele, "Liberation and the Crisis of Culture," in *Altered State? Writing and South Africa*, ed. Elleke Boehmer, Laura Chrisman, and Kenneth Parker (Sydney: Dangaroo Press, 1994), 1.

17. Njabulo S. Ndebele, *South African Literature and Culture: Rediscovery of the Ordinary* (Manchester: Manchester University Press, 1994), 151–52.

18. Ibid., 158.

19. For a fuller sense of South African writing during the period of late apartheid, see Stephan Clingman, "Revolution and Reality: South African Fiction in the 1980s," in *Rendering Things Visible: Essays on South African Literary Culture*, ed. Martin Trump (Athens: Ohio University Press, 1990), 41–60.

20. J. M. Coetzee, *Waiting for the Barbarians* (New York: Penguin, 1980), 153–54.

21. Ibid., 178.

22. J. M. Coetzee, *The Life and Times of Michael K* (New York: Penguin, 1983), 60.

23. Ibid., 47.

24. Ibid.

25. André Brink, *States of Emergency* (London: Fontana Paperbacks, 1989), 13.

26. For a discussion of the slippage from "emergency" to "emergence," see Madeleine Sorapure, "A Story in Love's Default: André Brink's *States of Emergency*," *MFS: Modern Fiction Studies* 37, no. 4 (Winter 1991): 659–75.

27. Brink, *States of Emergency*, 243.

28. Ibid., 244.

29. Elleke Boehmer, "Endings and New Beginning: South African Fiction in Transition," in *Writing South Africa: Literature, Apartheid, and Democracy, 1970–1995*, ed. Derek Attridge and Rosemary Jolly (Cambridge: Cambridge University Press, 1998), 45.

30. Gramsci, *Selections from Prison Notebooks*, 276.

31. Gramsci, *Prison Notebooks*, 3:209.

32. Agamben, *State of Exception*, 48.

33. Benjamin, *Reflections*, 286.

34. Slavoj Žižek, *Tarrying with the Negative* (Durham: Duke University Press, 1993), 1.

35. Walter Benjamin, *Illuminations*, trans. Harry Zohn (New York: Schocken Books, 1968), 262.

36. See Stephen Clingman, *The Novels of Nadine Gordimer: History from the Inside* (Amherst: University of Massachusetts Press, 1992); Kathrin Wagner, *Rereading Nadine Gordimer* (Bloomington: Indiana University Press, 1994); Andrew Vogel Ettin, *Betrayals of the Body Politic: The Literary*

Commitments of Nadine Gordimer (Charlottesville: University Press of Virginia, 1992).

37. Gordimer, *The Essential Gesture*, 264–65.

38. Ibid.

39. Ibid., 266.

40. Pearsall, "'Where the Banalities Are Enacted,'" 96.

41. Lazarus, "Modernism and Modernity," 155.

42. Gordimer, *The Essential Gesture*, 270.

43. R. Radhakrishnan, *Theory in an Uneven World* (Malden, MA: Blackwell, 2003), 127.

44. Michael Neill, "Translating the Present: Language, Knowledge, and Identity in Nadine Gordimer's *July's People*," *Journal of Commonwealth Literature* 25 (1990): 73.

45. Brian Macaskill, "Placing Spaces: Style and Ideology in Gordimer's Later Fiction," in *The Later Fiction of Nadine Gordimer*, ed. Bruce King (London: Macmillan, 1993), 62.

46. The salience of word uses and their relationship to history is in many ways at the crux of the debate between Jacques Derrida on the one hand and Rob Nixon and Anne McClintock regarding the word "apartheid." See Derrida, "On Racism's Last Word," *Critical Inquiry* 12, no. 1 (1985): 290–99; Anne McClintock and Rob Nixon, "No Names Apart: The Separation of Word and History in Derrida's 'Le Dernier Mot du Racisme,'" *Critical Inquiry* 13, no. 1 (1986): 155–70; and Derrida's response in "But Beyond . . . (An Open Letter to Anne McClintock and Rob Nixon)," trans. Peggy Kamuf, *Critical Inquiry* 13, no. 1 (1986): 155–70. For an assessment of this debate, see Christopher Fynsk, "Apartheid, Word and History," *Boundary2* 16, no. 2/3 (1989): 1–12.

47. For an account of this temporal disjuncture in late apartheid political discourse, see Leonard Thompson, *A History of South Africa* (New Haven: Yale University Press, 2001); Deborah Posel, "The Language of Domination, 1978–1983," in *The Politics of Race, Class and Nationalism in Twentieth-Century South Africa*, ed. Shula Marks and Stanley Trapido (London: Longman Group, 1987), 419–43.

48. Karl Marx, *The Eighteenth Brumaire of Louis Bonaparte* (New York: International Publishers, 1988), 15.

49. This gesture directly contrasts Bam's difficulty in letting go of his own vehicle. For example, Bam's masculinity is threatened when he becomes aware of the bakkie being driven off by July: "Bam got up and had the menacing aspect of maleness a man has before the superego has gained control of his body, come out of sleep. His penis was swollen under his rumpled trousers" (39). This directly contrasts with the children's ease in giving up their prized possessions. John Cooke has argued that the children in fact begin to see themselves as distinct from their parents: "In their new surroundings, the Smales children soon begin to equate their parents' treatments of the Africans and themselves. . . . The children change simply because they are young enough not to have been completely formed by the world of 'back there.'" "'Nobody's

Children': Families in Gordimer's Later Novels," in *The Later Fiction of Nadine Gordimer*, ed. Bruce King (London: Macmillan, 1993), 24–25.

50. Neill, "Translating the Present," 73.

51. For an extended discussion of place in *July's People* and South African writing more generally, see Rita Barnard, *Apartheid and Beyond: South African Writers and the Politics of Place* (Oxford: Oxford University Press, 2007).

52. Gramsci, *Prison Notebooks*, 2:33, emphasis added.

53. Nicholas Visser, "Beyond the Interregnum: A Note on the Ending of *July's People*," in *Rendering Things Visible: Essays on South African Literary Culture*, ed. Martin Trump (Athens: Ohio University Press, 1990), 65.

54. Ibid., 65–66.

55. Ibid., 66.

56. Keeping the World Bank's report on civil war in mind, it becomes possible to reread the arrival of the helicopter as not merely the arrival of domestic "saviors or murderers" but international intervention. Why have readers assumed that the contents of the helicopter are domestic agents—either black revolutionaries or the apartheid regime's military—and not an international peace-keeping force? Of course, because the markings on the helicopter and consequently identity of its inhabitants are kept from the reader, it is impossible to know. But in light of the World Bank's report, it seems reasonable to consider the possibility that the mysterious helicopter is a metaphor for international intervention.

CODA

1. Agamben, *State of Exception*, 2.

2. Schmitt, *Theory of the Partisan*, 34, 39.

3. Michael Hardt and Antonio Negri, *Multitude: War and Democracy in the Age of Empire* (New York: Penguin, 2004), 12.

4. Ibid., 59. See also Hans Magnus Enzensberger's account of "molecular civil wars" in *Civil Wars* (New York: The New Press, 1993).

5. Carlo Galli, *Political Spaces and Global War*, trans. Elisabeth Fay (Minneapolis: University of Minnesota Press, 2010), 171.

6. Ibid., 172.

7. V. S. Naipaul, "A Grotesque Love of Propaganda. Unspeakable Barbarity. The Loathing of Jews—and a Hunger for World Domination. In this Stunning Intervention, Literary Colossus V. S. NAIPAUL Says ISIS is Now the Fourth Reich," *Daily Mail*, March 21, 2015, accessed October 20, 2016, http://www.dailymail.co.uk/debate/article-3005882/A-grotesque-love-propaganda-Unspeakable-barbarity-loathing-Jews-hunger-world-domination-stunning-intervention-literary-colossus-V-S-NAIPAUL-says-ISIS-Fourth-Reich.html.

8. Ibid.

9. Ibid.

10. Ibid.

11. "Greece Far-Right Party Golden Dawn: 'We Are in a Civil War,'" BBC News, October 17, 2012. http://www.bbc.com/news/world-europe-19983571.

12. "The End of Tolerance? Anti-Muslim Movement Rattles Germany," *Der Spiegel* 51 (December 15, 2014).

13. Yves Mamou, "France: The Coming Civil War," July 16, 2016, Gateson Institute, https://www.gatestoneinstitute.org/8489/france-the-coming-civil-war.

14. Balibar, "In War."

15. See Étienne Balibar, "Europe and the Refugees: A Demographic Enlargement," *openDemocracy*, September 25, 2015, https://www.opendemocracy.net/can-europe-make-it/etienne-balibar/europe-and-refugees-demographic-enlargement.

16. In fact, Balibar has himself characterized the crisis of European national identity as an "interregnum" in the Gramscian sense of the term. See Étienne Balibar, "Out of the Interregnum," *openDemocracy*, May 16, 2013, https://www.opendemocracy.net/can-europe-make-it/etienne-balibar/out-of-interregnum. See also Zygmunt Bauman, "Times of Interregnum," *Ethics & Global Politics* 5, no. 1 (2012): 49–56; and Bauman, *Modernity and Ambivalence* (Cambridge: Polity Press, 1991).

17. Brief for Technology Companies and Other Businesses as Amicus Curiae, 4, State of Washington v. Donald J. Trump, 17-35105 (9th Circuit) 2:17.

18. Ibid.

19. Ibid., 5.

Works Cited

Achebe, Chinua. *Home and Exile*. New York: Anchor Books, 2000.

———. "An Image of Africa: Racism in Conrad's *Heart of Darkness*." In *Hopes and Impediments: Selected Essays*," 1–20. New York: Anchor Books, 1990.

Acton, John. *The History of Freedom and Other Essays*. London: Macmillan, 1907.

Adichie, Chimamanda Ngozi. *Half of a Yellow Sun*. New York: Anchor Books, 2006.

Adorno, Theodor. *Notes to Literature*. Vol. 1. Translated by Shierry Weber Nicholsen. New York: Columbia University Press, 1991.

Agamben, Giorgio. *Homo Sacer: Sovereign Power and Bare Life*. Translated by Daniel Heller-Roazen. Stanford: Stanford University Press, 1998.

———. *Stasis: Civil War as a Political Paradigm*. Translated by Nicholas Heron. Stanford: Stanford University Press, 2015.

———. *State of Exception*. Translated by Keven Attell. Chicago: University of Chicago Press, 2005.

Ahmed, Aijaz. *In Theory: Nations, Classes, Literatures*. London: Verso, 2008.

Althusser, Louis, and Étienne Balibar. *Reading Capital*. Translated by Ben Brewster. New York: Verso, 2009.

Amin, Shahid. *Event, Metaphor, Memory: Chauri Chaura, 1922–1992*. Berkeley: University of California Press, 1995.

Anderson, Benedict. *Imagined Communities: Reflections on the Origins and Spread of Nationalism*. Revised edition. London: Verso, 2006.

Anderson, Perry. "From Progress to Catastrophe: The Historical Novel." *London Review of Books* 33, no. 15 (July 2011): 24–28.

Anonymous. "Review of *London Labour and the London Poor*." *Christian Observer* 52 (1852): 234–48.

Arendt. Hannah. *On Revolution*. London: Penguin, 1963.

———. *The Origins of Totalitarianism*. New York: Harvest Books, 1976.

Armitage, David. *Civil War: A History in Ideas*. New York: Alfred A. Knopf, 2017.

———. "Every Great Revolution Is a Civil War." In *Scripting Revolution: A Historical Approach to the Comparative Study of Revolutions*, edited by Keith Michael Baker and Dan Edelstein, 57–68. Stanford: Stanford University Press, 2015.

———. "Greater Britain: A Useful Category of Historical Analysis?" *American Historical Review* 104, no. 2 (1999): 427–45.

Armitage, David, and Peter Burroughs. "John Robert Seeley and British Imperial History." *Journal of Imperial and Commonwealth History* 1 (1972): 191–211.

Armstrong, Nancy. *Desire and Domestic Fiction: A Political History of the Novel*. Oxford: Oxford University Press, 1990.

———. "Gender Must Be Defended." *South Atlantic Quarterly* 111, no. 3 (2012): 529–47.

Armstrong, Paul B. *The Challenge of Bewilderment: Understanding and Representation in James, Conrad, and Ford*. Ithaca: Cornell University Press, 1987.

Arnold, Matthew. *Culture and Anarchy*. Oxford: Oxford University Press, 2006.

Aslami, Zarena. *The Dream Life of Citizens: Late Victorian Novels and the Fantasy of the State*. New York: Fordham University Press, 2012.

Balibar, Étienne. "Citizen Subject." In *Who Comes After the Subject?*, edited by Eduardo Cadava, Peter Connor, and Jean-Luc Nancy, 33–57. New York: Routledge, 1991.

———. "Europe and the Refugees: A Demographic Enlargement." *openDemocracy*, 25 September 2015, https://www.opendemocracy.net/can-europe-make-it/etienne-balibar/europe-and-refugees-demographic-enlargement.

———. "The Genealogical Scheme: Race or Culture?" *Trans-Scripts* 1 (2011): 1–9.

———. "In War." *openDemocracy*, 16 November 2015, https://www.opendemocracy.net/can-europe-make-it/etienne-balibar/in-war.

———. "Marxism and War." *Radical Philosophy* 160 (2010): 9–17.

———. *Masses, Classes, Ideas: Studies on Politics and Philosophy Before and After Marx*. Translated by James Swenson. London: Routledge, 1994.

———. "Out of the Interregnum." *openDemocracy*, 16 May 2013, https://www.opendemocracy.net/can-europe-make-it/etienne-balibar/out-of-interregnum.

———. *Politics and the Other Scene*. Translated by Christine Jones, James Swenson, and Chris Turner. London: Verso, 2002.

———. "Reflections on *Gewalt*." *Historical Materialism* 17 (2009): 99–125.

Balibar, Étienne, and Immanuel Wallerstein. *Race, Nation, Class: Ambiguous Identities*. Translated by Chris Turner. London: Verso, 1991.

Banerjee, Sukanya. *Becoming Imperial Citizens: Indians in the Late-Victorian Empire*. Durham: Duke University Press, 2010.

Barnard, Rita. *Apartheid and Beyond: South African Writers and the Politics of Place*. Oxford: Oxford University Press, 2007.

Baucom, Ian. *Out of Place: Englishness, Empire, and the Locations of Identity*. Princeton: Princeton University Press, 1999.

Bauman, Zygmunt. *Modernity and Ambivalence*. Cambridge: Polity Press, 1991.

———. "Times of Interregnum." *Ethics & Global Politics* 5, no. 1 (2012): 49–56.

Bayly, C. A. *The Birth of the Modern World: 1780–1914*. Malden, MA: Blackwell, 2004.

Bell, Duncan. "Dissolving Distance: Technology, Space, and Empire in British Political Thought, 1770–1900." *Journal of Modern History* 77, no. 3 (September 2005): 523–62.

———. *The Idea of Greater Britain*. Princeton: Princeton University Press, 2007.

Benjamin, Walter. "Critique of Violence." In *Reflections*, translated by Edmund Jephcott, 277–300. New York: Schocken Books, 1986.

———. *Illuminations*. Translated by Harry Zohn. New York: Schocken Books, 1968.

———. *The Writer of Modern Life: Essays on Charles Baudelaire*. Edited by Michael W. Jennings. Cambridge, MA: Harvard University Press, 2006.

Benveniste, Émile. "Civilization: A Contribution to the History of the World." In *Problems in General Linguistics*, 289–96. Miami, OH: Miami University Press, 1973.

———. *Problèmes de Linguistique Générale*. Vol. 2. Paris: Gallimard, 1974.

Bernstein, Eduard. *The Preconditions for Socialism*. Translated and edited by Henry Tudor. Cambridge: Cambridge University Press, 1993.

Betensky, Carolyn. *Feeling for the Poor: Bourgeois Compassion, Social Action, and the Victorian Novel*. Charlottesville: University of Virginia Press, 2010.

Bethell, Leslie. *The Cambridge History of Latin America*. Vol. 4, *c. 1870–1930*. Cambridge: Cambridge University Press, 2008.

Bhabha, Homi K. *The Location of Culture*. London: Routledge, 1994.

———. "Naipaul's Vernacular Cosmopolitanism." *Chronicle of Higher Education*, 26 October 2001, B13.

———. *Nation and Narration*. London: Routledge, 1990.

Bigand, Karine. "French Historiography of the English Revolution Under the Restoration: A National or Cross-Channel Dialogue?" *European Journal of English Studies* 14, no. 3 (2010): 249–61.

Bivona, Daniel. *British Imperial Literature, 1870–1940: Writing and the Administration of Empire*. Cambridge: Cambridge University Press, 1998.

———. *Desire and Contradiction: Imperial Visions and Domestic Debates in Victorian Literature*. Manchester: Manchester University Press, 1990.

Blaber, Ronald. "'This Piece of Earth': V. S. Naipaul's *A Bend in the River*."

In *A Sense of Place in the New Literatures in English*, edited by Peggy Nightingale, 61–67. St. Lucia: University of Queensland Press, 1986.

Blum, Hester. "The Prospect of Oceanic Studies." *PMLA* 125, no. 3 (2010): 670–77.

Bodenheimer, Rosemary. *The Politics of Story in Victorian Social Fiction.* Ithaca: Cornell University Press, 1988.

Boehmer, Elleke. *Empire, the National, and the Postcolonial: Resistance in Interaction.* Oxford: Oxford University Press, 2002.

———. "Endings and New Beginning: South African Fiction in Transition." In *Writing South Africa: Literature, Apartheid, and Democracy, 1970–1995*, edited by Derek Attridge and Rosemary Jolly, 43–56. Cambridge: Cambridge University Press, 1998.

———. "The Worlding of the Jingo Poem." *Yearbook of English Studies* 41, no. 2 (2011): 41–57.

Booth, Martin. *The Doctor and the Detective: A Biography of Arthur Conan Doyle.* New York: Minataur Books, 1997.

Bossche, Chris R. Vanden. *Carlyle and the Search for Authority.* Columbus: Ohio University Press, 1991.

———. *Reform Acts: Chartism, Social Agency and the Victorian Novel, 1832–1867.* Baltimore: Johns Hopkins University Press, 2014.

Brantlinger, Patrick. *The Spirit of Reform.* Cambridge, MA: Harvard University Press, 1977.

———. *Victorian Literature and Postcolonial Studies.* Edinburgh: Edinburgh University Press, 2009.

Brennan, Timothy. "The Nation Longing for Form." In *Nation and Narration*, edited by Homi K. Bhabha, 44–70. London: Routledge, 1990.

Briggs, Asa. "Saxons, Normans and Victorians." In *The Collected Essays of Asa Briggs*, 2:215–35. Brighton: University of Sussex Press, 1985.

Brink, André. *States of Emergency.* London: Fontana Paperbacks, 1989.

Brontë, Charlotte. *Jane Eyre.* London: Penguin Classics, 2006.

Brooks, Peter. *The Melodramatic Imagination: Balzac, Henry James, Melodrama, and the Mode of Excess.* New Haven: Yale University Press, 1975.

———. *Reading for the Plot: Design and Intention in Narrative.* Cambridge, MA: Harvard University Press, 1992.

Bryce, James. *The Holy Roman Empire.* London: Macmillan, 1905.

———. *Studies in History and Jurisprudence.* New York: Oxford University Press, 1901.

Burn, W. L. *The Age of Equipoise: A Study of the Mid-Victorian Generation.* London: Allen and Unwin, 1964.

Burton, Antoinette. "Archive of Bones: *Anil's Ghost* and the Ends of History." *Journal of Commonwealth Literature* 38, no. 1 (2003): 39–56.

Buttigieg, Joseph. "Philology and Politics: Returning to the Text of Antonio Gramsci's *Prison Notebooks*." *Boundary2* 21, no. 2 (1994): 98–138.

Buzard, James. *Disorienting Fiction: The Autoethnographic Work of Nineteenth-Century British Novels.* Princeton: Princeton University Press, 2005.

Carlyle, Thomas. *"Chartism" and "Past and Present."* London: Chapman and Hall, 1843.

———. *Historical Essays.* Edited by Chris R. Vanden Bossche, Joel J. Brattin, and D. J. Trela. Berkeley: University of California Press, 2005.

Carlyle, Thomas, and John Stuart Mill. *The Nigger Question and the Negro Question.* Edited by Eugene R. August. New York: Appleton Century-Crofts, 1971.

Castoriadis, Cornelius. *The Imaginary Institution of Society.* Translated by Kathleen Blamey. Cambridge, MA: MIT Press, 1987.

Chakrabarty, Dipesh. *Provincializing Europe: Postcolonial Thought and Historical Difference.* Princeton: Princeton University Press, 2000.

Chakravarty, Gautam. *The Indian Mutiny and the British Imagination.* Cambridge: Cambridge University Press, 2004.

Chandler, Alice. *A Dream of Order: The Medieval Ideal in Nineteenth Century English Literature.* London: Routledge, 1971.

Chandler, James. *England in 1819: The Politics of Literature Culture and the Case of Romantic Historicism.* Chicago: University of Chicago Press, 1998.

Chatterjee, Partha. *Nationalist Thought and the Colonial World.* Minneapolis: University of Minnesota Press, 1986.

———. "Whose Imagined Community?" in *The Nation and Its Fragments*, 3–13. Princeton: Princeton University Press, 1993.

Cheah, Pheng. *Spectral Nationality: Passages of Freedom from Kant to Postcolonial Literatures of Liberation.* New York: Columbia University Press, 2003.

Childers, Joseph. "Carlyle's *Past and Present*, History, and a Question of Hermeneutics." *Clio* 13, no. 3 (1984): 247–58.

Clingman, Stephen. *The Novels of Nadine Gordimer: History from the Inside.* Amherst: University of Massachusetts Press, 1992.

———. "Revolution and Reality: South African Fiction in the 1980s." In *Rendering Things Visible: Essays on South African Literary Culture*, edited by Martin Trump, 41–60. Athens: Ohio University Press, 1990.

Clover, Joshua. *Riot. Strike. Riot: The New Era of Uprisings.* New York: Verso, 2016.

Coetzee, J. M. *The Life and Times of Michael K.* New York: Penguin, 1983.

———. *Waiting for the Barbarians.* New York: Penguin, 1980.

———. *White Writing: On the Culture of Letters in South Africa.* New Haven: Yale University Press, 1988.

Colley, Linda. "Britishness and Otherness: An Argument." *Journal of British Studies* 31, no. 4 (1992): 309–29.

———. *Britons: Forging the Nation: 1707–1837.* Revised edition. New Haven: Yale University Press, 2012.

Collier, Paul, and Nicholas Sambanis. "Understanding Civil War: A New Agenda." *Journal of Conflict Resolution* 46, no. 1 (2002): 3–12.

Conrad, Joseph. *Heart of Darkness.* London: Penguin, 2012.

———. *Nostromo: A Tale of the Seaboard.* Oxford: Oxford University Press, 2007.

Cooke, John. "'Nobody's Children': Families in Gordimer's Later Novels." In *The Later Fiction of Nadine Gordimer*, edited by Bruce King, 21–33. London: Macmillan, 1993.

Coovadia, Imran. *Authority and Authorship in V. S. Naipaul*. New York: Palgrave Macmillan, 2009.

Corbett, Mary Jean. *Allegories of Union in Irish and English Writing, 1790–1870: Politics, History, and the Family from Edgeworth to Arnold*. Cambridge: Cambridge University Press, 2000.

Corfield, F. D. *The Origins and Growth of the Mau Mau*. Nairobi, 1960.

Coundouriotis, Eleni. *The People's Right to the Novel: War Fiction in the Postcolony*. New York: Fordham University Press, 2014.

Crapanzano, Vincent. *Waiting: The Whites of South Africa*. New York: Random House, 1985.

Cromer, Evelyn Barring. "The Government of Subject Races." In *Political and Literary Essays: 1908–1913*, 3–53. London: Macmillan, 1913.

Cudjoe, Selwyn R. *V. S. Naipaul: A Materialist Reading*. Amherst: University of Massachusetts Press, 1988.

Culler, Jonathan. "Anderson and the Novel." In *Grounds of Comparison: Around the Work of Benedict Anderson*, edited by Jonathan Culler and Pheng Cheah, 29–52. New York: Routledge, 2003.

Dalley, Hamish. *The Postcolonial Historical Novel: Realism, Allegory, and the Representation of Contested Pasts*. London: Palgrave Macmillan, 2014.

Daly, Suzanne. *The Empire Inside: Indian Commodities in Victorian Domestic Novels*. Ann Arbor: University of Michigan Press, 2014.

Damstra, St. John. "Attacking the Boers in the Style of Kipling Sahib." *Kipling Journal* 82, no. 329 (2008): 10–25.

Datta, Pradip Kumar. "Interlocking Worlds of the Anglo-Boer War in South Africa/India." *South African Historical Journal* 57 (2007): 35–59.

de Certeau, Michel. *The Practice of Everyday Life*. Translated by Steven Randall. Berkeley: University of California Press, 1984.

de Tocqueville, Alexis. *Journeys to England and Ireland*. Translated by George Lawrence and K. P. Mayer. New Haven: Yale University Press, 1958.

Demory, Pamela H. "*Nostromo*: Making History." *Texas Studies in Literature and Language* 35, no. 3 (Fall 1993): 316–46.

Dennis, Richard. *English Industrial Cities of the Nineteenth Century: A Social Geography*. Cambridge: Cambridge University Press, 1984.

Derrida, Jacques. "But Beyond . . . (An Open Letter to Anne McClintock and Rob Nixon)." Translated by Peggy Kamuf. *Critical Inquiry* 13, no. 1 (1986): 155–70.

———. "Force of Law." In *Deconstruction and the Possibility of Justice*, edited by Drucilla Cornell, Michael Rosenfield, and David G. Carlson, 3–67. London: Routledge, 1992.

———. *Margins of Philosophy*. Translated by Alan Bass. Chicago: University of Chicago Press, 1982.

———. *Of Grammatology*. Translated by Gayatri Chakravorty Spivak. Baltimore: Johns Hopkins University Press, 1998.

————. "On Racism's Last Word." *Critical Inquiry* 12, no. 1 (1985): 290–99.

Desrosières, Alain. *The Politics of Large Numbers: A History of Statistical Reasoning.* Translated by Camille Naish. Cambridge, MA: Harvard University Press, 2002.

Dickens, Charles. *Bleak House.* London: Penguin, 1996.

————. *The Letters of Charles Dickens.* Vol. 8, *1856–1858,* edited by Graham Storey and Kathleen Tillotson. Oxford: Clarendon Press, 1995.

————. "The Niger Expedition." In *Miscellaneous Papers.* Cambridge: Cambridge University Press, 2009.

————. *Oliver Twist.* London: Penguin, 2003.

————. *Sketches by Boz.* London: Penguin, 1995.

Dilke, Charles Wentworth. *Greater Britain: A Record of Travel in English-Speaking Countries.* New York: Harper and Brothers, 1869.

————. *The Problems of Greater Britain.* London: Macmillan, 1890.

Disraeli, Benjamin. *Vindication of the English Constitution.* London: Saunders and Otley, 1835.

————. *Sybil, or, The Two Nations.* Oxford: Oxford University Press, 1981.

Doyle, Arthur Conan. *The Great Boer War.* London: Smith, Elder, & Co., 1901.

Elias, Norbert. *The Civilizing Process: Sociogenetic and Psychogenetic Investigations.* Translated by Edmund Jephcott. Malden, MA: Blackwell, 1982.

"The End of Tolerance? Anti-Muslim Movement Rattles Germany." *Der Spiegel* 51 (15 December 2014).

Engels, Friedrich. *The Conditions of the Working Class in England.* Oxford: Oxford University Press, 2009.

————. *The Role of Force in History: A Study of Bismarck's Policy of Blood and Iron.* Edited by Ernst Wangermann. New York: International Publishers, 1968.

Enzensberger, Hans Magnus. *Civil Wars.* New York: The New Press, 1993.

Esty, Jed. "Global Lukács." *NOVEL: A Forum on Fiction* 42, no. 3 (2009): 366–72.

————. *Unseasonable Youth: Modernism, Colonialism and the Fiction of Development.* Oxford: Oxford University Press, 2011.

Ettin, Andrew Vogel. *Betrayals of the Body Politic: The Literary Commitments of Nadine Gordimer.* Charlottesville: University Press of Virginia, 1992.

Fearon, James D., and David D. Laitin. "Ethnicity, Insurgency, and Civil War." *American Political Science Review* 97, no. 1 (February 2003): 75–90.

Feeley, Margaret Peller. "The *Kim* That Nobody Reads." *Studies in the Novel* 13, no. 3 (Fall 1981): 266–81.

Fido, Martin. "'From His Own Observation': Sources of Working Class Passages in Disraeli's *Sybil.*" *Modern Language Review* 72, no. 2 (1977): 268–84.

————. "The Treatment of Rural Distress in Disraeli's *Sybil.*" *Yearbook of English Studies* 5 (1975): 153–63.

Fleishman, Avrom. *Conrad's Politics: Community and Anarchy in the Fiction of Joseph Conrad.* Baltimore: Johns Hopkins University Press, 1967.

Fogel, Aaron. *Coercion to Speak: Conrad's Poetics of Dialogue.* Cambridge, MA: Harvard University Press, 1985.

Foucault, Michel. *The History of Sexuality, Volume 1: An Introduction.* Translated by Robert Hurley. New York: Pantheon Books, 1978.

———. *The Punitive Society.* Translated by Graham Burchell and edited by Bernard Harcourt. New York: Palgrave Macmillan, 2015.

———. *"Society Must Be Defended."* Translated by David Macey and edited by Mauro Bertani and Alessandro Fontana. New York: Picador, 2003.

Free, Melissa. "Fault Lines of Loyalty: Kipling's Boer War Conflict." *Victorian Studies* 58, no. 2 (2016): 314–23.

Froude, James Anthony. *Lord Beaconsfield.* London: Sampson Low, Marston, Searle and Rivington, 1891.

———. *Oceana: England and her Colonies.* London: Longmans, Green and Co., 1886.

Fynsk, Christopher. "Apartheid, Word and History." *Boundary2* 16, no. 2/3 (1989): 1–12.

Gallagher, Catherine. *The Body Economic: Life, Death, and Sensation in Political Economy and the Victorian Novel.* Princeton: Princeton University Press, 2006.

———. "George Eliot: Immanent Victorian." *Representations* 90, no. 1 (2005): 61–74.

———. *The Industrial Reformation of English Fiction.* Chicago: University of Chicago Press, 1985.

Galli, Carlo. *Political Spaces and Global War.* Translated by Elisabeth Fay. Minneapolis: University of Minnesota Press, 2010.

Garcha, Amanpal. *From Sketch to Novel: The Development of Victorian Fiction.* Oxford: Oxford University Press, 2008.

Gaskell, Elizabeth. *North and South.* London: Penguin Classics, 1996.

Gat, Azar. "Clausewitz and the Marxists: Yet Another Look." *Journal of Contemporary History* 27, no. 2 (1992): 363–82.

Gibbons, Luke. *Transformations in Irish Culture.* Notre Dame: University of Notre Dame Press, 1996.

Gikandi, Simon. *Maps of Englishness: Writing Identity in the Culture of Colonialism.* New York: Columbia University Press, 1996.

Gilbert, Pamela. *Mapping the Victorian Social Body.* Albany: State University of New York Press, 2004.

Glennie, Paul, and Nigel Thrift. "Reworking E. P. Thompson's 'Time, Work-Discipline and Industrial Capitalism.'" *Time Society* 5 (1996): 275–99.

GoGwilt, Christopher. *The Invention of the West: Joseph Conrad and the Double-Mapping of Europe and Empire.* Stanford: Stanford University Press, 1995.

Gooch, Joshua. "'The Shape of Credit': Imagination, Speculation, and Language in *Nostromo.*" *Texas Studies in Literature and Language* 52, no. 3 (Fall 2010): 266–97.

Goodlad, Lauren. *Victorian Literature and the Victorian State: Character and Governance in a Liberal Society.* Baltimore: Johns Hopkins University Press, 2003.

Gordimer, Nadine. *Conversations with Nadine Gordimer.* Edited by Nancy Topping Bazin and Marilyn Dallman Seymour. Jackson: University Press of Mississippi, 1990.

———. *The Essential Gesture.* Edited by Stephen Clingman. London: Penguin, 1988.

———. *July's People.* New York: Penguin, 1981.

———. *Loot and Other Stories.* London: Penguin, 2004.

Gorman, Daniel. *Imperial Citizenship: Empire and the Question of Belonging.* Manchester: Manchester University Press, 2006.

Gorra, Michael. *After Empire: Scott, Naipaul, Rushdie.* Chicago: University of Chicago Press, 1997.

Gourgouris, Stathis. *Dream Nation: Enlightenment, Colonization, and the Institution of Modern Greece.* Stanford: Stanford University Press, 1996.

Goux, Jean-Joseph. *Symbolic Economies: After Marx and Freud.* Translated by Jennifer Curtiss Gage. Ithaca: Cornell University Press, 1990.

Gramsci, Antonio. *Prison Notebooks.* Translated by Joseph A. Buttigeig. 3 vols. New York: Columbia University Press, 1991.

———. *Selections from the Prison Notebooks.* Translated and edited by Quintin Hoare and Geoffrey Nowell Smith. New York: International Publishers, 1971.

Grant, Hope. *Incidents in the Sepoy War: 1857–8.* Edinburgh: William Blackwood and Sons, 1873.

"Greece Far-Right Party Golden Dawn: 'We Are in a Civil War.'" BBC News, 17 October 2012, http://www.bbc.com/news/world-europe-19983571.

Gross, Erin M. "Reading Cant, Transforming the Nation: Carlyle's *Past and Present.*" In *Victorian Transformations: Genre, Nationalism and Desire in Nineteenth-Century Literature*, edited by Bianca Tredennick, 95–114. Farnham: Ashgate, 2011.

Grossman, Jonathan. *Charles Dickens's Networks: Public Transport and the Novel.* Oxford: Oxford University Press, 2013.

Guerard, Albert J. *Conrad the Novelist.* Cambridge, MA: Harvard University Press, 1958.

Guha, Ranajit. "The Colonial City and Its Time(s)." *Indian Economic and Social History Review* 45, no. 3 (2008): 329–51.

Hardt, Michael, and Antonio Negri. *Empire.* Cambridge, MA: Harvard University Press, 2001.

———. *Multitude: War and Democracy in the Age of Empire.* New York: Penguin, 2004.

Havely, Cicely Palser. "A Sahibs' War." *Kipling Journal* 68, no. 272 (December 1994): 12–22.

Headrick, Daniel R. *The Invisible Weapon: Telecommunications and International Politics, 1851–1945.* New York: Oxford University Press, 1991.

Hensley, Nathan K. *Forms of Empire: The Poetics of Victorian Sovereignty.* Oxford: Oxford University Press, 2016.

Herbert, Christopher. *The War of No Pity: The Indian Mutiny and Victorian Trauma.* Princeton: Princeton University Press, 2009.

Hewitt, Martin, ed. *An Age of Equipoise?: Reassessing Mid-Victorian Britain.* Burlington, VT: Ashgate, 2000.

Hobbes, Thomas. *Behemoth, or, The Long Parliament*. Edited by Ferdinand Tönnies. Chicago: University of Chicago Press, 1990.

———. *Leviathan*. London: Penguin, 1985.

Hobson, J. A. *Imperialism: A Study*. Ann Arbor: University of Michigan Press, 1965.

———. *The War in South Africa: Its Causes and Effects*. New York: Macmillan, 1900.

Hofmeyr, Isabel. "Universalizing the Indian Ocean." *PMLA* 125, no. 3 (2010): 721–29.

Hofmeyr, Isabel, and Michelle Williams, eds. "South Africa–India: Connections and Comparisons." Special issue, *Journal of Asian and African Studies* 44, no. 1–2 (2009): 1–165.

Holden, Philip. "Halls of Mirrors: Mimicry and Ambivalence in Kipling's Boer War Short Stories." *Ariel* 28, no. 4 (1997): 91–110.

Howe, Irving. *Politics and the Novel*. New York: Horizon Press, 1957.

Hudson, William Henry. *The Purple Land*. New York: Grosset and Dunlap, 1904.

Ismail, Qadri. "A Flippant Gesture Towards Sri Lanka: A Review of Michael Ondaatje's *Anil's Ghost*." *Pravada* 6, no. 9 (2000): 24–29.

Jaffe, Audrey. *The Affective Life of the Average Man: The Victorian Novel and the Stock Market Graph*. Columbus: Ohio State University Press, 2010.

Jameson, Fredric. *The Political Unconscious: Narrative as a Socially Symbolic Act*. Ithaca: Cornell University Press, 1981.

———. *A Singular Modernity: Essay on the Ontology of the Present*. London: Verso, 2002.

JanMohamed, Abdul R. *Manichean Aesthetics: The Politics of Literature in Colonial Africa*. Amherst: University of Massachusetts Press, 1983.

Jupp, Peter. "Disraeli's Interpretation of History." In *The Self-Fashioning Disraeli, 1818–1851*, edited by Charles Richmond and Paul Smith, 131–51. New York: Cambridge University Press, 1999.

Kalyvas, Stathis. "'New' and 'Old' Civil Wars: A Valid Distinction?" *World Politics* 54, no. 1 (October 2001): 99–118.

Katznelson, Ira. *Marxism and the City*. Oxford: Clarendon Press, 1992.

Kermode, Frank. *The Sense of an Ending: Studies in the Theory of Fiction*. New York: Oxford University Press, 1967.

Kerry, Paul E., and Marylu Hill. *Thomas Carlyle Resartus*. Teaneck, NJ: Fairleigh Dickinson University Press, 2010.

King, Bruce. *V. S. Naipaul*. 2nd ed. New York: Palgrave Macmillan, 2003.

Kipling, Rudyard. *The Collected Works of Rudyard Kipling*. 27 vols. New York: Doubleday, Doran and Company, 1941.

———. *Kim*. New York: Penguin Classics, 2011.

———. *The Letters of Rudyard Kipling*. Vol. 3, *1900–1910*. Edited by Thomas Pinney. Iowa City: University of Iowa Press, 1990.

Klotz, Michael. "Manufacturing Fictional Individuals: Victorian Social Statistics, the Novel, and *Great Expectations*." *NOVEL: A Forum on Fiction* 46, no. 2 (2013): 214–33.

Krebs, Paula M. *Gender, Race and the Writing of Empire: Public Discourse and the Boer War.* Cambridge: Cambridge University Press, 2003.

Kreilkamp, Ivan. *Voice and the Victorian Storyteller.* Cambridge: Cambridge University Press, 2005.

Krishnamurthy, Aruna. "'More than Abstract Knowledge': Friedrich Engels in Industrial Manchester." *Victorian Literature and Culture* 48, no. 2 (2000): 427–88.

Krishnan, Sanjay. "Edward Said, Mahmood Mamdani, V. S. Naipaul: Rethinking Postcolonial Studies." *Modern Fiction Studies* 58, no. 4 (Winter 2012): 818–36.

———. "V. S. Naipaul and Historical Derangement." *Modern Language Quarterly* 73, no. 3 (September 2012): 433–51.

Lane, Christopher. *Hatred and Civility: The Antisocial Life in Victorian England.* New York: Columbia University Press, 2004.

Lazarus, Neil. "Modernism and Modernity: T. W. Adorno and Contemporary White South African Literature." *Cultural Critique* 5 (1986–87): 131–55.

Lefebvre, Henri. *The Production of Space.* Translated by Donald Nicholson-Smith. Oxford: Blackwell, 1991.

Lenin, V. I. *The Essential Works of Lenin.* Edited by Henry Christman. New York: Dover, 1987.

———. "The Russian Revolution and Civil War." In *Collected Works.* Vol. 26. Moscow: Progress Publishers, 1972.

Lesjak, Carolyn. *Working Fictions: A Genealogy of the Victorian Novel.* Durham: Duke University Press, 2006.

Lester, Alan. *Imperial Networks: Creating Identities in Nineteenth-Century South Africa and Britain.* London: Routledge, 2001.

Lichtenstein, Alex, ed. *American Historical Review* 120, no. 5 (December 2015): 1682–1837.

Linebaugh, Peter, and Marcus Rediker. *The Many-Headed Hydra: Sailors, Slaves, Commoners and the Hidden History of the Revolutionary Atlantic.* Boston: Beacon Press, 2000.

Lloyd, David. *Anomalous States: Irish Writing and the Post-Colonial Moment.* Durham: Duke University Press, 1993.

———. *Irish Times: Temporalities of Modernity.* Dublin: Field Day Files, 2008.

———. *Nationalism and Minor Literature: James Clarence Mangan and the Emergence of Irish Cultural Nationalism.* Berkeley: University of California Press, 1987.

Loraux, Nicole. *The Divided City: On Memory and Forgetting in Ancient Athens.* Translated by Corinne Pache and Jeff Fort. New York: Zone Books, 2001.

———. "Reflections of the Greek City on Unity and Division." In *City-States in Classical Antiquity and Medieval Italy: Athens and Rome, Florence and Venice,* edited by Anthony Molho, Kurt Raaflaub, and Julia Emlen, 33–52. Stuttgart: Franz Steiner, 1991.

Lukács, György. *The Historical Novel.* Translated by Hannah Mitchell and Stanley Mitchell. London: Merlin Press, 1962.

———. *History and Class Consciousness: Studies in Marxist Dialectics.* Translated by Rodney Livingstone. Cambridge, MA: MIT Press, 1971.

Luxemburg, Rosa. *The Essential Rosa Luxemburg: "Reform or Revolution" and "The Mass Strike."* Edited by Helen Scott. Chicago: Haymarket Books, 2008.

Macaskill, Brian. "Placing Spaces: Style and Ideology in Gordimer's Later Fiction." In *The Later Fiction of Nadine Gordimer,* edited by Bruce King, 59–73. London: Macmillan, 1993.

Macaulay, Thomas. *The History of England from the Ascension of James II.* Vol. 2. London: J. M. Dent & Sons Ltd., 1906.

———. *Speeches by Lord Macaulay.* London: Oxford University Press, 2008.

Magee, Gary B., and Andrew S. Thompson. *Empire and Globalisation: Networks of People, Goods and Capital in the British World, 1850–1914.* Cambridge: Cambridge University Press, 2010.

Mamdani, Mahmood. "How Not to Intervene in Internal Conflicts." *Security Dialogue* 20, no. 4 (1989): 437–40.

———. "The Politics of Naming." *London Review of Books* 29, no. 5 (2007): 5–8.

———. *Saviours and Survivors: Darfur, Politics, and the War on Terror.* Cape Town: HSRC Press, 2009.

Mamou, Yves. "France: The Coming Civil War." July 16, 2016, Gateson Institute, https://www.gatestoneinstitute.org/8489/france-the-coming-civil-war.

Marcus, Stephen. *Engels, Manchester and the Working Class.* New York: Vintage, 1975.

Marroni, Francesco. *Victorian Disharmonies: A Reconsideration of Nineteenth-Century English Fiction.* Rome: John Cabot University Press, 2010.

Marx, John. *Geopolitics and the Anglophone Novel, 1890–2011.* Cambridge: Cambridge University Press, 2012.

———. *The Modernist Novel and the Decline of Empire.* Cambridge: Cambridge University Press, 2005.

Marx, Karl. *Capital: A Critique of Political Economy.* Vol. 1. Translated by Ben Fowkes. New York: Vintage, 1977.

———. *The Civil War in France: The Paris Commune.* New York: International Publishers, 1988.

———. *The Civil War in the United States.* New York: International Press, 1971.

———. *The Eighteenth Brumaire of Louis Bonaparte.* New York: International Publishers, 1988.

Marx, Karl, and Friedrich Engels. *Collected Works.* 50 vols. New York: International Publishers, 1975–2004.

———. *The Marx-Engels Reader.* 2nd ed. Edited by Robert Tucker. New York: W. W. Norton, 1978.

Mayhew, Henry. *London Labour and the London Poor.* London: Griffin, Bohn, and Company, 1861.

Mbembe, Achille. "Necropolitics." Translated by Libby Meintjes. *Public Culture* 15, no. 1 (2003): 11–40.

————. *On the Postcolony*. Berkeley: University of California Press, 2001.

McClintock, Anne, and Rob Nixon. "No Names Apart: The Separation of Word and History in Derrida's 'Le Dernier Mot du Racisme.'" *Critical Inquiry* 13, no. 1 (1986): 155–70.

Mengiste, Maaza. *Beneath a Lion's Gaze*. New York: W. W. Norton, 2010.

Menke, Richard. *Telegraphic Realism: Victorian Fiction and Other Information Systems*. Stanford: Stanford University Press, 2008.

Metcalf, Thomas R. *Imperial Connections: India and the Indian Ocean Arena, 1860–1920*. Berkeley: University of California Press, 2007.

Mieszkowski, Jan. "How to Do Things with Clausewitz." *Global South* 3, no. 1 (2009): 18–29.

Mill, John Stuart. *The Contest in America*. Boston: Little, Brown, 1862.

Miller, D. A. *The Novel and the Police*. Berkeley: University of California Press, 1988.

Miller, J. Hillis. *Reading Narrative*. Norman: University of Oklahoma Press, 1998.

————. *Victorian Subjects*. Durham: Duke University Press, 1991.

Moore, Grace. *Dickens and Empire: Discourses of Class, Race, and Colonialism in the Works of Charles Dickens*. Aldershot: Ashgate, 2004.

Moretti, Franco. *Atlas of the European Novel: 1800–1900*. London: Verso, 1998.

————. *Signs Taken for Wonders: Essays in the Sociology of Literary Forms*. London: Verso, 1983.

Mundy, Jacob. "Deconstructing Civil Wars: Beyond the New Wars Debate." *Security Dialogue* 42, no. 3 (2011): 279–95.

————. *Imaginative Geographies of Algerian Violence: Conflict Science, Conflict Management, Antipolitics*. Stanford: Stanford University Press, 2015.

Nagai, Kaori. *Empire of Analogies: Kipling, India and Ireland*. Cork: Cork University Press, 2006.

Naipaul, V. S. *A Bend in the River*. New York: Vintage, 1989.

————. "Conrad's Darkness and Mine." In *Literary Occasions: Essays*, 162–80. New York: Vintage, 2003.

————. "A Grotesque Love of Propaganda. Unspeakable Barbarity. The Loathing of Jews—and a Hunger for World Domination. In this Stunning Intervention, Literary Colossus V. S. NAIPAUL Says ISIS is Now the Fourth Reich." *Daily Mail*, 21 March 2015, http://www.dailymail.co.uk/debate/article-3005882/A-grotesque-love-propaganda-Unspeakable-barbarity-loathing-Jews-hunger-world-domination-stunning-intervention-literary-colossus-V-S-NAIPAUL-says-ISIS-Fourth-Reich.html.

————. *In a Free State*. New York: Vintage, 2002.

————. *The Loss of Eldorado: A Colonial History*. New York: Vintage, 1997.

————. "A New King for the Congo." *New York Review of Books*, 26 June 1975.

Ndebele, Njabulo S. "Liberation and the Crisis of Culture." In *Altered State? Writing and South Africa*, edited by Elleke Boehmer, Laura Chrisman, and Kenneth Parker, 1–36. Sydney: Dangaroo Press, 1994.

———. *South African Literature and Culture: Rediscovery of the Ordinary*. Manchester: Manchester University Press, 1994.

———. "Turkish Tales and Some Thoughts on South African Fiction." In *South African Literature and Culture: Rediscovery of the Ordinary*, 17–40. Manchester: Manchester University Press, 1994.

Neill, Michael. "Translating the Present: Language, Knowledge, and Identity in Nadine Gordimer's *July's People*." *Journal of Commonwealth Literature* 25 (1990): 71–97.

Nightingale, Peggy. *Journey Through Darkness: The Writing of V. S. Naipaul*. St. Lucia: University of Queensland Press, 1987.

Nixon, Rob. *London Calling: Postcolonial Mandarin*. Oxford: Oxford University Press, 1992.

Nora, Pierre. "Between History and Memory: *Les Lieux de Mémoire*." Translated by Marc Roudebush. *Representations* 26 (1989): 7–24.

O'Kell, Robert. "Two Nations or One?: Disraeli's Allegorical Romance." *Victorian Studies* 30, no. 2 (1987): 211–34.

O'Malley, Seamus. *Making History New: Modernism and Historical Narrative*. London: Oxford University Press, 2015.

Ondaatje, Michael. *Anil's Ghost*. New York: Vintage International, 2000.

O'Shaughnessy, Andrew Jackson. *An Empire Divided: The American Revolution and the British Caribbean*. Philadelphia: University of Pennsylvania Press, 2000.

Palmerston, Henry John Temple. "On the Affairs in Greece." In *The Life and Correspondence of Henry John Temple Viscount Palmerston*. Vol. 2. Edited by Evelyn Ashley. London: Richard Bentley and Son, 1879.

Parrinder, Patrick. *Nation and Novel: The English Novel from Its Origins to the Present Day*. Oxford: Oxford University Press, 2006.

Parry, Benita. *Conrad and Imperialism: Ideological Boundaries and Visionary Frontiers*. London: Macmillan, 1983.

Pasquiano, Pasquale. "Political Theory of War and Peace: Foucault and the History of Modern Political Theory." *Economy and Society* 22, no. 1 (1993): 77–88.

Pearsall, Susan. "'Where the Banalities Are Enacted': The Everyday in Gordimer's Novels." *Research in African Literatures* 31, no. 1 (Spring 2000): 95–118.

Perloff, Marjorie. *Differentials: Poetry, Poetics, Pedagogy*. Tuscaloosa: University of Alabama Press, 2004.

Plotz, John. *The Crowd: British Literature and Public Politics*. Berkeley: University of California Press, 2000.

———. *Portable Property: Victorian Culture on the Move*. Princeton: Princeton University Press, 2008.

Pocock. J. G. A. *Barbarism and Religion*. Vol. 4. Cambridge: Cambridge University Press, 2005.

———. *Virtue, Commerce, and History*. Cambridge: Cambridge University Press, 1985.

Poole, Robert. "'By the Law of the Sword': Peterloo Revisited." *History* 91, no. 302 (2006): 254–76.

Poovey, Mary. *Making a Social Body*. Chicago: University of Chicago Press, 1995.

Posel, Deborah. "The Language of Domination, 1978–1983." In *The Politics of Race, Class and Nationalism in Twentieth-Century South Africa*, edited by Shula Marks and Stanley Trapido, 419–43. London: Longman Group, 1987.

Potter, Simon J. "Webs, Networks, and Systems: Globalization and the Mass Media in the Nineteenth and Twentieth Century British Empire." *Journal of British Studies* 46, no. 3 (July 2007): 621–46.

Prescott, Linda. "Past and Present Darkness: Sources for V. S. Naipaul's *A Bend in the River*." *Modern Fiction Studies* 30, no. 3 (Autumn 1984): 547–59.

Puckett, Kent. *Bad Form: Social Mistakes and the Nineteenth-Century Novel*. Oxford: Oxford University Press, 2008.

Radhakrishnan, R. "Derivative Discourse and the Problem of Signification." *European Legacy* 7, no. 6 (2002): 783–95.

———. *Theory in an Uneven World*. Malden, MA: Blackwell, 2003.

Ramirez, Luz Elena. *British Representations of Latin America*. Gainesville: University Press of Florida, 2007.

Regan, Patrick. *Civil Wars and Foreign Powers: Outside Intervention in Intrastate Conflict*. Ann Arbor: University of Michigan Press, 2002.

Renan, Ernst. "What Is a Nation?" In *Nation and Narration*, edited by Homi Bhabha, 8–22. London: Routledge, 1990.

Ricoeur, Paul. *History, Memory, Forgetting*. Translated by Kathleen Blamey and David Pellauer. Chicago: University of Chicago Press, 2004.

———. "The Metaphoric Process." *Critical Inquiry* 5, no. 1 (1978): 143–59.

———. "Narrative Time." *Critical Inquiry* 7, no. 1 (1980): 178–79.

———. *Time and Narrative*. Vol. 1. Chicago: University of Chicago Press, 1990.

Rigney, Ann. *Imperfect Histories: The Elusive Past and the Legacy of Romantic Historicism*. Ithaca: Cornell University Press, 2001.

Robinson, Alan. *Imagining London, 1770–1900*. New York: Palgrave Macmillan, 2004.

Rosenberg, John D. *Carlyle and the Burden of History*. Cambridge, MA: Harvard University Press, 1986.

Rosenfield, Claire. *Paradise of Snakes: An Archetypical Analysis of Conrad's Political Novels*. Chicago: University of Chicago Press, 1967.

Rosenthal, Jesse. "The Large Novel and the Law of Large Numbers, or, Why George Eliot Hates Gambling." *ELH* 77, no. 3 (Fall 2010): 777–811.

Ross, Stephen. *Conrad and Empire*. Columbia: University of Missouri Press, 2004.

Roy, Anindyo. *Civility and Empire: Literature and Culture in British India, 1822–1922*. London: Routledge, 2005.

Runia, Eelco. *Moved by the Past: Discontinuity and Historical Mutation*. New York: Columbia University Press, 2014.

Said, Edward W. *Beginnings: Intention and Method*. New York: Columbia University Press, 1975.

———. *Culture and Imperialism*. New York: Vintage, 1994.

———. *Orientalism*. New York: Vintage, 1979.

———. *Reflections on Exile, & Other Literary and Cultural Essays*. Cambridge, MA: Harvard University Press, 2002.

———. "Secular Criticism." In *The World, the Text, and the Critic*, 1–30. Cambridge, MA: Harvard University Press, 1983.

Sambanis, Nicholas. "What Is Civil War? Conceptual and Empirical Complexities of an Operational Definition." *Journal of Conflict Resolution* 48, no. 6 (December 2004): 814–58.

Sampson, Jennifer. "*Sybil*, or the Two Monarchs." *Studies in Philology* 95, no. 1 (1998): 71–119.

Schmitt, Cannon. "Rumor, Shares, Novelistic Form: Joseph Conrad's *Nostromo*." In *Victorian Investments: New Perspectives on Finance and Culture*, edited by Nancy Henry and Cannon Schmitt, 182–201. Bloomington: University of Indiana Press, 2008.

Schmitt, Carl. *The Concept of the Political*. Translated by George Schwab. Chicago: University of Chicago Press, 1996.

———. *The Nomos of the Earth: In the International Law of the Jus Publicum Europeanum*. Translated by G. L. Ulmen. New York: Telos Publishing, 2003.

———. *Theory of the Partisan: Intermediary Commentary on the Concept of the Political*. Translated by G. L. Ulmen. New York: Telos Publishing, 2007.

Schwarz, Daniel R. *Disraeli's Fiction*. New York: Palgrave Macmillan, 1979.

Scott, David. *Conscripts of Modernity: The Tragedy of Colonial Enlightenment*. Durham: Duke University Press, 2004.

Scott, Walter. *Ivanhoe*. Oxford: Oxford World's Classics, 2010.

Seeley, J. R. *The Expansion of England: Two Courses of Lectures*. London: Macmillan, 1914.

Simmons, Claire A. *Reversing Conquest: History and Myth in Nineteenth-Century British Literature*. New Brunswick, NJ: Rutgers University Press, 1990.

Small, Melvin, and J. David Singer. *Resort to Arms: International and Civil Wars, 1816–1980*. Beverly Hills, CA: Sage, 1982.

Smith, Malvern van Wyk. *Drummer Hodge: The Poetry of the Anglo-Boer War, 1899–1902*. Oxford: Oxford University Press, 1978.

———. "Telling the Boer War: Narrative Indeterminacy in Kipling's Stories." *South African Historical Journal* 41 (1999): 349–69.

Smith, Peter. *Public and Private Value: Studies in the Nineteenth Century Novel*. Cambridge: Cambridge University Press, 1984.

Smith, Shiela M. *The Other Nation: Poor in English Novels of the 1840s and 1850s*. Oxford: Clarendon Press, 1980.

———. "Willenhall and Wodgate: Disraeli's Use of Blue Book Evidence." *Review of English Studies* 13, no. 52 (1962): 368–84.

Snow, Donald M. *UnCivil Wars: International Security and the New Internal Conflicts*. Boulder, CO: Lynne Rienner, 1996.

Sorapure, Madeleine. "A Story in Love's Default: André Brink's *States of Emergency*." *MFS: Modern Fiction Studies* 37, no. 4 (Winter 1991): 659–75.

Sorel, Georges. *Reflections on Violence*. Edited by Jeremy Jennings. Cambridge: Cambridge University Press, 1999.

Spivak, Gayatri Chakravorty. *A Critique of Postcolonial Reason: Toward a History of the Vanishing Present*. Cambridge, MA: Harvard University Press, 1999.

———. *Nationalism and the Imagination*. Kolkata: Seagull Books, 2010.

Steinlight, Emily. "Dickens's 'Supernumeraries' and the Biopolitical Imagination of Victorian Fiction." *NOVEL: A Forum on Fiction* 43, no. 2 (2010): 227–50.

Stewart, David. "Orality in Kipling's *Kim*." *JNT: Journal of Narrative Technique* 13, no. 1 (Winter 1983): 47–57.

Stewart, Garett. *Reading Voices: Literature and the Phonotext*. Berkeley: University of California Press, 1990.

Stokes, Anthony. *A View of the Constitution of the British Colonies in North America and the West Indies at the time the Civil War Broke Out on the Continent of America*. London: B. White, 1783.

Stoler, Ann Laura. *Race and the Education of Desire: Foucault's "History of Sexuality" and the Colonial Order of Things*. Durham: Duke University Press, 1995.

Subrahmanyam, Sanjay. "Where Does He Come From?" *London Review of Books* 29, no. 21 (November 2007): 7–9.

Swift, Roger. "Thomas Carlyle, *Chartism*, and the Irish in Early Victorian England." *Victorian Literature and Culture* 29, no. 1 (2001): 67–83.

Tabli, Laura. "A Homogeneous Society? Britain's Internal 'Others' 1800–Present." In *At Home with the Empire*, edited by Catherine Hall and Sonya O. Rose, 53–76. Cambridge: Cambridge University Press, 2007.

Thierry, Augustin. *History of the Conquest of England by the Normans: Its Causes and Consequences, in England, Scotland, Ireland, and on the Continent*. Translated by William Hazlitt. 2 vols. London: David Bogue, 1847.

Thiong'o, Ngũgĩ wa. *Weep Not, Child*. Johannesburg: Heinemann, 1987.

Thompson, E. P. *Making History: Writings on History and Culture*. New York: New Press, 1994.

———. *The Making of the English Working Class*. New York: Vintage, 1966.

———. "Time, Work-Discipline, and Industrial Capitalism." *Past and Present* 38 (1967): 56–97.

Thompson, Leonard. *A History of South Africa*. New Haven: Yale University Press, 2001.

Tönnies, Ferdinand. *Community and Civil Society*. Translated by Jose Harris and Margaret Hollis. Cambridge: Cambridge University Press, 2001.

Trotter, David. "Modernism and Empire: Reading *The Waste Land*." *Critical Quarterly* 28, no. 1–2 (1986): 143–53.

Trump, Martin. "Part of the Struggle: Black Writing and the South African Liberation Movement." In *Rendering Things Visible: Essays on South African Literary Culture*, edited by Martin Trump, 161–85. Athens: Ohio University Press, 1990.

Tse-Tung, Mao. *On Protracted War.* 3rd ed. Peking: Foreign Languages Press, 1967.

Tsing, Anna Lowenhaupt. *Friction: An Ethnography of Global Connection.* Princeton: Princeton University Press, 2005.

Tucker, Albert. "Disraeli and the Natural Aristocracy." *Canadian Journal of Economics and Political Science* 28, no. 1 (1962): 1–15.

Ulrich, John M. *Signs of Their Times: History, Labor, and the Body in Cobbett, Carlyle, and Disraeli.* Athens: Ohio University Press, 2002.

Vardoulakis, Dimitris. "The Ends of Stasis: Spinoza as a Reader of Agamben." *Culture, Theory and Critique* 51, no. 2 (2010): 145–56.

Visser, Nicholas. "Beyond the Interregnum: A Note on the Ending of *July's People.*" In *Rendering Things Visible: Essays on South African Literary Culture,* edited by Martin Trump, 61–67. Athens: Ohio University Press, 1990.

———. "Crowds and Politics in *Nostromo.*" *Mosaic* 23, no. 2 (1990): 1–15.

Wagner, Kathrin. *Rereading Nadine Gordimer.* Bloomington: Indiana University Press, 1994.

Wahrman, Dror. *Imagining the Middle Class: The Political Representation of Class in Britain, c. 1870–1840.* Cambridge: Cambridge University Press, 1995.

Ward, David. "Victorian Cities: How Modern?" *Journal of Historical Geography* 2, no. 1 (1975): 135–51.

Watt, Ian. *Joseph Conrad: Nostromo.* Cambridge: Cambridge University Press, 1988.

White, Hayden. *Figural Realism: Studies in the Mimesis Effect.* Baltimore: Johns Hopkins University Press, 1999.

———. *Metahistory: The Historical Imagination in Nineteenth-Century Europe.* Baltimore: Johns Hopkins University Press, 1973.

Wilder, Gary. *The French Imperial Nation-State: Negritude and Colonial Humanism Between the Two World Wars.* Chicago: University of Chicago Press, 2005.

Williams, Raymond. *Culture and Society: 1780–1950.* New York: Columbia University Press, 1983.

Winter, Yves. "Violence and Visibility." *New Political Science* 34, no. 2 (2012): 195–202.

World Bank. *Breaking the Conflict Trap: Civil War and Development Policy.* Washington, DC: World Bank, 2003.

Worth, Aaron. "Imperial Transmissions: H. G. Wells, 1897–1901." *Victorian Studies* 53, no. 1 (2010): 65–89.

Žižek, Slavoj. *Tarrying with the Negative.* Durham: Duke University Press, 1993.

Index

 FLASHPOINTS